DATE DUE

MR 1998			

DEMCO 38-296

IMPROVING
R&D PERFORMANCE
THE JURAN WAY

Improving R&D Performance the Juran Way

AL ENDRES

John Wiley & Sons, Inc.

New York ■ Chichester ■ Weinheim ■ Brisbane ■ Singapore ■ Toronto

ISBN: 0-471-16370-8

Printed in the United States of America

10 9 8 7 6 5 4 3 2 1

*This book is dedicated to Diane and Alyson,
my wife and daughter, without whose encouragement,
and willingness to frequently sacrifice our family weekends,
this material could not have been completed.*

CONTENTS

CONTENTS

CONTENTS

CONTENTS

FOREWORD

Based on my experiences at Eastman Chemical Company, I am convinced that Total Quality Management (TQM) is the most powerful management process available to modern managers. There is no doubt in my mind that TQM can be successfully applied in Research and Development to significantly improve bottom-line results. My leadership team and I used TQM to help double Eastman Chemical Company Research output and productivity and to significantly improve overall R&D performance. This breakthrough improvement in R&D performance is annually worth tens of millions of dollars to Eastman Chemical Company. Using TQM to successfully improve R&D results requires an understanding of TQM and how to make it work in R&D. We at Eastman Chemical R&D know this very well because the first three years we used TQM little or no improvements in performance were obtained. Even though there were some minor benefits from TQM during these first three years, the costs outweighed the benefits. We were not getting a significant improvement in research performance because we were not applying TQM correctly.

We wasted a lot of time and money during those first three years, which you should be able to avoid by reading *Improving R&D Performance the Juran Way*. We at Eastman Research learned the hard way and could have reduced our learning time and efforts substantially if we had been able to read this book. The author has used both personal observations and lessons from case studies of leading R&D organizations to define and develop the critical QM concepts and practices that make TQM successful in an R&D environment.

We found that the critical QM concepts described by the author are the keys to successfully using TQM:

- Top management leadership
- Focusing on outputs that are important to the customer
- Measuring the output

- Setting goals
- Improving the vital few work processes that deliver the output

These concepts are fairly easily understood; however, implementation of TQM in R&D is not easy and requires top management commitment, leadership, and communication, communication, and more communication. Dr. Endres has included valuable hints, including several case studies illustrating successful implementation of TQM. Advice and directions on successful implementation of TQM gleaned from this book should be invaluable in helping you implement TQM to significantly improve R&D performance.

TQM has become the way R&D is managed at Eastman Chemical Company and is not considered a separate program. TQM is the only management system used and it is the way we have been able to substantially improve results. *Improving R&D Performance the Juran Way* describes and illustrates the key principles, concepts, and practices needed to make TQM pay off in improved performance. I know these concepts and principles work because of my personal experience using them at Eastman.

I am convinced that using TQM properly to manage/lead an R&D organization will in the long run provide a competitive advantage over those not using TQM or using it improperly. Reading and applying the lessons, principles, and concepts discussed in this book can accelerate your journey for successfully using TQM to significantly improve the performance of your R&D organization. It should also help you avoid some of the frustrations, costs, and wasted time that we at Eastman experienced before we got on the right track.

Jerry D. Holmes
(retired 1/1/97)
Vice President R&D
Eastman Chemical Company

PREFACE

The genesis of this book occurred while I was working as a vice president at Juran Institute. The Institute had been receiving an increasing number of queries and requests relative to materials and workshops on applying Dr. Juran's concepts within R&D environments. Although the Institute's database had a plethora of materials on traditional manufacturing examples and a significant number of examples from service and administrative applications, there was ample opportunity to enlarge the R&D "folder."

In order to expand our R&D folder and share the results, I proposed that we sponsor a symposium devoted to the discussion of applying TQM concepts, processes, and tools to improve R&D performance. The proposal was accepted, and much to my delight, I was given the assignment of "beating the bushes" to broaden our understanding of the most important subjects and lessons being learned.

During my introductory remarks to the first symposium, I mentioned that I truly believed that the presenters were pioneers who were developing and marking R&D quality trails for others to follow. With a few exceptions, the first symposium's papers tended to focus more on broad definitions and concepts (e.g., defining customers for R&D quality). This was particularly evident for the "R" papers. Some of the most useful early papers discussed why the R&D environment was different, and how those differences should be taken into account in *measuring* R&D quality and designing implementations strategies for *improving* R&D quality. With subsequent symposia came a natural evolution of papers reporting on the implementation of quality *systems* (e.g., Baldrige, ISO, and papers identifying the key R&D processes, measures, and *results*). The importance of reporting beneficial results cannot be overemphasized. Those papers not only *marked* the best trails, but also demonstrated the benefits achievable from *following* those trails.

The six years of symposia proceedings have provided an extraordinary basis for the design and completion of this work. Organization was aided by feedback from the symposia. The feedback helped identify those questions that were asked most frequently (e.g., "What is research quality?"). The feedback also helped identify those topics that were of the greatest interest, such as measuring and assessing R&D quality status. Correspondingly, the content has been significantly enriched from the real-world examples contained in the selected symposia papers or excerpts from those papers. The papers and the excerpts were chosen to provide *benchmark* examples of the development of the applications of the concepts, processes, and tools discussed throughout the book.

CHAPTER 1

HOW TO THINK ABOUT R&D QUALITY

R&D Is Key to Business

Driven by the need to decrease costs and cycle times, organizations have become increasingly focused on improving the performance of their key processes, such as product design, marketing, order processing, manufacturing, and customer service. These organizations recognize that the performance of core processes directly affects their ability to meet their goals for revenue growth, cost reduction, and increased market share. Analysis of organization strategies and business processes indicate that, in order to sustain their growth and profitability via product innovation, organizations must significantly improve their R&D processes. A survey by Hall and Associates (1996) concluded that "there is increasing emphasis in U.S. high-technology *product* companies to get R&D closer to the customer, and to have that R&D reflect the needs of the market. Processes for R&D in these companies are becoming increasingly focused on support of the business units of the company to stay ahead of the competition, be first to market where possible, and satisfying the customer. R&D and business strategies are becoming increasingly aligned, with the company CEO frequently playing an important role in R&D decisions."

Similarly, Roussel, Saad, and Erickson (1991) emphasized that to effectively manage third-generation R&D, organizations must align R&D's priorities with their business strategies. Aligning R&D with the company's overarching business strategy is achieved by identifying and assigning *strategic* goals to R&D, and regularly evaluating progress against the goals. The need to manage for R&D quality has therefore become a *strategic* issue rather than solely a process issue. In fact, strategies for improving R&D's effectiveness are being addressed globally. A *Wall Street Journal* article (Ascarelli, March 15, 1996) reported that European R&D labs' scientists are now required to think in terms of research projects' relevance to corporate strategies and their projected contributions to the bottom line. On the Eastern front, Uchimaru, Okanmoto, and Bunteru

(1993) discuss the opportunities and progress made in using TQM to improve NEC's IC Microcomputer Systems Corporation's design process.

Managing for Quality: The Road from Manufacturing to R&D

A handful of organizations have made significant progress in improving their overall performance by applying a quality management approach to their key processes. Many of the more successful organizations, such as AT&T, Federal Express, IBM, Motorola, and Xerox, have reported significant gains from utilizing the concepts, processes, and tools of Total Quality Management (TQM) in managing their entire organization.

Juran's (1974) original perspective of TQM was defined in the context of the *quality function,* where he used the term to identify "the entire collection of activities through which we achieve fitness for use, no matter where these activities are performed."

For a manufacturing organization, Juran depicted the quality function in his "Spiral of progress in quality" (Figure 1.1).

The Spiral demonstrates the progression of events throughout which quality must be managed to assure that the resultant products are "fit for use."[1]

The implementation of quality management systems in business evolved through several phases. At first, organizations initiated TQM by attacking the costs of the Spiral's relatively high volume processes in manufacturing or the backroom operations for financial services. Ad hoc quality improvement teams were trained to diagnose and remedy the causes of rework, scrap, warranty, and customer complaints. After recognizing the importance of managing process quality, increasing numbers of organizations assigned *permanent* process owners and teams to plan, control, and improve the company's core business processes.[2]

---

[1] It is useful to divide the research function on the Spiral into *market research,* focused on determining customers' needs, and *internal research,* focused on providing knowledge for developing new technologies and products. Both Sony's Walkman® and 3M's Post-it® notes originated from the ideas of individuals *within* the organizations. These two sources of product ideas are respectively defined as *market pull* and *technology push.*

[2] When the results of either the ad hoc or permanent team approach indicated that the *total* process needed to be replanned, the subsequent replanning activities gained notoriety under the banner of "process reengineering."

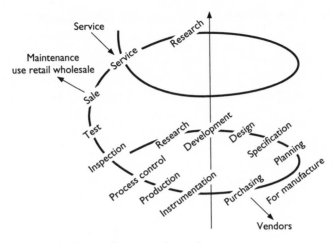

Figure 1.1   Juran's Spiral of progress in quality.

Improvements and lessons learned in key operations areas led to corresponding applications in high-volume *administrative and support* processes (e.g., order entry, invoicing, and accounts payable). Corresponding successes in these areas, combined with organizational strategies focused on enhancing revenues from *new* products, have led to a third phase of TQM implementation in the relatively low volume and long-lead-time processes of *research and development* (R&D). The early lessons learned from applying TQM to the downstream processes of manufacturing, distribution, and service have evolved to include upstream application to R&D.

Improvements stemming from managing for quality in R&D can be significant. Corning Laboratories saved $21 million over a four-year period while pushing out new products faster and with lower costs (Boath 1992). Eastman Chemical's Research Organization used TQM to double the net present value of new/improved product and process *concepts* accepted for commercialization (Holmes and McClaskey 1992). Shell's Development Company discussed an R&D quality improvement team that reduced the product development cycle by 12 months by improving Shell's research projects' requirements development process (Jenson and Morgan 1990). AT&T (Mayo 1994) reported that from 1991–1993 software development intervals for the 5ESS switching system were cut by 50 percent, with an associated tenfold decrease in faults found by customers.

Concepts Required for Managing R&D Quality

Before attempting to implement TQM into R&D organizations and departments, some fundamental concepts need to be discussed. Understanding these concepts is an important prerequisite for designing, developing, and implementing a TQM process tailored for R&D environments. The primary concepts are as follows:

1. R&D's mission
2. R&D's products
3. R&D's key processes
4. R&D's key customers
5. R&D quality

The Mission of Research and Development

To establish a common basis of understanding for managing R&D quality, it is useful to distinguish among various types of R&D. The Industrial Research Institute (IRI) (July 1996) has divided R&D into the following categories:

- *Basic or fundamental research* consisting of original experimental and/or theoretical investigations conducted to advance human knowledge in scientific and engineering fields.
- *Directed basic or exploratory research* for original scientific or technical work that advances knowledge in relevant (as applied to corporate business strategies) scientific and engineering fields or that creates useful concepts that can be subsequently developed into commercial materials, processes, or products and, thus, makes a contribution to the company's profitability some time in the foreseeable future. It may not respond directly to a specific problem or need, but it is selected and directed in those fields where advances will have a major impact on the company's future core businesses.
- *Applied research* for investigations directed toward obtaining specific knowledge related to existing or planned commercial products, processes, systems, or services.

IRI has defined *development* as "the translation of research findings or other knowledge into a plan or design for new, modified, or improved products/processes/services, whether intended for sale or use. It includes the conceptual formulation, design, and testing of product/process/service alternatives, the construction of prototypes, and the operation of initial, scaled-down systems or pilot plants."

Based upon these perspectives, and building from Roussel, Saad, and Erickson (1991), it will be helpful to think of *research* as the process used by an organization to acquire new scientific or technical information and knowledge, and *development* as the process used to apply technical or scientific information and knowledge for product or process designs required to meet the needs of the organization or its customers (Endres 1996).

These concepts are broad, but useful, and have been purposely designed to incorporate the word *process*. Juran (1992) has used the word *process* to mean a "systematic series of actions directed to the achievement of a goal."

One of the mandates of TQM is to focus on continuously improving key processes that result in products meeting the needs of internal and external customers. This directive will be used in our further discussions of the products and processes of R&D.

The Products of R&D

Juran (1992) has defined a product as "the output of any process," and noted that the word *product* can refer to either goods or services. All the previously listed definitions for research and development state that a final output of the R&D processes is *knowledge*.[3] The products of the research or the development processes may be either *final* or *intermediary* outputs. A final output of a research project is a report conveying the knowledge and information required to develop a promising technology.[4] Correspondingly, final outputs of the product development process are product and process specifications needed to proceed with full-scale manufacturing. A possible intermediate, or in-process, output of the research project is a formula, or calculations. Intermediate outputs of the development process would include models, prototypes, and pilot plants.

---

[3] Knowledge results from an understanding of the implications of information, and information results from the analysis and synthesis of data.

[4] *Technology* is defined by Roussel et al. as "the application of scientific and engineering knowledge to achieve a practical result."

Table 1.1   Differences between Manufacturing
and R&D Processes (Hooper 1990)

Manufacturing Processes	R&D Processes
Fast—short cycle time	Slow—long cycle time
Defined and visible	Poorly defined, opaque
Clear ownership, roles, responsibilities	Extend across organizations creating unclear ownership roles, responsibilities
Managed	Not managed
Process data collected	Little process data collected
Controlled	Control not maintained
Improvements pursued and implemented	Improvements slow and sporadic

The Processes of R&D

Table 1.1 (Hooper 1990) summarizes some important distinctions between typical manufacturing and R&D processes. To successfully implement TQM in R&D organizations, these distinctions must be understood and addressed.

Key Research Processes

In their work on improving Eastman Chemical Company's (ECC's) R&D processes, Holmes and McClaskey (1992) provided additional insights into R&D's products and processes. They also contributed valuable insights into defining key research *subprocesses* and their intermediary products. Figure 1.2 represents the total innovation process ECC uses to originate, develop, and commercialize ideas and concepts for new processes and products.

The first four steps of Figure 1.2 reflect the research subprocesses resulting in the "new/improved product and process concepts" in step 5. The last step of the process can be thought of as the macro-level development process that yields new or improved products or processes. After identifying the key outputs of their research process, Holmes and McClaskey (1994) focused on identifying and analyzing the "vital few" subprocesses that had the "most potential for improving the performance of research's major outputs." The vital few subprocesses that they identified and improved were as follows:

1. Needs validation and revalidation (including prioritization)
2. Interaction with business units (project status reviews)

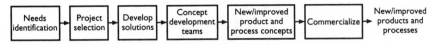

Figure 1.2   Eastman Chemical Company's innovation process.

3. Concept development (including project management)
4. Technology transfer (including commercialization focus and follow-through)

Figure 1.3 (Holmes and McClaskey 1994, updated for 1996) demonstrates the benefits ECC enjoyed as a result of improving these key subprocesses. The net present value of new/improved product and process *concepts* originating from ECC research more than doubled.

Phased Technology and Product Development Process

Juran's Spiral of progress (1974, 1992) is useful to portray the general progression of events and the cast of characters in the product development process. Many organizations have also used what is generally called the *phase concept* to model and control the Spiral's progression of events. A phased product development process is used to divide the Spiral's activities into several phases or

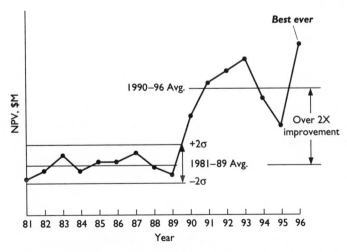

Figure 1.3   Estimated value of new/improved product and process concepts.

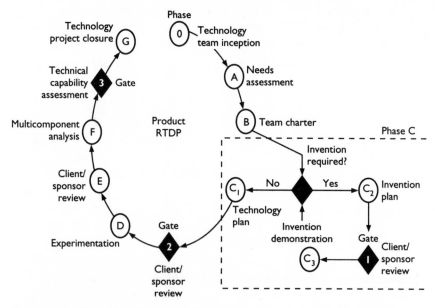

Figure 1.4 Kodak's robust technology development process for product technologies.

stages. At the end of each phase, the project must pass through technical and business reviews (referred to as *gates*) that are conducted to determine if sufficient progress has been made to proceed to the next phase.[5] Altland (1995) of Kodak discussed how the phased concept is used to develop *robust technologies* that are "relatively insensitive to factors that cannot be eliminated or controlled—and which are less likely to cause problems late in product commercialization." Kodak has named this phased process its *robust technology development process* (RTDP). Figure 1.4 and Table 1.2 explain Kodak's RTDP for new product technologies.[6]

Hammer and Champy (1993) recognized that Kodak improved its product development process through implementing CAD/CAM (computer-aided design/manufacturing) and an associated integrated product design database. The database enabled engineers to communicate current design status and pre-

[5] Juran and Gryna (1993) discuss the use of the "early warning concept" (e.g., design reviews and prototype testing for controlling the product design process).

[6] Altland (1995) also references a similar model for *process* technologies.

Table 1.2 Phases and Gates for Kodak's Robust Technology Development Process for Products

Phase/Gate	Description
Phase 0 Technology team Inception—product	Description of what must occur before RTDP teams are formed.
Phase A Needs assessment	Customer, consumer, client needs translated into technology needs. A justification document prepared.
Phase B Team charter	Product technology team defined. Leader designated. Leader selects team members. Team appropriately staffed and funded.
Phase C Technology/invention plan	C1—Technology Plan. Product technology and what it is addressing described and development issues addressed. C2—Invention Plan. Invention concept
Gate 1 Client/sponsor review	document prepared. Commitment to the invention plan sought.
Phase C—continued	C3—Invention Demonstration. Implement invention plan. C1—Technology Plan. Complete technology plan.
Gate 2 Client/sponsor review	Commitment to technology plan sought; includes the decision makers for Gate 3.
Phase D Experimentation	Experiments performed to identify which technologies to be developed for TCA (Gate 3).
Phase E Client/sponsor review	Technical status review. Needs, priorities, and team focus reviewed.
Phase F Multicomponent analysis	Team determines how various new technologies and other product components fit together.
Gate 3 Technology capability assessment (TCA)	The technology demonstrated to be robust to meet needs. Is documented and ready for commercialization through Kodak materials commercialization process.
Phase G Technology project closure	Implementation and documentation of technology reviewed and, if appropriate, technology project closed.

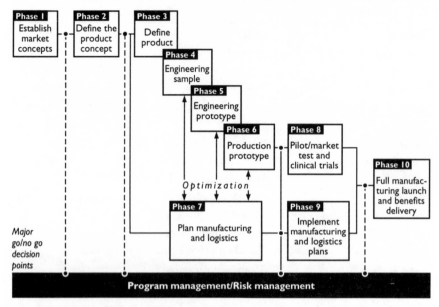

Figure 1.5 A redesigned product development process.

vent or resolve potential design problems. Concurrent engineering was used to nearly halve the time (from a typical 70 weeks to 38 weeks) Kodak needed to go from concept to production of its first single-use 35-millimeter camera and thus effectively respond to Fuji's 1987 single-use camera announcement.

Boath (1993) presented the results shown in Figure 1.5 for a reengineering project to redesign an organization's product development process. The redesigned process contained ten phases, four "major" gates, and resulted in a 25 percent increase in the efficiency of the organization's resource utilization.

R&D's Customers

Juran (1992) defined a *customer* as "anyone who is impacted by the product or process." He further stratified customers into external and internal customers, where *external customers* are those affected by the product (or process[7]) but

---

[7] Customers are most likely to be immediately affected by delivery operations in service environments (e.g., ATM customers are concerned for their safety, or fast-food customers are concerned with courtesy and cleanliness).

Table 1.3 R&D's
Customers (Darby 1990)

Internal	External
Manufacturing	Direct customer
Marketing	Customer's customer
Business unit	
Corporation	

who are not members of the organization that provides the product, and *internal customers* are those effected by the product (or process) and who also are members of the organization that provides the product.

In concert with these concepts, Darby (1990) of Du Pont stated that "R&D has at least as many customers as any other function. . . . Internal customers are just that—customers. It serves no useful purpose for R&D to look at them in any other way. . . . From my experience, our (R&D's) internal Du Pont customers are at least as hard-nosed and demanding as external customers, and usually for good reason." Table 1.3 is Darby's list of R&D's major internal and external customers.

In Table 1.4, Shipley (1991) of Dow Chemical summarizes R&D's respective responsibilities and needs in its roles as a supplier and customer to its "vital few" internal customers: manufacturing and commercial (sales).

Table 1.4 R&D's Internal
Customer/Supplier Relationships (Shipley 1991)

	R&D Interaction As	
	Customer	Supplier
Commercial	Marketing data	Finished projects and products
	Market focus/direction	Technology focus
	Funding	
Manufacturing	Scale-up site	Process support
	Finished product	Technology improvements
	Process capabilities	

Defining R&D Quality

Du Pont (Darby 1990) has defined *quality R&D* as "creating, anticipating, and meeting customer requirements." Hooper (1990) at AT&T's Bell Laboratories, an R&D powerhouse, defined quality as "the degree to which a product or service meets evolving customer expectations. Quality includes cost, performance, and timely availability." According to Wiley (1993) of Battelle's Memorial Institute, "In addition to creativity, innovation, and conformance to the scientific process, quality means meeting our customers' needs, creating a supportive working environment, and improving efficiency."

A general definition of quality is provided by Juran and Gryna (1993), who have defined quality goods and services as those that are "fit for use." Juran (1992) has suggested that fitness for use be determined from two primary dimensions: product features and freedom from deficiencies.

- *Product features* are inherent product properties that are intended to meet certain customer needs, and thereby result in *customer satisfaction.*
- *Product deficiencies* are product failures that produce *customer dissatisfaction.*

Research Quality

Research quality can be defined from both the perspective of customer satisfaction with the knowledge and information the products or services provide, and the absence of associated deficiencies. General Electric (Garfinkel 1990) has defined four features of research quality:

- *Technical quality:* Conformance to good research practices
- *Impact:* "Game changer" versus incremental
- *Business relevance*
- *Timeliness:* Early or late relative to the targeted market release.

Godfrey (1991) views the general features of quality as it pertains to information as timeliness, completeness, usability, and accuracy. (An additional important dimension of information quality is its cost.)

Research product deficiencies result in customer dissatisfaction (and increased costs). The previously defined product of research is the information and knowledge that enable technology, process, and product development. Deficiencies can occur in either the research process or its final products. Deficiencies in the research *process* require process rework or scrap (e.g., having to reissue a progress report because of a wrong formula, or scrapping the results of an experiment because an investigation of aberrant results revealed that laboratory equipment was not properly calibrated). Examples of final research product deficiencies include information and knowledge that are late, inaccurate, or don't provide the information required by sponsors.

Process Quality for Development

The development process results in new or improved product and process designs. *Development process quality* can be thought of as the extent to which the features of the resulting products and processes reflect the customers' and organization's needs and are capable of meeting targeted design goals (e.g., for cycle times, cost, process capability, or product reliability).

When defining product requirements, it is beneficial to think of product and process features from the perspective of Juran's (1992) "Big Q." Big Q thinking occurs when the needs of not only end users, but individuals, organizations, or communities potentially affected by the products or processes are addressed. For example, Port (1996) discusses the growing importance of environmentally friendly products and processes. In Germany, regulators are compelling designers to provide product features that meet the requirement for manufacturers to accept all packaging returned after use in product transport. (Port also references a requirement in the Netherlands for manufacturers to accept old or broken appliances for recycling.)

Deficiencies in the development process are problems occurring either during or at the end of the process that require rework or scrap. Examples include early design changes required because of missing or incomplete design requirements documents, and having to totally change a design concept that manufacturing, during a design review, reported would be too expensive to produce.

Perry and Westwood (1991) reflect similar perspectives of process quality in development. They report that "measures of the quality of the product of the [development] process include meeting technical targets, i.e., meeting specific process capability targets . . . [and] the percent and degree of customer needs that are met, and the number of problems discovered at various stages of the product development process."

Implementing TQM in R&D: Avoiding Common Barriers and Errors

Having discussed the concepts required for managing R&D quality, it is important to anticipate common barriers and errors that prevent successful TQM

Table 1.5 Cultural and
Organizational Barriers to Quality
Improvement in R&D (Hooper 1990)

Cultural Barriers	Organizational Barriers
Arrogance	Strong hierarchical management (structure)
Self-image and values	Insulated from customers and the business
Independent	Manage the "whats" but not the "hows"
Creative	No responsibility for quality improvement
Unique	
Never fail	
Belief that technology solves all problems	
Belief in large-scale versus incremental improvements	

implementation. It is equally, if not more, important to understand how organizations have successfully addressed these challenges.

Common Barriers to TQM Implementation

Hooper (1990) has provided a list of barriers to quality improvement in R&D encountered during AT&T's introduction of TQM concepts at AT&T's Bell Laboratories. Table 1.5 lists both cultural and organizational barriers discussed by Hooper.

Similar TQM implementation barriers are associated with researchers' predilections for being team-adverse, fearing perceived quality controls, and loathing creativity-stifling bureaucracy (Endres [1992]). Mizuno (1989) stated that "research and development people tend to scorn quality control because they believe research requires inspiration, and inspiration is not to be had in the midst of standardized, organized, and regulated control activities. . . ." However, Mizuno then counters these positions by stating that "the collection and analysis of data to spark the individual's inspiration" must be done "efficiently and effectively." Hence, training researchers to more efficiently design experiments and analyze data can help them maximize the information and knowledge gained from each experiment. Mizuno also proposes that an "individual who participates in a group effort to solve a problem finds the interplay of ideas stimulates him to be more creative."

Common Implementation Errors

Common errors of upper managers and quality professionals who attempt to introduce TQM into research organizations are as follows:

- Not relating TQM to the organization's mission
- Introducing arcane language or TQM-speak
- Delegating and disappearing[8]

It is therefore valuable to discuss how these pitfalls can be avoided.

Focusing TQM on the Mission of R&D

Introducing TQM into any R&D organization should focus on helping the organization fulfill its mission. Eastman Chemical's Research organization (1992) has defined its mission as follows: "Provide new and improved product and process concepts which will better satisfy customer needs and better fulfill ECC's strategic and business objectives."

ECC used this goal to focus their TQM initiatives on those processes that would improve the net present value of new and improved product and process concepts.

A resultant goal of applying TQM to a research organization is the improved availability of resources needed by research managers and specialists to complete projects linked to their company's mission. An international petroleum company addressed this requirement by asking its researchers to identify what they considered to be the barriers preventing them from conducting and completing more useful research. Similarly, Corning's initial research projects addressed problems researchers were having in procuring laboratory equipment and filling requisitions for research assistants. These types of pilot projects can provide relevant answers to researcher's questions of "What's in it for me?" and help allay fears of stifling creativity.

---

[8] The author was first introduced to this phrase during a consulting assignment in Canada. Canada's analogue to the U.S. Department of Defense (DOD) is the Department of National Defense (DND). When asked what DND meant, the troops responded, "Delegate 'n disappear."

Speaking the Language of R&D

Improving the processes and products of research and development can be facilitated by communicating and training in the language of the research organization. According to Shear (1991) at the Brookhaven National Laboratory:

> *Quality assurance professionals are now attempting to bring our message to the research scientist, and like many zealous missionaries we are trying to impose our own dogma and language while ignoring the existing culture. As a result, we are misunderstood and resented, and in our innocent zeal we wonder why. Those of us who have gone through this type of rejection have a tendency to blame the "uninformed" without really trying to understand the basic reasons.*
>
> *There is also a tendency on the part of many practitioners not to take the human aspect of quality assurance into account. Since we are the ones who are entering into what may be considered foreign territory for us to try to sell our ideas, it behooves us to try to learn the language and terminology of the people who inhabit that territory. We should communicate in terms that are familiar to the people we are trying to convince. We should not try to force the quality assurance terminology developed in industry on researchers.*

An example of TQM-speak that researchers have found particularly grating is the use of banners and other paraphernalia that exhort "Do it right the first time!" Although in manufacturing and service operations, the "it" is usually well defined, in R&D the "it" and the value of "it" must often be discovered. Both scientists and engineers are more likely to relate to the objective of conducting R&D by utilizing the scientific method and proven processes for project management.

Providing Resources and Support

In any organization, the success of a TQM implementation is directly linked to its executives and managers understanding, and then meeting, their responsibilities in managing for quality. These responsibilities include the following:

- Receiving and providing TQM training
- Assessing the status of quality
- Defining and deploying quality goals
- Prioritizing TQM projects
- Providing project support

- Reviewing progress[9]
- Providing reward and recognition

This list is certainly not unique to R&D organizations. Juran (1989) provides a similar task list for upper managers. Each of the responsibilities is necessary for the success of a quality initiative. Juran (1990) stated that "I am unable to point to a single instance in which stunning results were gotten without the active and personal leadership of the upper managers."

The following chapters will provide further insights into these responsibilities. These insights reflect the experience and research of the author, as well as the terrain traversed by multiple pioneers who have generously shared their experiences (both good and bad) in papers that contain the lessons learned from implementing the concepts, processes, and tools of TQM into R&D.[10]

---

[9] An executive at the "cutting edge" of R&D progress reviews is Alfred Zeien, chairman and chief executive of Gillette. *Investor's Business Daily* (1995) reported that to assess the potential for Gillette's Sensor razor for women, Zeien used it to shave his face and the back of his hands.

[10] These papers were presented at Juran Institute's *Symposia on Managing for Quality in Research and Development,* which were organized and chaired by the author.

CHAPTER 2

ORGANIZING FOR QUALITY IN R&D

The Need for Organization

Understanding the benefits of improving R&D quality is one thing. Starting and sustaining an R&D quality process is another. The continued success of any quality initiative requires *organization* (e.g., councils, teams) and *processes* for planning, problem solving, reviewing, and rewarding progress. The need for developing organization and support processes was defined by Cole (1990) at Kodak, who stated, "... the management team must develop the vision, strategic direction, and goals. They must develop leadership, *organizational structure,* and the environment for innovation to allow the people to meet the goals. This includes *processes* for customer interface and for the linking of the technical strategy to the business strategy." Figure 2.1, from Juran Institute's (1991) TQM implementation "road map" contains the two primary subject areas for this chapter: organizational infrastructure and pilot projects.

The Role of Upper Managers

As discussed in Chapter 1, to improve R&D quality, upper management must understand how to think about R&D quality. R&D upper management must also understand their roles and responsibilities in improving R&D quality. A primary responsibility of R&D senior management is to ensure that organizational elements and processes for initiating, expanding, and sustaining R&D quality are designed, developed, and implemented. Juran (1990) called this framework an "infrastructure for improvement." Elements of this infrastructure are as follows[1]:

---

[1] During the start-up phase, these elements are typically treated as separate tasks required to manage quality. However, after reviewing and acting upon the results of the initial projects, these elements must be integrated with ongoing business planning and operations. They must become viewed as a part of the "way we do business."

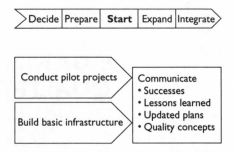

Figure 2.1   Activities for starting TQM (from Juran Institute's TQM road map).

1. A quality council to assess quality status, establish goals, and track progress
2. A process for identifying and prioritizing projects
3. Teams to tackle the projects
4. Facilitators[2] to support the teams
5. Training (facilitators, team leaders, team members, and individuals)
6. A scorecard of measures for determining R&D quality status[3]
7. A process for *communicating* plans, goals, and progress
8. A process for recognizing and rewarding teams and individuals meeting quality goals[4]

The Role of Middle Managers

After upper managers define the priorities for a quality infrastructure, middle managers must design, implement, communicate, and support the priorities. Middle managers' support is required in the following ways:

1. Serving on task forces for developing plans and procedures for
   a. The total quality initiative
   b. Elements of quality infrastructure

---

[2] The paper by Konosz and Ice (1991) of Alcoa's Technical Center, which describes the responsibilities, selection, and training of facilitators in an R&D environment, is included at the end of this chapter.

[3] Chapter 3 discusses the development and use of quality measures for R&D.

[4] Chapter 3 also provides discussion on measuring individuals' contributions to R&D quality.

2. Nominating projects (pilot and follow-on)
3. Screening project nominations
4. Participating on quality teams
5. Supporting their employees' training; participation on teams

Since middle managers often represent the largest source of resistance to quality initiatives,[5] obtaining and rewarding their input and participation is essential to the success of quality in R&D. Middle-management support can be obtained through several strategies:

1. Start with volunteers.
2. Select pilot projects that will provide visible benefits to middle managers.
3. Recognize and reward (R&R) exemplary participation and support.
4. Mandate participation as a required element of job responsibility.[6]

This chapter will provide examples of how upper and middle R&D managers have developed and supported the infrastructure required to manage R&D quality.

Councils and "White-Space" Management

Managing for quality in R&D requires the orchestration of multifunctional processes. Figure 2.2 was excerpted and presented by Cole (1990) to demonstrate the multifunctional flows in Kodak's R&D planning process.

The top row of boxes identifies the participants in the process. Experience has shown the multiple organizational handoffs in such processes are breeding grounds for problems. Rummler and Brache (1995) have referred to these troublesome handoff points as the *white spaces* of the organization.

To manage the white spaces, Kodak developed an organizational architecture of interlocking councils. Figure 2.3 was presented by Cole as Kodak's organizational structure responsible for "planning R&D, linking plans to business activity, and defining the improvement processes used by the R&D community worldwide."

[5] Main (1994), in *Quality Wars,* has a section titled "The Forgotten Player: The Middle Manager," which provides lessons learned from Southern Pacific Railroad and Motorola in excluding and including managers in their quality initiatives.

[6] Irrespective of start-up strategy, the last two elements, R&R and mandatory participation, are critical success factors for the perpetuation of any quality process.

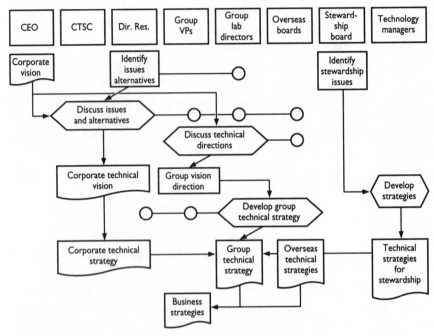

Figure 2.2 Flowchart (partial) of Kodak's R&D planning process (1990).

Research organizations have developed analogous interlocking councils to coordinate the processes and projects that cut across multiple research departments. Figure 2.4 from Holmes and McClaskey (1992) is an example of the organizational architecture developed at Eastman Chemical Company's research organization.

Menger (1993) discussed how Corning's World Class Quality (WCQ) committee oversees the quality process implementation within its technology group. (Corning's technology group includes research, development, and engineering functions.)

> This committee is comprised of high-level executives from the organization.
> Twice a year, this group visits each of the 15 units in the Technology Group to
> review the key results indicators,[7] to assess progress against their stated objec-

---

[7] *Key results indicators* (KRIs) are defined as "those four or five areas where improvement could have the greatest impact."

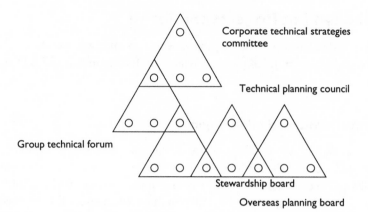

Figure 2.3 Kodak's interlocking R&D planning and improvement structure (1990).

tives, and to discuss plans to improve on those Key Results Indicators where little progress has been evidenced. The WCQ fosters cooperation among the units so that the best ideas of each can be shared. Each unit receives feedback from the WCQ committee on an individual unit basis before the sharing session so the "best of breed" practices are clearly identified.

Taylor and Jule (1991) of Westinghouse's Savannah River Laboratory provided further insights into how quality councils can be used to integrate quality goals into an R&D organization's annual business plan. Their paper (see page 25) also provides a good example of a strategy for involving middle managers in integrating business and quality planning.

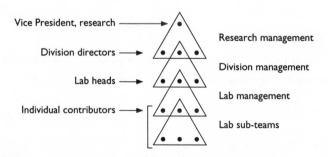

Figure 2.4 Eastman Chemical Company's research organization's structure.

Selecting Pilot Projects and Teams

Chapter 1 discussed the use of project teams to improve operations quality. Juran's project-by-project approach is also useful for initiating R&D quality improvement.

Identifying Potential Pilot Projects

Concurrently with the development of quality infrastructure, it is important to choose, initiate, and successfully conclude some pilot projects. The purpose of the pilot projects is to demonstrate that the quality process works in R&D and that it can produce significant benefits. Another objective for the pilot projects is to learn how to improve training methods and management support to preclude premature infrastructure standardization and expansion.

Juran (1989) provides the following criteria for selecting *pilot* quality improvement projects:

1. They should represent chronic problem areas.
2. They should be bite-size (i.e., highly likely to be successful after a team has worked on the problem for three to six months[8]).
3. They should be recognized as being significant.
4. The results can be easily measured in terms of both money and technology.

Another useful criterion for pilot-project selection is that both the diagnosis of the problems' causes and their likely remedies can be conducted and implemented totally within the organization (research). This guideline is useful for avoiding likely delays associated with obtaining resources and support from outside functions.

Classifying the Projects

Before the council finalizes the selection of pilot projects, it must review the project list to identify the most likely type of team required for each of the

Continued on page 37

[8] Most organizations have organized teams whose members average three to six hours per week on project-related assignments. Other organizations have formed "blitz teams" whose members work full-time on the pilot projects.

Implementing Total Quality at Savannah River Laboratory

Dr. Dennis H. Taylor
Senior Total Quality Process Specialist
Westinghouse Savannah River Company
Aiken, South Carolina

Dr. Willard E. Jule
Manager, Quality Resource Section
Westinghouse Savannah River Company
Aiken, South Carolina

Abstract

The cornerstone of the Total Quality (TQ) effort is a partnership between the laboratory Quality Council, composed of the laboratory director and his department heads, and the Quality Resource Section, comprising a total quality manager and a team of total quality resources, one for each department head. The Quality Council provides the line management champions for quality improvement, while the Quality Resource Section provides the TQ know-how. Working together, these groups develop an annual Quality Improvement Plan. Each Council member chooses a quality "area of emphasis" to sponsor for the coming year and develops a plan to address the issues within that area of emphasis assisted by his departmental total quality resource. Information on the morale of the laboratory and quality issues that need addressing is provided to the Quality Council by the Quality Resource Section.

Critical to the operation of these two groups are information gathering systems such as Total Quality Fitness Reviews (a Westinghouse-developed measurement instrument), continuous Total Quality skills training, and accountability through effective indicators and measures.

Introduction

The Savannah River Laboratory, referred to as SRL, is one of many Divisions comprising the Westinghouse Savannah River Company, contractor to the

U.S. Department of Energy for the Savannah River Site. The Savannah River Site, known as the "Site," is part of the nuclear weapons complex owned by the U.S. Department of Energy. The Site covers approximately 300 square miles along the Savannah River in South Carolina and employs in excess of 25,000 people. The Savannah River Laboratory, SRL, supports the operations of the Site in the areas of Reactor operation, waste processing and environmental remediation. It has approximately 1400 employees, consisting of scientists, engineers and support personnel. There is a Site-wide total quality effort, but this paper only describes the TQ activities at SRL.

The cornerstone of the Total Quality (TQ) effort at the SRL is a partnership between the laboratory Quality Council, composed of the Laboratory Director and his department heads, and the Quality Resource Section (QRS) comprising a total quality manager and a team of total quality resources. Working together, these groups develop and implement an annual Quality Improvement Plan for SRL that is a principal element in developing a TQ culture within the Laboratory.

The 1991 SRL Quality Improvement Plan described in this paper is the second annual QIP developed for SRL and has drawn heavily on lessons learned from the 1990 QIP. The 1991 SRL Quality Improvement Plan envisions Total Quality as a business strategy. It does not envision achieving a Total Quality culture by focusing on training in TQ principles and processes per se. Rather it focuses on making improvements in our key business activities using TQ principles and processes. As recognizable success is continuously achieved a TQ culture will automatically follow.

This business focus is crucial to implementing the QIP. It is the department managers who must implement the plan. Often in trying to create a total quality culture resistance is met at the manager level. The reasons underlying this resistance commonly include: (1) managers do not see that spending time and effort with TQ enhances their performance rating; (2) they do not view TQ as an effective business strategy, but rather as a program imposed upon them that increases their administrative load and keeps them from "getting on" with their "real" work; (3) they do not understand TQ principles and processes or know how to use them to create improvement in their own performance as well as that of their organization.

These three reasons are interrelated, of course. If managers felt upper management seriously expected them to learn about and use TQ, they would willingly do it in order to enhance their performance rating. But, as they infused TQ into their business practices and realized increasing success, they would appreciate that TQ is an effective business strategy that can improve their performance of "real" work and increase their career opportunities.

At SRL the above three reasons for resistance have been addressed through the process for developing the QIP. Successful implementation of an annual QIP by the department managers year after year will lead to strong acceptance of TQ by the managers and a strong TQ culture among the employees themselves. Therefore, the thrust of the QIP development process is to help the managers achieve success through implementing the QIP.

The elements of the QIP process are depicted in Figure 2.5. There are three principal elements: The Quality Council, which provides the line authority to *do* total quality; the Quality Resource Section, which provides the *how* to do TQ; and the supporting information systems used to help management select the *what* to target for improvement, i.e., what are some of the critical business needs. These elements are explained in more detail below.

Structure of the Quality Council and Quality Resource Section

SRL Quality Council

- Chairman
    Laboratory Director (level 1 manager)
- Members
    Department heads (level 2 managers, Laboratory Director's
        direct reports). At Savannah River Laboratory there are six
        departments.
    Two senior research fellows
- Secretary
    Laboratory Total Quality Manager who is also manager of the
        Quality Resource Section.

Department/Section Quality Councils

- Chairperson
    Department/section manager

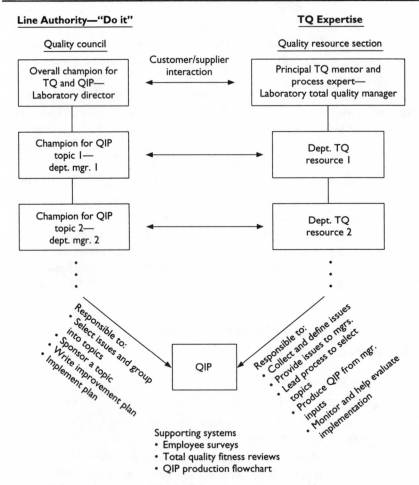

Line Authority—"Do it"

Quality council

Overall champion for
TQ and QIP—
Laboratory director

Customer/supplier
interaction

Champion for QIP
topic 1—
dept. mgr. 1

Champion for QIP
topic 2—
dept. mgr. 2

TQ Expertise

Quality resource section

Principal TQ mentor and
process expert—
Laboratory total quality manager

Dept. TQ
resource 1

Dept. TQ
resource 2

Responsible to:
• Select issues and group into topics
• Sponsor a topic
• Write improvement plan
• Implement plan

QIP

Responsible to:
• Collect and define issues
• Provide issues to mgrs.
• Lead process to select topics
• Produce QIP from mgr. inputs
• Monitor and help evaluate implementation

Supporting systems
• Employee surveys
• Total quality fitness reviews
• QIP production flowchart

Figure 2.5   Development of the SRL quality improvement plan.

■ Members
    Department/section staff
■ Although not specifically described in this paper, these quality
    councils function in relation to their departments and sections in
    the same way that the SRL Quality Council functions in relation
    to the laboratory as a whole.

Quality Resource Section

- Manager
  - Personal TQ resource to Laboratory Director
  - TQ resource to Quality Council as a body
  - Mentor to departmental and sectional TQ resources
  - Laboratory Total Quality Manager. As such he is the laboratory representative on the Site-wide council of Total Quality Managers led by the Site Total Quality Process Department.
  - Selection criteria: highly motivated toward TQ; exceptional people skills; experienced manager; good grasp of TQ principles, processes and practices
- Senior Total Quality Specialist
  - Full-time in TQ activities
  - Reports directly to the QRS manager
  - Degreed, technical background
  - Selection criteria: expressed desire; demonstrated aptitude in people skills and TQ process knowledge
- Departmental TQ Resources
  - Full-time
  - Non-exempt (fortuitously all women)
  - One assigned for each department manager
  - Functionally report to QRS Manager and interact directly with department managers
  - Administratively supervised by the department they were selected from, which may or may not be the department they serve as a TQ resource
  - Selection criteria: expressed desire; demonstrated aptitude in people skills; willingness to accept responsibility; willingness to accept criticism (not always constructive) by others and to engage in intense self-improvement activities; demonstrated TQ attitude
- Sectional TQ Resources
  - Some large departments have TQ resources assigned for the next administrative division, called sections.
  - Not full-time

Chosen from within the section they serve and interact directly with the section manager

Within their section, they function the same way as the departmental TQ resources

Quality Council

Role of the Laboratory Director

Having a strong TQ champion at the Director level is critical to developing a total quality culture in any environment, but perhaps more so in an R&D environment where traditional thinking asserts that R&D is different than manufacturing. The Laboratory Director has provided strong championship of total quality in two forms: leadership and management of the QIP process. As a leader, the Director has firmly established that TQ is a critical business strategy at SRL. His philosophy is that R&D is essentially similar to manufacturing: both have customers, and both have processes that TQ principles and tools can help improve.

The Director has continually asserted to his managers and everyone else in SRL that "Total Quality is not an addition to our work, it is the way we *do* our work. We use TQ because it works. It is nothing more than good scientific practice. Our goal is to use TQ practices in all our activities. Implementation of the SRL Quality Improvement Plan is the key step in achieving our goal." As emphasis to this theme, he continually asks project leaders a simple question, "Can you use a TQ process to improve the efficiency or effectiveness of this project?" This single question alone has resulted in several significant process improvements.

As a manager of the process, the Director commissioned the Quality Council. He chartered a team to prepare the QIP and organized a meeting of the Quality Council with the QIP team to review TQ progress from the past year and select topical areas for improvement in the coming year based on employee input gathered by the QIP preparation team. Each Department Manager was requested to act as sponsor for one of the topical areas and to write an improvement plan to address the issues included within that topical area by the Quality Council. These improvement plans were compiled by the QIP team into the SRL QIP. During the preparation of the QIP, the Director held several follow-up meetings with the Quality Council to check on their progress in preparing their plans.

As mentioned earlier many total quality efforts falter because managers do not perceive that engaging in TQ will matter to their performance rating. However, at SRL, the Laboratory Director has sent the message that managers on the Quality Council will be held accountable for their participation in TQ.

Role of the Department Manager on the Quality Council

The department managers meet to review the status of TQ at the laboratory and to select critical issues for the next year's QIP from among the issues gathered by the QIP preparation team. They organize these issues into broad topics and then assign themselves as a sponsor for one of the topics. As a sponsor, they develop a quality improvement plan for the issues within their topic and implement this plan throughout the laboratory during the year. The individual topic plans are combined to form the SRL QIP. Therefore, implementing the QIP is implementing their plans not someone else's. The department managers also have the responsibility to develop quality improvement plans within their own departments and to identify, recognize and reward TQ efforts by their employees.

Quality Council members have accepted responsibility for developing and implementing the QIP. By being responsible for the content of the QIP plan, the department managers assure that the effort they expend in TQ is directed at helping them do their "real" work.

Quality Resource Section

Role of TQ Manager

Equal in importance to the Laboratory Director in developing the Quality Improvement Plan is the Total Quality Manager. The TQ manager has taken the time to acquire extensive knowledge of TQ principles, processes and practices and has actively applied all these in his role as manager of the Quality Resource Section. As a result, the Quality Resource Section has become a model TQ culture and an effective training ground for the Total Quality resources.

An important product arising out of this QRS in-house training is the customer/supplier interaction shown in Figure 2.5. Acting as suppliers to the Laboratory Director and the department managers, the Total Quality Manager and departmental TQ resources supply the Quality Council with information and training on TQ ideas, tools, and management style—sharing the experience and success they have already achieved through having developed an effective, state-of-the-art TQ culture in the QRS. They also provide feedback on the progress of TQ implementation, effective guidance for team problem solving and support for all TQ activities in the departments. An important question each resource constantly asks of his manager/customer is, "What can I do for your success?"

In return, the manager, acting as a supplier to his resource/customer tells them what his business needs are, gives feedback on the effectiveness of help and training they have provided, recognizes and appreciates their efforts, and supports them in their continuing development as TQ resources.

The TQ Manager holds weekly four-hour training meetings with the TQ resources in which they build team spirit, share learnings and develop skills.

Role of Departmental TQ Resources

The TQ resources provide assistance throughout their assigned departments. In addition to the service to the department managers already mentioned, the TQ resources serve TQ functions for the laboratory as a whole and occasionally for the entire site. Help provided to the site includes production of site-wide TQ related conferences and teaching personal development classes. To enhance TQ awareness and expertise at SRL they also conduct monthly TQ one-hour training meetings for interested employees.

Role of the Senior TQ Specialist

A key role of the TQ specialist is to continually search for new TQ ideas and applications. He evaluates these and brings those with high potential for improving the SRL TQ effort back to the QRS. He acts as a mentor to the TQ resources and serves as a process consultant to task teams working on laboratory-wide improvement projects. He also serves as SRL representative to many TQ related committees and initiatives around the Site to ensure that SRL contributes to and remains in harmony with Site-wide TQ efforts.

QIP Information Systems

Total Quality Fitness Reviews (TQFR)

A total quality fitness review is a development of the Westinghouse Corporate Productivity and Quality Center in Pittsburgh. A TQFR is a total quality culture audit performed on an organization by a team consisting of one or two total quality experts from the Productivity and Quality Center and three or four other Westinghouse employees, some from other divisions at the Site, and some from other Westinghouse companies. The fitness review is voluntary and the results, in the form of identification of strengths and recommendations for improvements, are non-binding. They are also confidential to the requesting organization. However, because the review provides such a comprehensive picture of the business effectiveness of the organization, most managers welcome the recommendations and use them as the basis for their own quality improvement plans.

The fitness review lasts one week. For the first three days, each member of the review team interviews from six to seven employees per day. Interviewees are a mix from all levels of the organization. The interview itself is structured around the Twelve Conditions of Excellence upon which the Westinghouse total quality effort is based. These twelve conditions are customer orientation, employee participation, employee development, employee motivation, total quality of products and services, total quality in processes and procedures, quality of information and information systems, effective interaction with suppliers, TQ culture (knowledge of TQ principles, processes and practices), TQ in strategic and financial planning, effective communications, accountability (effective use of measures for total quality).

On the fourth day, the review team consolidates its findings and recommendations and prepares its report. On the fifth day the team presents its report to management and supervision of the organization. As part of this report, the review team compares its TQ fitness score with the self-assessment score the organization made of itself prior to the arrival of the TQFR team. Differences between the TQFR score and the self-assessment score as well as any of the findings and recommendations are discussed for understanding and clarity.

SRL-Wide Total Quality Employee Survey

This survey was designed to evaluate the TQ status of the laboratory in five areas: (1) customer orientation; (2) employee knowledge of TQ principles; (3) employee work ethic; (4) TQ work environment, i.e., the extent to which people, processes or systems exist that help or hinder implementing improvements in our work; (5) Culture to enable change in the work environment as needed.

For SRL the results of this survey revealed that employees generally had a strong desire to please their customers, a good knowledge of TQ principles, and a strong desire to do quality work. However, employees strongly felt that they were prevented from doing their best work by the people, processes and systems of the work environment and that they were powerless to bring about beneficial change in the work environment.

An important finding on customer orientation was as follows. Although most employees knew their customers, barely half felt that their customers expectations had been clearly communicated to them and barely half had asked their customers what aspect of their work needed improvement in order to meet the customers needs. Moreover, barely a third of employees had asked their customer if there were aspects of the products or services they were providing to their customers that were non-value-added. The anomaly is that in spite of this lack of effective communication with their customers, 84% of employees felt they normally do satisfy their customer's expectations and 86% said they look for ways to give customers more than they asked for.

Based on the results of this survey, the TQFR results and many other information sources the 1991 QIP has focused strongly on improving customer/supplier communication, on removing barriers to effective work and on creating the culture to more easily implement changes and improvements.

Organization of the QIP

Each section of the QIP was organized as follows to respond to the input provided by employees.

- Needs/issues
    What are the needs and issues being responded to in this section that we at SRL identified?
- Actions
    What actions are being taken to address those needs and issues?
- What you (the employee) can expect
    As a result of these actions, you should see the following changes.
- What you (the employee) can do
    In addition to the actions being taken by the organization, these are things you, the employee, can do to help bring about the needed changes you recommended.

Accountability

The Laboratory Director reports the Total Quality progress at SRL semi-annually to the Site Quality Council. During the year the SRL Quality Council, assisted by the department TQ resources, will perform continual self-assessments of progress in implementing the QIP. At the end of the year, the laboratory will again be surveyed for an overall perception of how well the QIP was implemented. These two assessments will be compared and be used as input into the 1992 QIP.

Additionally, a tear-out questionnaire will be included with the QIP asking for employee feedback on their perceptions of (1) the importance of the issues addressed in the QIP in helping them do their work better; (2) the appropriateness of the actions taken or going to be taken; (3) the usefulness and quality of the QIP itself.

Summary

In the environment at Savannah River Laboratory, our current level of success in developing a TQ culture has come from, and, it is expected, our future success will come from

- A strong commitment from the Laboratory Director

- A Quality Resource Section that is a TQ model of excellence and as such provides effective, personal TQ resources to the Laboratory Director and each department manager
- A laboratory wide Quality Improvement Plan that reflects the business needs of the laboratory
- A commitment from the department managers to sponsor and implement part of the QIP.

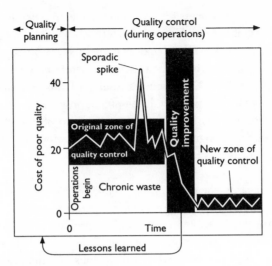

Figure 2.6 The Juran Trilogy.

candidate projects. Classifying pilot projects is a crucial activity. Pilot projects have failed because untrained councils have naively assumed that all problems require the same solution process. This one-size-fits-all blunder has led to the same training being given to all project teams—a prescription for failure. For example, intuition would suggest that training a team to *replan* the product development process would differ from the training needed to discover and remedy the causes of delays in test results. Juran (1986, 1989) developed the Juran Trilogy® to assist in problems' classification and solution. Figure 2.6 represents the Juran project-classification scheme. Projects are classified as being associated with either *quality planning, quality control,* or *quality improvement* opportunities.[9]

Quality planning/replanning (QP) projects arise from either of the following situations:

1. The complete *absence* of a needed product or process. An example would be the requirement to plan a laboratory equipment calibration procedure where none currently exists.

---

[9] The "lessons learned" arrow represents feedback to the product planners on the results of completing quality improvement or quality control projects. Juran (1992), referring to the philosopher, George Santayana ("Those who cannot remember the past are condemned to repeat it"), has called the feedback process "Santayana reviews."

2. A current product/process that is so *chronically and pervasively deficient* that the only acceptable remedy is to completely replan or reengineer it. Bastian and Miller (1994) at the Los Alamos National Laboratory reported on a QP project for replanning the process for allocating discretionary research funds. In another example, Boath (1993) discusses Boeing's Ballistic Systems Division's decision to redesign its new product development process. The project resulted in reducing design analysis times from two weeks to 38 minutes, while also reducing the number of engineering changes per drawing from a high ranging between 15 and 20 changes to a low of 1.

Note that in both cases, the *cause of the problem is either not an issue, or the cause is known to be pervasive process inadequacies.*

Quality control (QC) problems are sporadic problems that occur during a research project or any other process. Examples would include software bugs that periodically result in wrong stress calculations or computer crashes, and laboratory equipment that drifts out of calibration. Here the cause(s) of the spike must be determined to *return* the process to its *previous* level of performance. The basic question that must be answered for a quality control problem is: What has *changed?*

Quality improvement (QI) problems are associated with processes that are operating at chronically unacceptable levels and for which the problems' cause(s) must be determined. To determine the causes of QI problems, the most cogent question that can be asked is: What is the underlying source(s) that has continuously lead to this unacceptable level of performance? (Note that once the causes of the chronic deficiency level have been determined, the *remedy* may require replanning the process or product.) Here the team's mission is to diagnose the causes and develop a remedy that will result in a *breakthrough* in process performance.

As stated, the problem-solving process a team must follow depends on the type of project the team has been assigned (QP, QC, QP). Juran (1986, 1989, 1992) provides and describes the relevant road map for each of the three types of projects.[10]

The purpose of pilot projects is to demonstrate significant benefits in a relatively quick time frame. Since quality improvement projects can be expected to produce larger returns than quality control projects, and are likely to be completed more quickly than quality planning projects, *pilot-project* selection

---

[10] Various tools have also been found useful for each type of project. For example, Zeidler (1993) describes the use of quality function deployment (QFD) for planning and designing a new Voice Response Unit at Florida Power & Light Company.

should be biased toward quality improvement. Examples of QI pilot projects undertaken by research organizations have included the following:

1. Reducing reference publication acquisition time
2. Reducing the turnaround time for obtaining results from experiments
3. Reducing laboratory equipment requisition time
4. Increasing the percentage of research proposals resulting in contracts
5. Improving cash-flow management of research grants
6. Increasing the percentage of on-time research reports
7. Increasing the percentage of on-time design packages to the lab shop

Selecting Team Members

Although the selection of team members may appear to be an easy task, it is an important task. Team members should be selected based on their ability to provide one or more of the following:

1. Knowledge of one or more process areas requiring improvement
2. Identification of the cause(s) of the process problems
3. Development and implementation of a remedy
4. Diagnostic (e.g., experiment-design) skills the team will require

Training Teams and Facilitators

Yoest (1991) of Sverdrup Technology has discussed the importance of training teams at Arnold Air Force Base's Engineering Development Center. Yoest discussed the results obtained from three pilot teams. One team received no formal training. The second team had only one member with prior TQM training. The third team received two days of problem-solving training, participated in the development of their mission statement, and were led and supported by a team leader and a facilitator, both of whom had received formal training in problem solving and team facilitation. After reviewing the three teams' results, Yoest concluded:

> Organizations that attempt to launch quality improvement teams without the benefit of training for the team or the team leader generally waste resources by either inefficiently solving problems or totally failing in solving them. The use of trained facilitators is beneficial and cost-effective in that the teams will more efficiently achieve their goals. It is generally necessary to have both a trained

team leader and a trained facilitator. The trained team leader should accept ownership of the project, and the facilitator should accept the ownership of the quality improvement process.

Implied in this summary is the message to provide training to team leaders and facilitators *prior* to beginning a project. This training will establish a mutual understanding of the relative roles of the team leader and the facilitator to preclude misunderstandings and promote more effective team meetings. The facilitator, being the process and tools expert, can work with the team leader to determine the most beneficial time during the project to introduce a required tool (e.g., Pareto analysis). This type of just-in-time team training has been found to be more effective than training everyone in everything, "just-in-case."

Konosz and Ice (1991) at Alcoa's Technical Center have provided additional insights into the responsibilities, selection, and training of R&D team facilitators. Their paper, presented at Juran Institute's 1991 *Symposium on Managing for Quality in R&D*, is included at the end of this chapter.

Once the pilot projects and the infrastructure have been completed, the quality council(s) can prioritize *subsequent* projects by reviewing R&D quality indicators and quality system status. Since quality measurement and assessment are key elements of quality infrastructure, separate chapters will be devoted to each. Methods and examples for measuring R&D process quality will be presented in Chapter 3. Methods and examples of assessing R&D quality status will be presented in Chapter 4.

Facilitation of Problem-Solving Teams

Donald L. Konosz
Manager, Quality
Alcoa Laboratories
Alcoa Center, PA 15069

James W. Ice
Coorindator, Professional Development
Alcoa Laboratories
Alcoa Center, PA 15069

Abstract

Alcoa Technical Center is the research and development facility for the Aluminum Company of America (Alcoa). A highly educated community of scientists, engineers and technical support groups makes up the population of the Technical Center (approximately 1300 employees total). As part of a corporate-wide effort to improve our commitment to quality, the Technical Center has been actively addressing the issues of implementation of quality principles and practices.

One of the most powerful tools in the quality process is team problem solving. The successful implementation of problem-solving teams and quality improvement processes requires three critical components: (1) Management Leadership and Involvement, (2) Team Training and (3) Process Facilitation. A lot has been written about the need to have management's commitment to successfully implement quality processes. Management "buy-in" and ownership of the processes is fundamental to successful implementation. The benefits of proper training have been clearly demonstrated as training in problem-solving methodologies, group process and quality tools have resulted in better solutions and more efficient processes. Much less is known about the third component we believe to be critical to the success of team problem solving, "process facilitation." Much of the success of Quality Improvement efforts, as well as employee involvement activities, is reported to depend on the group process being "facilitated" (Bywaters, 1986; Harman, 1989). Process facilitation is still a mystery to most managers. Even though the word has recently become very popular, most of us do not understand what is so "magical" about facilitation. This paper will address why we believe process facilitation to be critical to the successful implementation of quality improvement efforts and discuss some of the factors that should be considered (selection, job design, training, etc.) when utilizing this methodology to help implement change.

What Is Process Facilitation?

To "facilitate" is "to make easier" (Merriam-Webster, 1988). Problem solving is difficult and working in teams is even more difficult. The role of a team facilitator is to make the process of team problem solving easier. It is important to understand that the function of facilitation is to make problem solving easier *not* to solve the team's problems. At first this might seem a bit contradictory, but the distinction is important to understand. Parents illustrate this distinction when they try to help their children make good decisions. The parent resists the temptation to solve the child's problem so that children learn how to solve problems for themselves. To solve the problem for them might direct them to the "right solution" but providing the solution may not make them better problem solvers. In a similar fashion, a facilitator attempts to provide the right information, tools and environment to enable to team to solve its own problems and, therefore, make the members better problem solvers. All too often, well-intentioned managers (or "Quality Professionals") have attempted "to help" teams by directing them to the "right solution." Those same managers wonder why the "right solution" is never implemented, why the team is unable to solve any problem on its own, and why quality improvement efforts fail.

The role of "Process Facilitator" is complex. The job requires knowledge and skills in applying quality tools and processes, impacting group and interpersonal dynamics, applying consulting principles, and impacting change. Within each team interaction there exist two realities: how the interaction is contributing to progress on the task and how the interaction is impacting the relationships between the members of the team. Quality improvement processes (identifying opportunities for improvement, problem solving, understanding customer needs and expectation) and tools (cause-effect diagrams, process flow diagrams, Pareto charts, house of quality) are enablers that a skilled facilitator provides to assist teams to solve problems. Most of us are good at assessing the progress we are (or are not) making toward accomplishing the team's task, but few of us understand the impact of the "maintenance" of the group relationships on team performance. In fact, we often deceive ourselves into thinking that if we just work harder on the task, we can overcome any relationship obstacles. A skilled facilitator knows when attention *must* be given to relationship issues in order "to make easier" task accomplishment. Every team has its own unique culture. Each team has different behavior patterns, norms, social and interpersonal dynamics. In order to make the team's process easier, the facilitator must understand how to help the team use, and/or challenge, its behavior patterns, norms and expectations to improve how the team members work together to solve problems. The skilled process facilitator understands the balance between task and maintenance within the teaming *process*. A facilitator must not allow himself/herself to be caught in the trap of becoming hypnotized by the problem the team is working on. When the facilitator focuses his/her attention on the "content" of the problem, instead of the "process" the team is using to solve the problem, he/she becomes a problem solver and is no longer making the "process" of problem solving easier. In fact, the addition of another problem solver usually adds to the complexity and confusion of the process. This might be the most difficult part of being a facilitator, turning off the natural desire to solve the problem or share your opinion, in order to attend to the process of *how* the team is solving the problem.

Another role of a Process Facilitator is to help a group recognize when old behavior patterns (methods/habits) are no longer effective and need to be changed. To facilitate is to be an agent for change. One of the few things that does not change about humans is that we don't like to change. A facilitator is often called upon to help teams and individuals change behaviors, attitudes, standard operating procedures, problem solving/data collection methods and even personal paradigms in order to make the team task "easier." The ability to adopt a "peer-to-peer relationship" with the team, its leader(s) and its sponsor(s) is critical to successfully accomplishing the role of "change agent" (Block, 1981). Process Facilitation is a combination of "Science" and "Art," the science of applying the appropriate quality and facilitation tools and the art of working with complex human interactions, conflicts and expectations.

Why Are Process Facilitators Important?

Skilled Facilitators are process experts. In the same way as we look to a manufacturing process expert to help us learn and improve the manufacturing process, a team process facilitator knows how to monitor, measure and recommend adjustments in group processes. Skilled facilitators are also quality and problem-solving-tool experts, equipped with a "toolbox" of methods for analyzing and impacting team task and maintenance issues. The nature of the team's expectations or "informal contract" with the facilitator allows her/him to challenge the team, its assumptions and behaviors, in an agreed upon, non-threatening manner. Another powerful advantage of a facilitator working with a problem-solving team is the opportunity to model desired behaviors/methods for the team. In any large-scale change effort, as most quality improvement efforts are, the impact of a messenger (change agent) in the field, who has the respect of employees, is directly related to the success of the change effort (Rogers and Shoemaker, 1971). The change agent is able to illustrate the need for change, and can demonstrate successful applications of new methods. We will now turn our attention to the factors that should be considered when implementing process facilitation methodologies.

How Do You Select Good Process Facilitators?

The selection process for Process Facilitators involves three major decision areas: the job design, the method of selection, and the criteria (attributes) for selection. There are several important questions which, when answered, will help you design the strategy for implementation of process facilitator to support quality improvement efforts. Below are listed several of these questions and a brief discussion of how each question was addressed at Alcoa Technical Center.

Job Design

1. What model of process facilitation is most appropriate in your organizational culture?

Several perspectives and orientations exist regarding models, or styles, of facilitation. Facilitation means different things to different people. It is critical to clarify for yourself and others what you want process facilitation to look like in your improvement effort. One common way to describe facilitation models is along the "directive–non-directive" continuum. At one end of the continuum is a directive approach, where the facilitator acts as a "leader/manager" of the team process. This style is demonstrated by the facilitator who designs the process (team meeting activities) ahead of time and runs the team meeting by directing the team through the designed process. This style is often characterized by telling/directing behaviors demonstrated by the facilitator. At the other end of the continuum is the non-directive approach, characterized by extensive coaching of the team leader behind the scenes and a less visible role of the facilitator during team meetings. The interventions during meetings are usually worded in the form of a question to cause the team to think about important issues, but do not imply one answer is better than another. Obviously, there are other styles that fall in between, or move back and forth between these two extremes. The model that is best for your situation depends on the cultural expectations and situational requirements. Another important issue to address is the expectation of the team regarding the facilitator's role capturing the minutes of the meeting. Some models of facilitation include this responsibility, others deliberately do not, in order that the facilitator will be free to focus attention on monitoring the group process.

After benchmarking several organizations and conducting a focus group session with experienced process facilitators, it was decided that we would adopt a model of facilitation that was closer to the non-directive approach than the directive approach. Directive approaches, while perhaps solving the problem at hand, often do not result in team member mastery of the problem solving processes; instead, they often build a reliance on the facilitator. Additionally, teams facilitated using the "directive" approach frequently lack the ownership in the generated solution. Using a non-directive approach does not imply that directive behaviors never are used by the facilitators, but that the facilitator continually strives to transfer the responsibility for facilitating its own process. Over time, non-directive facilitation becomes almost transparent to the team. Consistent with this approach, the role of facilitator becomes not that of a leader, content expert, or even note taker but a process consultant. Focusing on the team process (both task and maintenance) and in the role of the consultant to the team, the facilitator is *not* a team member but an enabler to make problem solving easier. The ultimate objective of this effort is to transfer the technology of facilitation to team members so that more people are equipped "to make the problem-solving process easier."

2. What is the best way to structure the job to have the biggest impact (i.e., reporting relationships, full or part-time assignment, length of assignment)?

The way a job is designed, positioned and advertised has strategic implications on the ultimate success of the project. Creating and evaluating a job description (i.e., job duties, salary ranges, etc.) will send a message to the community about management's perception of the anticipated value these individuals will add to the organization. Where the job falls on the organization chart also has implications on how the individuals within those jobs will be perceived by the team members with whom they will be working. Every detail of creating and filling these roles must be analyzed in light of the impact each alternative would have on the success of the change effort.

This question raised some unique challenges for us at the Technical Center. Central to job design was the fact that every action and decision *must* be consistent with the quality principles and practices we are trying to implement. Benchmark data illustrated that some organizations that employ full-time "professional facilitators" created an environment where teams relied on the facilitator to solve the problem instead of taking ownership for the problem and its solution. Using quality professionals as facilitators often set up a situation where the facilitator was viewed by the team as someone imposing his/her personal priorities and bias upon the team. In order to create an environment where teams feel that they are in control of their own processes and to help legitimize the role of this outsider to the team, we implemented a unique job design. We began with the following assumptions:

■ The responsibility for quality is shared by *everyone* in the organization, and any quality improvement effort will fail unless employees take *personal responsibility* for quality improvement,

- In the research environment it is important that facilitators be viewed as technical contributors,
- The knowledge and skill required of a Process Facilitator is a unique blend of disciplines, and is not something that comes naturally, therefore, a developmental process must be designed to prepare individuals for the challenges of facilitating problem-solving teams, and
- A diverse workforce and cross section of job levels and areas of expertise would provide a better chance for the implementation to succeed.

The job of a Quality Facilitator at Alcoa Technical Center is a two-year, part-time assignment of individuals from a cross section of the technical community. Fifty percent of the facilitator's time is spent dedicated to the quality implementation effort and 50 percent is dedicated to the job he/she currently holds. This job design was intended to allow the job candidates to remain current in the technology of their current jobs as well as to build and apply facilitation skills in this new assignment. The goal was to maintain each candidate's technical reputation and to deliberately avoid creating full-time facilitation career paths. In an attempt to impact change in the organizational culture, the job of Quality facilitator is a two-year assignment. The objectives of this job design are twofold: (1) to return trained facilitators to where they can make the biggest impact on the changing attitudes and behaviors in their technical disciplines, and (2) to provide the opportunity for training to a greater number of individuals. These objectives recognize the fact that change takes time and the more change agents in the organization the easier it is to change the culture. As facilitators are trained and then return to their technical areas full-time, they become agents for change. Vision statements and training programs are important ingredients in changing cultures, but it has been shown time after time that, in themselves, they are not enough. Change requires vision, strategy, leadership, training, goal setting (metrics), an awareness of the social and personal implications of change and, most of all, time. The role of Process Facilitator must be designed in harmony with these other factors. Functionally, the facilitators report to the Manager, Quality and administratively to their technical Managers.

Method of Selection

1. Who is eligible to be a Process Facilitator?

Based on the job description, all Technical Center employees were eligible for this assignment. The initial letter requesting candidates for the position of Quality Facilitator was sent from P. R. Bridenbaugh, Vice President—Research and Development to every Technical Center employee. His letter communicated that this activity was a high priority and that responsibility for quality processes and improvement is not dependent on organizational level. The initial selection screening criteria were as follows: (1) employee interest in this new opportunity (self-screening), and (2) current/expected workload, as negotiated between the employee and his/her supervisor. Over 50 individuals applied for 12 positions. The commitment to choose only those individuals who it was believed could succeed in this unique job caused the selection committee to choose only 10 facilitators instead of the original goal of 12. The selected individuals were representative of various organizational levels (i.e., engineers, scientists, managers, technicians, and secretarial), technical disciplines (i.e., analytical chemistry, fabricating technology, molten metal processing, computer science), educational backgrounds (high school to postdoctorate), and the diversity of the Technical Center community (race, sex, ethnically).

2. What Process was to be used to select the Facilitators?

A selection process must model quality principles. It should be free of bias, based on a process with established validity and reliability. The process should also provide opportunities for information exchange and data gathering.

A selection committee designed and conducted the selection activities. The Human Resources department, the Quality department, the Education and Training department and the Organizational Development group were represented on the selection committee. Each member either had extensive facilitation experience or clearly understood the impact facilitation has on team progress. The first step in the screening process was a blind analysis (no names attached) of human resource data (performance reviews, etc.) for each candidate. This produced a list of candidates to be interviewed. A basic assumption the selection committee held was that the best predictor of future behavior is past behavior. Therefore, each interview was designed to explore specific situations and how each candidate handled that situation. We used an available software package to identify the attributes believed to be essential for the success of a facilitation candidate and to help organize the interview process.

Selection Attributes

1. What previous knowledge and skills are prerequisite for selection?

We began with the assumption that no specific knowledge or skills were prerequisite for selection. An extensive education and training curriculum, described later in this paper, was designed to address the learning needs of the facilitators.

2. What criteria (attributes) will be used to select the Facilitators?

What sets one candidate apart from the others? What causes this individual to be selected and another not to be selected? These answers should be directly tied to the requirements and goals of the job. Central to identifying these job requirements and goals are the answers to questions raised earlier:

- What model of process facilitation is most appropriate in your organizational culture?
- What is the best way to structure the job to have the biggest impact (i.e., reporting relationships, full or part-time assignment, length of assignment, etc.)?

Eighteen candidates were interviewed and evaluated on the following attributes:

- Adaptability—maintaining effectiveness in varying environments, tasks, responsibilities, and with various types of people
- Initiative—active attempts to influence events to achieve goals: self-starter
- Oral Communication/Presentation—effective expression in individual and group situations

- Sensitivity—actions that indicate a consideration for the feelings and needs of others
- Planning and Organizing—establishing a course of action for self and/or others and organization
- Work Standards—setting high standards of performance for self, others and organization
- Analysis Skills—ability to break a problem into solvable parts and to apply various methods/tools of problem solving

How Do You Train Process Facilitators?

Traditionally, education and training programs for facilitators, if they exist at all, have been based upon "rules of thumb" and not a systematic understanding of the knowledge and skills required to accomplish with those facilitators. They expect the facilitators to effect change but do not have a clear picture of what role the facilitator should play within the team. The facilitator is appointed to help teams solve problems but then is not given the education and training needed to "make the team's problem-solving process easier." If making the team's problem-solving process easy were obvious, then teams could facilitate themselves. The process of facilitation is not obvious. It requires knowledge and tools taken from many disciplines (quality assurance, quality improvement, group dynamics/psychology, communication, organizational development education, etc.). In the same manner that one does not expect a new employee to be able to run a complex machine or process without proper training, we shouldn't expect someone who is not trained in process facilitation to be able to "wing it." There are few processes more complex than human interaction.

Two major content areas were addressed in our facilitator training curriculum: (1) quality tools and concepts, and (2) group facilitation tools and concepts. Each of these two areas contains numerous learning objectives which must be mastered to become a skilled Process Facilitator. Customer requirements and expectations were gathered from problem-solving teams to help us articulate how facilitators could best improve team performance. Subject matter experts in the areas of quality and facilitation were used to help identify the learning goals for facilitator training. An extensive list of facilitator knowledge and skills requirements directed the design and delivery of training.

What are the entry knowledge and skill levels of the facilitators? As discussed earlier, the decision was made not to require prerequisite knowledge or skills for candidate selection. However, assessing the entry-level skills and knowledge of the new facilitators allowed the training designers to know where each incumbent would begin his/her journey toward accomplishing the stated curriculum goals.

Training Design and Delivery:

1. What instructional strategies will be used to deliver training?

Instructional delivery strategies must be developed to educate the facilitators. It is important to realize that not all people learn the same way. Research has demonstrated that not all information is best communicated using the same delivery method. Gone are the days when classroom lecture style instruction is used to teach everything. At Alcoa Technical Center we used a variety of delivery methods to address individual learning styles and the wide range of knowledge and skills required to be taught. The following list illustrates some of the delivery styles used in our facilitator training program: classroom instructor-led instruction, facilitation laboratories, self-paced instruction, simulations, case studies, co-facilitation, etc. The curriculum is designed to last the entire two-year assignment, encouraging the facilitators to continually improve their process of facilitation.

The complexity of today's problems requires more and more input into decision making. It is rare in today's business world to find an individual who has all the required information to make the "right" decision. Teams are increasingly required to gather enough data and knowledge to solve today's tough problems. The skills of trained Process Facilitators are more important today than ever.

Mission of Process Facilitators of Problem-Solving Teams

The mission of the Process Facilitators is to: offer guidance to Quality Improvement Teams through the Alcoa Eight Step Quality Improvement Process; provide coaching and guidance in applying quality tools and concepts; assist in the planning and evaluation of team meetings; influence team dynamics by process intervention; continually seek to improve the Quality Improvement Process and its implementation; and, positively impact the implementation of quality principles/practices throughout the technical community.

CHAPTER 3

MEASURING R&D QUALITY

If you wait for perfect metrics, you'll be waiting the rest of your life.

—Ray Waddoups, Director, R&D,
Motorola's Government Electronics Group[1]

Measures for R&D Quality: Challenges and Classification

In Chapter 2 we discussed the need to develop an infrastructure for implementing, expanding, and institutionalizing an R&D quality process. A key element of that infrastructure is a hierarchy of quality measurements. This chapter will provide various perspectives and examples of developing, classifying, and aligning measures of R&D quality. It is equally important that measures for quality be reviewed regularly for both their *use* and their *utility*. For example, at Corning, Luther (1993) reported that of some 200 key results indicators (KRIs) used by Corning in early 1991, "over 100 have been replaced with different ones. This is good news because it says that improvement is happening. . . ."

Challenges and Responses for Measuring R&D Quality

Among the challenges of measuring research quality is the *mistaken* belief that research quality cannot be measured. It is often argued that because each

---

[1] Comment made by Dr. Waddoups during his presentation at Juran Institute's 1991 *Symposium on Managing for Quality in Research and Development.*

research program is unique, different measures are required for each new program and project. Furthermore, since successful research requires human innovation, any resultant quality measures must be highly subjective. This argument fails to recognize that, as Wiley (1993) of Battelle put it, "Good science is good quality." That is, although the objectives of research programs and projects may differ, the *process by which research is planned and conducted* should follow accepted good management and good research practices (e.g., sound requirements planning and use of the scientific method). Admittedly, research and development quality cannot be measured as *easily* (or as precisely) as manufacturing/operations process quality. However, this chapter contains multiple examples of actual quality measures used by R&D organizations to plan, control, and improve their programs, processes, and projects. The chapter also provides examples of processes for *developing* quality measures for R&D organizations.

Classifying Quality Measures

Quality measures' use and utility can be assessed from several major perspectives: *timeliness, application,* and *completeness*. Measures for timeliness can be classified as being either *lagging, concurrent,* or *leading* indicators. Application categories are determined with respect to the measurements' usage for quality planning (strategic and operational), quality control, or quality improvement (Juran's Trilogy). Finally, key measures must be reviewed to ensure that they are comprehensive and logically linked/connected to drive and support desired R&D performance goals. The *combination* of being comprehensive and connected is referred to as *completeness*. Measures' completeness will be discussed from the perspective of what Juran (1964) has called an "instrument panel for executives," or what Kaplan and Norton (1992) have called the "balanced scorecard."

Measures' Timeliness

Chapter 1 discussed the evolution of quality management from the high-volume, low-cycle-time environments of operations to the low-volume, long-lead-time environment of research and development. Garfinkel (1990), in GE's corporate R&D center, has reported on the challenges of obtaining timely measurements of research quality. Garfinkel concluded:

1. The most accurate measures for research quality are retrospective (e.g., revenues from products that emanated from research) or estimated revenues from technology that has been transitioned to GE businesses.

Although results data may be used to estimate returns on research investments, they cannot *directly* be used to improve future research.

2. Another useful (but lagging) indicator is the percentage of R&D funding that is obtained from R&D internal business units customers. "Our ability to raise funds for future work from GE's businesses is a direct measurement of their satisfaction with our past work and expectations of the future." Constructive feedback from internal business unit customers can be used to define and improve *future* programs and projects.

3. Patent productivity measures (applications and awards) have also been used to get closer to measuring real-time R&D performance (e.g., the ratio of patents to total R&D expenditures, or patents per million dollars of R&D spending). Potential pitfalls associated with patents and associated ratios are that the patents may or may not have business relevance (e.g., patents per megabuck may be inflated by potentially lethal decreases in R&D expenditures) and that patent productivity is dependent upon an effective patent application process.[2] Patent data can be used to benchmark and diagnose differences with other R&D organizations. GE reported "about 1.25 patents" per megabuck, and found that most of its major advanced technology competitors in the United States were substantially below that figure.

Developing Leading Indicators

We have previously discussed the use of R&D results data to measure return on research investments. However, in the spirit of Juran's Santayana review, results data may also be used as a basis to help determine correlates for *predicting*, controlling, and improving outcomes from *future and current* research. Garfinkel reported on GE's use of retrospective studies "for recognizing the reasons programs that initially sound promising turn into dogs. In this case, the ones we looked at, the list of reasons projects were *not* successful reads like this:

1. Inability to meet market timing requirements
2. Product late to market
3. Mismatch between technology and market life cycles
4. Product cost performance not in line with market requirements

---

[2] Chapter 5 discusses the use of TQM for improving intellectual property management processes.

Garfinkel also provided corresponding variables believed to be correlated with projects' *successes:*

1. Developing project plans and goals with GE's business units
2. Working closely with leaders, engineering, and manufacturing of the business units
3. Organizing interdisciplinary expertise (cross-functional teams)

These findings can then be used to help measure, predict, and control the likelihood of success for proposed or existing research projects.

Figure 3.1 provides an example of a corresponding concept for the *product development process* that was provided by Cole (1990) at Kodak. The vertical axis is the reported score on various key measures taken *during* the product development process, and the horizontal axis is the corresponding reported length (presumably years) of time to complete the development cycle.

The use of historical reviews for improving IBM's Rochester, Minnesota, software development process was reported by Rocca (1991). "Historical data is used to build a defect-removal profile of the software development process. With this profile, a model is established to track progress in program development and accurately predict the number of defects yet to be removed at each step in the process. Goals set for entry and exit of each stage are met before entering the next stage." Figure 3.2 (Rocca) demonstrates the model's forecast performance versus actual defects per thousand lines of code during the software development pro-

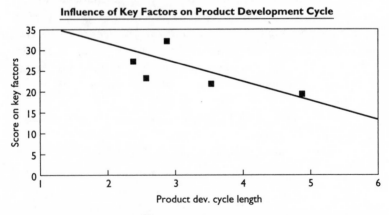

Figure 3.1 Measuring the influence of key factors on Kodak's product development cycle.

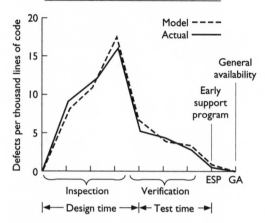

Software Defect Removal Modeling

Figure 3.2   Forecast versus actual software faults (IBM Rochester).

cess. Rocca reported that "combining the effects of hardware simulation and software modeling efforts has allowed us to reduce the debug portion of the overall development effort by 80 percent, thereby allowing us to enter verification tests and manufacturing earlier than through previous efforts."[3]

Measures for R&D Features and Deficiencies

As discussed in Chapter 1, Juran has defined two dimensions of quality: *features* (which *increase* customer satisfaction) and *deficiencies* (which *decrease* customer satisfaction). We have previously discussed the utility of Juran's Trilogy (Chapter 2, Figure 2.6) in preventing, categorizing, and solving quality problems. When properly implemented, the Trilogy *drives* the development and use of measures. The quality *planning* process drives the development of measures and goals for product and process features. The quality *control*[4] and *improvement* processes drive the development and use of measures and goals for deficiencies.

[3] From 1980 through 1988 IBM Rochester reduced overall development cycle time from five years to 28 months.

[4] Juran (1995) discusses a painting found in an Egyptian tomb circa 1450 B.C. The painting portrays two Egyptians, one a worker dressing a pyramid stone block, the other an inspector using a piece of string to measure the stone's flatness. This painting has been used by Juran to represent one of the earliest known examples of the use of measurement for quality control.

What Is Quality?

Figure 3.3 The features and deficiencies dimensions of quality.

A Process for Measuring and Analyzing Research Portfolio Features

As shown in Figure 3.3, the features dimension of quality is associated with "doing the right things." At the highest level of the research organization, a major determinant of doing the "right things" is the process for planning and analyzing research portfolios. Within the general context of quality planning, the work by Lander, Matheson, and Ransley (1994) on page 59 discusses the use of benchmarking to identify and develop measures for best practices for planning research portfolios.[5]

Measurement Processes for R&D Customer Satisfaction

The previous section discussed the use of benchmarking to measure and improve the performance of R&D *planning.* This section will be focused on processes for determining and measuring the key features of R&D performance that drive internal and external customer satisfaction (and dissatisfaction). (Refer to the symposium paper by Ferm et al. on page 67.)

Continued on page 81

[5] The paper by Matheson, Matheson, and Menke (1994) at the end of this chapter provides additional insights into the design of the benchmarking study and the use of the resultant measures to identify portfolio improvement opportunities.

IRI's Quality Directors' Network Takes R&D Decision Quality Benchmarking One Step Further

Lynn H. Lander
Director, Total Quality Management
Unilever Research U.S.
45 River Road
Edgewater, NJ 07020

David M. Matheson
Senior Associate
Michael M. Menke
Principal
Strategic Decisions Group
2440 Sand Hill Road
Menlo Park, CA 94025

Derek L. Ransley
Senior Quality Consultant
Chevron Research & Technology Co.
P.O. Box 1627
Richmond, CA 94802

Abstract

The Quality Directors' Network (QDN) of the IRI is involved in a number of activities related to R&D quality management. One of those is benchmarking. Last year, the QDN conducted a benchmarking study of R&D decision-making practices that built upon the groundbreaking work by Strategic Decisions Group. The QDN study reveals traits and processes that are common to organizations recognized for excellence in their R&D decisions. It also offers a seven-step agenda for QDN members to successfully implement these practices in their own organizations, with the ultimate objective of improving R&D decision quality.

Background

In July of 1992, the Industrial Research Institute (IRI) formed the Quality Directors' Network (QDN). The purpose was to bring together quality-management professionals from IRI-member companies to share experiences and discuss quality-related issues. The QDN has been well received, growing from 15 founders to more than 100 members in less than two years.

The QDN's initial effort has focused on four areas: analyzing approaches for the pervasive deployment of quality in R&D, developing performance measures and metrics to evaluate R&D effectiveness, assessing the impact of process reengineering on R&D, and conducting benchmarking studies. With our benchmarking work, our primary objective was to gain a better understanding of how companies use quality strategic decision-making practices to improve the selection of R&D projects. Just as important, we wanted to help QDN members learn how to effectively implement these decision-making practices in their own organizations.

When we started our research, we were aware that Strategic Decisions Group (SDG), a Menlo Park–based consulting firm was nearing completion of a comprehensive study of the same subject. We chose SDG's study to serve as a springboard for our work, with representatives of SDG actively participating in the QDN effort.

The QDN benchmarking study consisted of two phases. In Phase I, the total QDN membership was surveyed about the frequency of use, performance, implementation, and impact of 20 decision-quality practices. Our results validated the SDG study, coming to the following conclusions:

- There is ample opportunity for improving R&D decision quality in most organizations.
- For every practice, a number of organizations feel that they are using it very well.
- The goal is to implement these practices as part of a cohesive, well-integrated plan.

In Phase II of the study, we narrowed our focus and conducted in-depth interviews with these "best-practice" companies on the implementation of four key quality practices: (1) Measuring R&D's contribution to strategic objectives; (2) Using decision-quality tools and techniques to evaluate an

R&D portfolio; (3) Coordinating long-range business and R&D plans; and (4) Agreeing on clear, measurable goals. These practices were selected from the original 20 primarily because there was a relatively large gap between the companies that rated themselves highly and the median for the group as a whole.

For our Phase II interviews, we pursued companies that in Phase I of the study claimed to actualize the best decision-making practices well. These companies included: AT&T, Avery Dennison, Chevron, Du Pont, Elf Atochem, Exxon, Grumman, and Henkel, among others.

Traits That Lead to Decision Quality

The first thing we learned from the QDN study was that companies which are excellent at the four decision-making practices have several traits in common. These traits represent powerful enablers for achieving high decision quality. They include:

1. Establishing an explicit decision process that focuses on aligning R&D with corporate strategy and creating economic value.
2. Using metrics that measure this alignment and value creation.
3. Maintaining a fertile organizational setting that supports decision quality and the implementation of change efforts.

Our findings did not depend on the specific practice or practices under consideration. In every interview, we found the four practices working together to support excellence in decision making. Shades of one practice—for instance, measuring contributions to strategic objectives—were clearly evident in another, such as coordinating long-range business and R&D plans.

As we looked at how decision quality practices are applied, we discovered the best companies not only have common traits, but follow a similar path to their goals as well. (See Figure 3.4.)

Establishing an Explicit Decision-Making Process

The decision-making process starts with input derived from either corporate strategy or surveys of customer needs. Next, these corporate or cus-

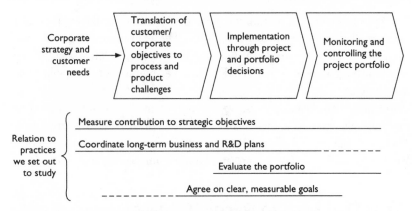

Figure 3.4 The four "best" R&D decision-quality practices work together to support a process that focuses on value creation through project and portfolio decisions.

tomer objectives must be *translated* into process and product assignments that are meaningful to R&D. This is followed by *implementing* an R&D program through specific project and portfolio decisions. Finally, to keep the process on track, the best companies consistently *monitor and control* project portfolios.

The four decision-quality practices we studied play different roles at various points in this process. For example, *measuring R&D's contribution to strategic objectives* is important throughout the entire process. *Coordinating long-range business and R&D plans* is especially critical from the start of the process through project and portfolio decision making, then less important during monitoring and control. The practice of thoroughly *evaluating the portfolio* is obviously used only during the final two steps. *Agreeing on clear, measurable goals* has some value through the early stages, but is crucial from project and portfolio decision making through monitoring and control.

Translation—We found that at each of the stages, several organizations had developed noteworthy techniques that contributed significantly to higher decision quality. For example, for translating business and customer objectives into R&D guidelines, one company we studied makes detailed maps linking research to end-customer value, then models these links quantitatively. This ensures that research is always directed toward customer needs, even if it's too early to clearly identify a specific market.

Implementation—During implementation when critical funding decisions are made, one company uses a formal stage-gate process, with different criteria to pass through each gate; another uses portfolio grids with dimensions defined by standardized, culturally accepted values and an evaluation process that's enforced through spirited debates with colleagues; while a third empowers each project team to make its own decisions, but demands that teams follow a rigorous process for decision making with strong involvement from R&D's business-unit "customers."

Monitoring and control—Finally, for monitoring, control, and continuous improvement of project activities and results, noteworthy techniques included using cross-functional teams to negotiate their own milestones and regularly reevaluate project decisions; establishing formal "exit" criteria for each project from the moment it is chartered; terminating those that do not perform; and using R&D revenue-contribution scorecards created by business units to determine a project's viability.

Using Measures and Metrics

In our interviews, we found a number of specific measures and metrics that support R&D decision quality. These varied from one organization to another and tended to be situation-specific—that is, they were designed to meet a given set of implementation and methodology requirements. In general, useful measures and metrics drive organizational behavior in helping to align R&D objectives with corporate strategy and value creation.

The QDN study identified several distinctions about measures and metrics that are important to understand their design and application.

Activity versus results measures—Measures of activity, such as the use of portfolio grids, achievement of stage gates, or holding of joint R&D and marketing meetings, can help determine if a process is being used or a practice is being implemented. However, these measures can be misleading by focusing attention on activities rather than results.

Measures of results—such as the percentage of revenue from new products, the expected net present value of projects or portfolios, and development cycle times—focus on achieving the desired outcomes. The best companies used only a few general results measures (tailored to specific situations) to avoid losing focus on important strategic issues.

Quantitative versus qualitative measures—Quantitative measures enable tracking and continuous improvement through verifiable, mathematical means. However, because of the difficulty of devising measurables that are crucial to every type of R&D project at every stage, the best organizations also use qualitative measures, such as the chief executive officer's assessment of R&D's contributions. Qualitative measures can gauge the value of many R&D efforts long before there are quantitative business results to measure.

Prospective versus retrospective measures—Prospective measures are predictions, such as the ultimate commercial potential of an R&D project or a five-year forecast of new product revenue. These measures are essential for effective decision making and control. Retrospective measures are historical—for instance, a summary of new product revenue from the past five years. These measures are important for feedback and monitoring.

In our study, we found that *combining* these two types of measures produced a particularly powerful metric—for example, new product revenue reported on a five-year lagging basis and projected on a five-year leading basis using the current portfolio of R&D projects.

The best measures and metrics express the views of internal customers on the quality, speed, value, and cost of R&D efforts. These measures take full advantage of the experience of managers and staff in both R&D and business areas, providing valuable feedback on what is important at any given moment.

Maintaining a Fertile Organizational Setting

All of the outstanding companies we studied have fertile organizational settings that support high decision quality. Those companies surveyed in Phase I that were less successful at implementing the four R&D decision-making practices usually lacked important elements of this setting.

To help QDN members create an organizational setting conducive to quality R&D decisions, we developed a checklist organized around seven questions that are key to implementing these decision-making practices.

1. *How good is your quality foundation?* The companies we benchmarked all had internalized quality principles, which pro-

vides a common language for applying decision quality techniques to R&D decision making. Customer focus was another common thread. These organizations are accustomed to measuring customer responses to products and services and learning from them. In addition, the top performers in our sample use flowcharts extensively—in some instances, literally covering their walls with them. This encourages people to talk about the processes and find innovative ways of improving them.

2. *Do you have an agent of change?* All the companies we studied had at least one individual leading the change program. Often, a new head of research initiated the effort. In some cases, the CEO drove it, with the head of R&D providing the local vision. And in at least one instance, a middle manager with no formal authority but with broad respect in R&D got the ball rolling. But in every case, there was an identifiable agent of change.

3. *Do you have a case for action?* For the companies we benchmarked, the driving force behind the undertaking was either defensive or offensive—from a real threat to survival, to a company vision in which quality decision making was a key component. For some organizations, a significant decline in customer satisfaction provided the necessary motivation to take action.

4. *Do you get feedback on proposed changes?* To succeed in any change program, feedback is essential. R&D organizations need to regularly measure the satisfaction of both internal (business unit) and external customers. The most successful companies in our study have highly structured joint planning processes between R&D and business units. It is also important to solicit and respond to comments and suggestions on the proposed process changes themselves. For example, in one company we looked at, a design team developed a plan for a broad restructuring, publicized that plan, then made sure those affected were aware that the plan had been adapted in response to staff feedback.

5. *Do your business partners participate?* Company business units aren't only your customers, they should own the decision-making process—ensuring that strategic R&D decisions always address their needs. We found that the best R&D results were achieved by organizations in which participation in key decisions includes all

levels and functions. In several cases, the ready access R&D management has to higher levels of business management facilitated the alignment of R&D strategy with business goals.

6. *How well are your decision-making practices integrated with your customer?* The QDN study made it clear that it is important to develop an integrated system. Don't suboptimize by focusing on one part of the process over another. As you might expect, there were some differences between larger organizations and smaller ones. Large companies typically have highly structured decision-making processes that require a relatively longer time cycle. Smaller organizations have shorter planning cycles and select projects at a higher level, but empower cross-functional teams to set project goals.

7. *Do people see the value added in the process?* Although R&D is a long-lag-time business, people need to see or feel the value of a change program as soon as possible. In our study, this was apparent through comments such as, "The first trial use of the program showed cycle-time reduction," "business units now understand R&D better," and "customer satisfaction measures are increasing." This positive environment gives people the confidence to continue with the change program.

The Next Step

A lot of what we learned in the QDN study may seem like common sense. But as business people discover every day, practicing common sense in an increasingly competitive, constantly changing environment can be a difficult challenge indeed.

As Edward S. Finein, president of Edward S. Finein & Associates and former vice president and chief engineer of Xerox Corporation said, "The important message (of benchmarking) is that by taking measure of your own firm's use of the best practices . . . you will develop a clear road map of practices that will contribute the most value to improving the quality of R&D decisions in your organization.

"The key challenge is to use these results to clarify what you need to be doing, ask yourself why you are not doing them, and get on with it."

Developing a Customer Orientation in a Corporate Laboratory Environment

P. Ferm, S. Hacker, T. P. Izod, G. R. Smith
AlliedSignal Inc., Research & Technology
P. O. Box 1021, 101 Columbia Road
Morristown, New Jersey 07962-1021

M. Israelow
Mulberry Hill Associates
835 Hardscrabble Road
Chappaqua, New York 10514

Introduction

In 1990, a new Polymer Science Laboratory (PSL) was established within the Corporate Research & Technology (R&T) laboratories of AlliedSignal Inc. This group was charged with the objective of developing a much strengthened interaction with AlliedSignal's business units, particularly those which were a part of its Engineered Materials Sector (EMS).

A previous role model for R&T at AlliedSignal had been to generate completely new business opportunities, largely outside the current business strengths of the Corporation. However, it had been recognized at a Corporate management level that this was not leading to an adequate strengthening or broadening of existing businesses. The objectives set down for PSL were designed to accelerate this process. (See Tables 3.1 and 3.2.)

This paper presents a description of how the management and staff of the PSL approached the development of a customer orientation with their EMS internal customers, of how they effectively made measurements of their progress with their key internal customers, and, finally, of how they have developed improved and greatly enhanced strategic research planning and implementation approaches, jointly with the management of business units and EMS sector.

Table 3.1 PSL Mission

Provide value to AlliedSignal through the application of polymer science and technology.

A 5-Year Vision

The PSL at AlliedSignal is a "world-class" performance polymer R&D group, known for
    the quality of its R&D programs
    its ability to rapidly integrate research successes and commercial opportunities through its partnership with business units
    the quality and reputation of its staff

Mission and Objectives

During 1990, the PSL established a focus group among its members. This team worked, assisted by an external organizational consultant, Marvin Israelow, to create a Mission, Vision, a broad statement of objectives, and four key strategies (see Tables 3.1 to 3.3).

The team then worked to develop a buy in to these statements by all members of the laboratory, by R&T management, by PSL's business unit customers and also by the Sector management of EMS.

Thereafter, PSL established three teams which developed approaches (i) to improve teaming—within our laboratory and with other AlliedSignal technical and business groups, (ii) to build a well-understood planning process, and (iii) to develop job roles that met the planning and project execution requirements.

Table 3.2 Program Definition

Provide solutions for key SBU needs.
Define scientific bases for strategic businesses. Solve defined technical problems. Create commercial opportunities.
Understand evolving science/markets in strategic fields to develop exploratory programs providing "futures" options for AlliedSignal.

Table 3.3 Four Key Strategies

Development of strong business interactions with AlliedSignal's SBUs

People and their development

Technology definition/program development

Organization of PSL to achieve mission

Later, a fourth team was established to deal with identified technical training needs.

In 4Q1991, a year after the new PSL process was established, a customer satisfaction survey was developed to determine how well this process was perceived by PSL's customers, and in which areas they most urgently desired improvements from the PSL.

Two of the authors of this paper (Drs. Hacker and Ferm) undertook the development and assessment of this survey as part of a postgraduate research management course with the Stevens Alliance for Technology Management (SATM, Stevens Institute of Technology, Hoboken, New Jersey).

Creation of Survey

The goal of this survey was to create a broad, generic measure of customer satisfaction across AlliedSignal's SBUs and then to use the feedback to identify improvement opportunities, to assess internal perceptions of quality, and to set a baseline for the level of PSL research conformance to customer requirements. This was intended to be used as an internal benchmark for succeeding years. By keeping the survey generic, we were able to distribute it to all of PSL's then current SBU customers, as well to have it available for future, then unidentified, customers. It was also designed so that additional sections could be added to probe specific SBU concerns in future re-surveys.

After considerable revision, the final survey contained eight main sections, together with a section for comments. The categories [Project Definition (two subtopics), Project Proposals (four subtopics), Communication (nine subtopics), Teamwork (three subtopics), Technical Achievements (three subtopics), Overall PSL Assessment (three subtopics), Quality Process (four main questions)] contained, in addition to asking for an overall response, the above indicated numbers of detailed questions which further probed more specific items.

Each question was posed in the form "To what extent did the PSL . . . ?" and asked for responses from 1, corresponding to "Not at All," to 5, corresponding to "Very Much." A separate entry, NA, was included for those who did not know how to respond to a certain question, or who decided it to be inapplicable.

The survey and results presented here are the second iteration of this survey. During the fall of 1991, a first "Questionnaire of Customer Satisfaction" was prepared and distributed to just one business unit for testing and debugging. Only 8 out of 24 solicited responses were returned in this preliminary survey.

This "dry run" allowed us to gain valuable experience in the writing of an effective questionnaire and in evaluating the potential pitfalls involved— especially with regard to the inclusion of biased questions and to the achievement of a significant response level. Furthermore, since our hope had been to use the questionnaire in future years to measure our progress, it was very desirable for us to develop a robust survey.

The 1991 preliminary questionnaire was submitted to Professor Nancy DiTomaso of Rutgers University who offered substantial comments, particularly with regard to the removal of bias from the questionnaire. She advocated drafting questions such that customers are encouraged to rate an assessment of "facts" rather than of opinions or attitudes. Thus, we used the term "To What Extent" to propose questions throughout the survey. Professors Don Merino and Seymour Adler of SATM also made a number of useful comments during the final development of our survey.

An area of concern for us was how should SBU customers complete this questionnaire in a case where they had multiple projects with the laboratory. We saw several possibilities, including the following:

(i) asking them to rate their latest project,
(ii) rating both the best and the worst project they had experience with,
(iii) giving their "overall" impression of the PSL and the quality of work.

We decided to ask for their overall impression [i.e., (iii)] which effectively limited an individual's response to only one questionnaire (hopefully resulting in a higher return rate) and reduced the bias toward an evaluation of only the latest project—which may have been abnormally "better" or "worse" than previous experiences. However, several respondents, who had both good and bad past experiences, said that they had difficulty rating an overall impression. We now believe that, in future, respondents with both strongly negative and positive experiences should fill out two separate questionnaires for the survey.

The survey was distributed to all of PSL's internal SBU customers (ten SBUs). To achieve a much higher response rate than we had received for the preliminary (dry run) survey, invitations to respond to the survey were sent out under the joint letterhead of the PSL laboratory director, Dr. Smith, and the technology director of each individual SBU. These directors also acted as "clearinghouses" for incoming questionnaire responses. The joint letterhead was found to be an effective solution. It applied internal SBU pressure to complete the survey. An SBU return rate of 50% was achieved.

The survey was also distributed within the PSL to compare the internal perception of PSL SBU customer satisfaction with the business units responses. Here a 100% return was achieved.

After analyzing the data, we conducted brief, selected, telephone follow-ups to gain better understanding of one particular source of customer dissatisfaction—the perceived "value" of PSL research to its customers. This later personal contact was found to be extremely helpful. It is discussed further below.

Survey Data and Results

The data was inputted to an Excel database. We constructed a worksheet which enabled us to run searches on the database, to tabulate overall responses, particular SBU's responses, and/or other factors or multiple factors. With 60 total SBU responses, reasonably good statistical analyses, such as Pareto analyses, means and standard deviations, can be applied to the overall results. While the data was also broken down by individual SBU and examined, the limited number of responses for some SBUs made statistical analysis suspect. However, the underlying data is certainly valid and can be used to see how each SBU rates PSL performance within each particular questionnaire category.

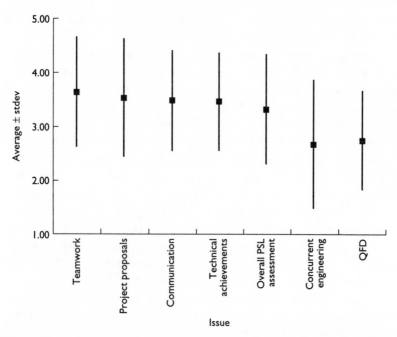

Figure 3.5 Summary of questionnaire results [average ($\pm$ 1 std. dev.)].

A summary of all results is presented in Figure 3.5. Average results are shown ($\pm$ 1 Standard Deviation). The use of the standard deviation in this manner assumes that the results form a normal distribution. However, as the results of Figure 3.5 suggest, there is a skewness towards the high end of the 1 to 5 range of the possible scores. Thus, in further analysis of the data, we have chosen to examine only indications of dissatisfaction—i.e., data from responders who rated the PSL a 1 or 2 for any particular question. An example of such a data treatment is shown in Figure 3.6.

Figure 3.6 is a Pareto diagram ranking the major issues by dissatisfaction. The major source of dissatisfaction (a response of 1 or 2) concerned "To what extent do you believe concurrent engineering between your SBU and the PSL is in place?" This accounts for 27% (17 responses) of the total of 63 dissatisfied responses. That the SBUs wanted concurrent engineering in place between themselves and the PSL is evident by their overall response to the question "To what extent would you like concurrent engineering in place between your SBU and the PSL?" where a 4.0 average was noted.

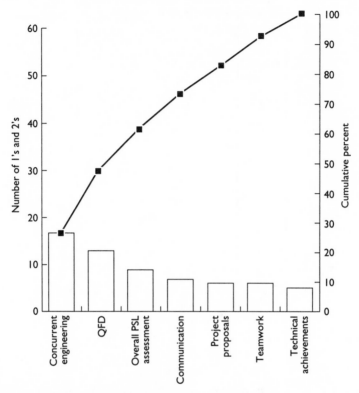

Figure 3.6   Pareto chart of major sources of dissatisfaction.

Concurrent engineering within AlliedSignal's current structure is, by necessity, multi-organizational in nature because Corporate Research & Technology and individual business units are divided by organizational and also, sometimes, geographic lines. The second most prevalent source of dissatisfaction involved "To what extent has the PSL staff identified your requirements for a product and the characteristics of comparable competitive products? (Quality Functional Deployment)." Thirteen customers expressed dissatisfaction (i.e., responded 1 or 2), corresponding to an additional 21% of the total dissatisfaction level.

The third largest source of dissatisfaction shown in Figure 3.6 is the overall PSL assessment issue. Breaking this down further, consider the Pareto chart in Figure 3.7. This Pareto contains the three subtopics under "Over-

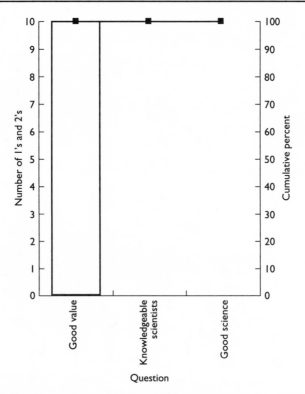

Figure 3.7 Comparison of SBU and PSL responses on key issues.

all PSL Assessment" which are abbreviated as "good value for your money," "knowledgeable scientists," and "performs good science."

Figure 3.7 dramatically shows that the issue of "value for your money" represents the overwhelming source of dissatisfaction. The level of confidence in the PSL scientists is not a registered concern. This issue clearly is a critical one for PSL (and R&T) to consider.

In order for a customer to "buy" a good or service, it must have sufficient value to that customer. Why do PSL customers feel that PSL does not provide value? For example, does the PSL perform good work but is just too expensive, or does the PSL conduct research that is incongruent with the SBU's expressed needs? These were questions we recognized to be in need of answers.

Thus, we followed up this "value" issue with personal telephone calls to elicit more specific information as to the source of dissatisfaction. First, ten customers who responded 1 or 2 were retrieved from the database. Nine of them had voluntarily provided their names while answering the questionnaire. We attempted to contact each individual by telephone and to ask what was the specific source of their dissatisfaction. In this manner, we received direct feedback from six of the nine respondents.

The respondents' most salient comments were as follows: "process was not well thought out and did not scale well," projects "are not adequately focused and results are not commercialized rapidly enough," "the amount charged for the work is too high . . . there is too much overhead," "would like more of the business needs taken into consideration," "Once a program gets into [PSL] domain, it loses its identity and time focus."

Some people who we interviewed thought that PSL did not give enough thought and consideration to commercialization aspects of their work. This raised a fundamental issue for us. The PSL's process of developing a Mission and Objectives statement and then identifying work processes to achieve a close partnership with SBU customers had been clearly addressed and (we had assumed) accepted by the SBUs over the previous two years. We had viewed commercialization leadership as an SBU responsibility. As a result, in our interactions with SBUs, we have since re-emphasized the questions: What differences are there in the role of PSL for each individual SBU? What mix of fundamental research and specific commercialization endeavors should the PSL be involved in, and how do they vary for each individual SBU?

It is interesting to directly compare the level of dissatisfaction of our SBU customers with the levels of dissatisfaction within SBUs—as perceived by PSL staff. Figure 3.8 shows this dual histogram for the seven major issues. The PSL also perceives concurrent engineering and QFD as the two biggest problem areas. While the ordering of the remaining issues is quite different from SBU responses, the distribution is fairly flat. Thus the differences do not seem as significant as the fact that dissatisfaction is present. Interestingly, the PSL perceives teamwork with the SBUs to be much worse than the SBUs think it is.° It may be indicative of a level of

---

° Note that PSL had addressed teamwork with SBUs as a key strategic issue for its planning process. That may have created higher expectations for PSL staff in this area.

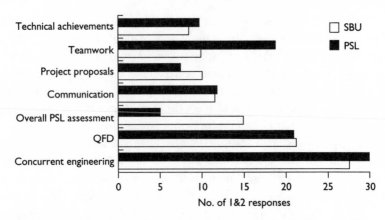

Figure 3.8 Comparison of dissatisfaction sources for SBU versus PSL responders.

frustration that some PSL members have discussed regarding their interactions with SBUs. These data have since proven very useful in opening lines of communication with our customers.

The data of Figure 3.9 depict the major communication dissatisfiers identified from the survey. Most concern was expressed about the level of detail in monthly reports and the conformance of these reports to customer requirements. The frequency of communication between PSL and relevant SBU personnel and the quality of review meetings were also seen to be significant issues. Though less significant an issue, some responders were also concerned about the inability of PSL staff to respond to feedback they received from SBU personnel.

A final forward-looking question was posed: "To what extent would you like to review quality-related issues of each project at its completion (whether successful or not)?" The SBU responses agreed extremely strongly, showing the highest average overall score in the questionnaire of 4.4. By comparison, the PSL response, though not as strongly positive, was also at its highest at 4.0.

Thus, the questionnaire offers valuable insight into sources of PSL customers' dissatisfaction. It is fair to comment that these analyses do remain subjective. Note that we have essentially weighted all questions equally, from "concurrent engineering," to "detail of monthly reports." This, strictly

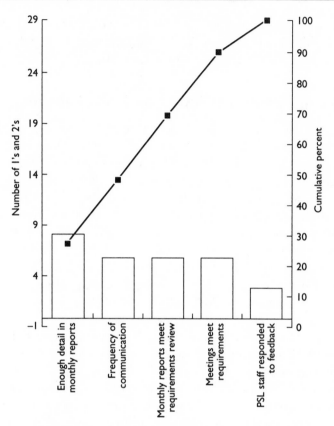

Figure 3.9 Major communications dissatisfiers.

speaking, is not a valid approach. Furthermore, there are different ways of calculating dissatisfaction, or of organizing questions, which result in different priority lists and Pareto charts. We believe these to be semantic issues, at this point. Most important, the analysis offers real opportunities for action and improvement. Thus the quality improvement teams which have been formed since the survey have used these survey results as guidelines and have added their own sense of which problem is either easiest to tackle first or which has the largest possible payback.

While a concentration on customer dissatisfaction has been emphasized in this report, do note that we have also been able to retrieve a very significant positive feedback from a number of our SBU customers. This is indicated by the results of Figure 3.5. We have also used these positive indications to build on our interactions with other SBUs.

TQ Improvements Based on Survey Results

The results of the survey were published broadly across AlliedSignal during the second quarter of 1992. As a direct result, several total quality teams were established between PSL and key business unit customers in order to develop improved approaches to the achievement of strategic program planning and execution. (Note that, more recently, these TQ teams have been further developed to encompass research activities across all of R&T.)

One particular SBU had registered some very real and particular concerns in the survey (both within its technical and senior management ranks). In response, a joint PSL/SBU TQ team was established. This group has now delineated an entire customized planning process, particular to PSL (and other R&T) interactions with that SBU, and a process for ongoing interaction. This approach has resulted in truly collaborative programs with this SBU in which members of various laboratories in the Corporate R&T organization take on certain of the research activities, while others are handled, as most appropriate, within the SBU technology organization. This has resulted in shared timelines, objectives and a jointly understood motivation for success in the research program PSL is undertaking with this SBU.

In another TQ teaming activity, PSL managers were asked to work with the business management and technical directors of a particular EMS division to determine the value and likelihood of success of that Division's 1992 technical program (including its R&T performed components). The outcome of this activity has been a much better focusing and alignment of all 1993 R&D endeavors with the strategic plans of each SBU within that Division.

Early in 1992, AlliedSignal undertook to train its entire organization in "Total Quality Leadership" via a four-day course and the subsequent completion of TQ team-based problem-solving exercises by every attendee. As of today, around 50% of AlliedSignal's employees have completed TQL training, while all of R&T's employees completed TQL by late 1992.

TQ-based procedures are now the norm in all meetings between R&T and its business unit customers. PSL's earlier development of a teaming and strategic planning orientation with these businesses has served it extremely well during this transformation to TQ across the company. Easier, more rapid and candid communications are evident at all organizational levels between SBU and PSL personnel. While a few sore points do remain with some customers, the acceptance of TQ, the PSL customer satisfaction survey, and the rapidly accumulating evidence of marked improvements in the quality and effectiveness of interactions with the majority of PSL's SBU customers, provide guidelines for those late acceptors of a multifunctional, interorganizational, teamwork orientation to research and development.

For 1993, the scope of TQ teaming with SBUs as a means to most effectively achieve Corporate Research & Technology's programs has been broadened beyond that practiced within PSL. It now encompasses *all* R&T programs with *all* AlliedSignal business units. The highly interactive teams of PSL researchers already established with SBU business and technical people do offer a role model for this activity.

The further development of PSL's original approach to now encompass all of AlliedSignal's Corporate Research & Technology organization does bring with it some issues for the longer term value of the customer satisfaction survey we described above. While the results of the PSL/SBU study have proven extremely useful, it is now clear to us that the next customer satisfaction survey in which we participate should encompass the entirety of R&T's customer base. We do believe that the PSL survey offers valuable guidelines for this activity. However, we also recognize that the survey itself would require very significant modifications in order to satisfy this larger R&T-wide requirement.

Concluding Remarks

Our TQ-based strategic planning approach continues to develop rapidly. For the Polymer Science Laboratory, a very different 1993 program portfolio has emerged with the EMS Divisions and Business Units with whom we had built key interactions. Joint teams, encompassing R&T and EMS personnel, are now the accepted mode of research operation and planning. These multifunctional program teams are responsible for the development of detailed plans and the achievement of programs objectives. These program objectives had previously been broadly outlined in the strategic descriptions that overview joint R&T/SBU TQ teams developed and then gained approval for with business management.

R&T (and PSL) now has a living process which is overwhelmingly accepted by EMS business unit managers and technologists. The involvement of EMS senior management in the definition, approval and support of these strategic programs has helped R&T to maintain a balance across three different technology types; which have been defined as Core, Enabling or Emerging. As a result, there is a better shared understanding and a balancing of AlliedSignal's R&D portfolio across the range of short-, medium-, and long-term research activities in which R&T is involved. Appropriately, this balance is becoming increasingly dependent upon, and aligned with, the individual business and technology strategies of each of the business units with which R&T interacts.

The introduction of a Total Quality program Corporate-wide at AlliedSignal and the very rapid assimilation of TQ across EMS have provided the catalyst which has enabled R&T's (and, initially, the PSL's) planning approach to be achieved so effectively. This is continuing to evolve in 1993 as the entire company embarks upon another TQ based skills development experience, this time focusing upon "Total Quality Through Speed."

It is notable that many high-level TQ teams are active across AlliedSignal, in EMS and in R&T. These (and our past PSL) initiatives are continuing to drive our activities toward greater strategic impact and to a significantly increased emphasis upon issues related to time and cost-effectiveness.

Customer Satisfaction Measurement at AlliedSignal's Polymer Science Laboratory

Measurement processes for determining internal customers' satisfaction with R&D have been discussed by Ferm et al. (1993) of AlliedSignal's Polymer Science Laboratory. The paper beginning on page 67 discusses Allied's use of focus groups and surveys to develop laboratory *mission and vision statements* and obtain feedback on actual performance from the lab's business unit customers and lab's staff members.

Developing Measures for Customer Satisfaction at Alcoa's Technical Center

Hersh et al. (1993) at Alcoa's Technical Center (ATC) have also reported on using customer surveys to identify, prioritize, and develop performance measures for Alcoa's research, development, and engineering's (RD&E's) customers' requirements. Table 3.4 summarizes the four major requirement categories (e.g., *Link technology and business strategies,* with the associated needs for each category).

Wasson (1995) discussed the use of the survey data to develop the new ATC vision and mission statements with associated measures for judging progress in mission completion:

> Vision: *Alcoa Technical Center will be a competitive technical organization that creates value through the rapid and effective transfer of integrated technology products and processes to our customers.*
>
> Mission: *Alcoa Technical Center will create a competitive advantage through the application of technology based on understanding our customers' current and future requirements. We will accomplish this through a commitment to customer satisfaction, respect for people, value of work, and shortening time to commercialization.*

Measures of Customer Satisfaction

> *As a team and individuals we will meet all of our mutually agreed-to project/program commitments and deliverables on time and within budget.*
> Measures:
>
>> 1. *Percentage of deliverables delivered. Deliverables are specific outputs that have been mutually agreed to by ATC and customers. The decision as to completion of a deliverable will be mutually determined with the customer.*

Table 3.4 Alcoa Technical Center's Customers' Requirements

Link Technology and Business Strategies	Priority
1. Collaborate with business units to develop a technical . strategy linked with business unit milestones.	7
2. Have a corporate technology portfolio linked with the corporation's strategy.	13
3. Develop a competitive advantage through significant differentiation of products, processes, and services.	4
4. Continuously improve Alcoa's current products, processes, and services.	9
5. Provide a technical basis for new business opportunities.	14
Build Strong Customer Relationships	
6. Develop productive team relationships with the business units.	14
7. Communicate effectively with the business unit personnel to develop mutual understanding.	16
8. Provide cross-functional training (ATC at plants/plants at ATC).	10
9. Team with marketing and sales to develop relationships with external customers.	19
Manage Technology Effectively	
10. Work with our internal customers to systematically assess and satisfy external customer needs.	4
11. Have focused RD&E° efforts on problems identified jointly with the business units.	3
12. Assume accountability for attaining mutually determined project objectives.	1
13. Manage resources effectively (direction, pace, roles, budget).	11
14. Use technology, from whatever the source, to Alcoa's advantage.	8
15. Provide solutions that fully meet agreed-to customer requirements.	4
16. Meet customer cost and performance expectations.	2
Provide Socially and Legally Acceptable Solutions	
17. Comply with legal and corporate requirements.	18
18. Protect Alcoa's proprietary technology.	16
19. Use standard corporate tools.	11

° RD&E represents the ATC's research, development, and engineering functions.

2. *Percentage of technical results achieved.*
3. *(Results of) customer satisfaction survey.*

Measure of Cost Reduction/System Simplification

As an organization, we will maintain our costs.
Measure: *Average hourly billable rate.*

Shorten the Time to Commercialization

Implement the ATC Technology Development Cycle methodology on all projects.
Measure: *All development cycle gates and hurdles defined for the approved projects.*

Measuring Performance at IBM's Research Division

Van der Hoeven of IBM and Whetten of Los Alamos Laboratories (1993) discuss IBM's research division's development and use of a customer scorecard for the research division's performance. Factors used to score the lab's performance are as follows:

1. Technical and scientific results
2. Effectiveness
3. People
4. Internal processes
5. Quality progress

Figure 3.10 provides additional scorecard details, including the associated customer review processes, mechanisms, and measurements.

To facilitate understanding of the scorecard, the following text has been excerpted from Van der Hoeven and Whetten's symposium paper:

"Scorecard" Processes and Measurements

Each element of the scorecard has identifiable key processes and measurements. For example the first two items on the scorecard, technical and scientific results and effectiveness, have three well-defined processes and measurements. They are the annual accomplishments review, the relationship assessment report card, and the *external effectiveness measurements* (EEM). Annual accomplishments, which are significant new, completed results in relevant areas of science tech-

Research Division Scorecard

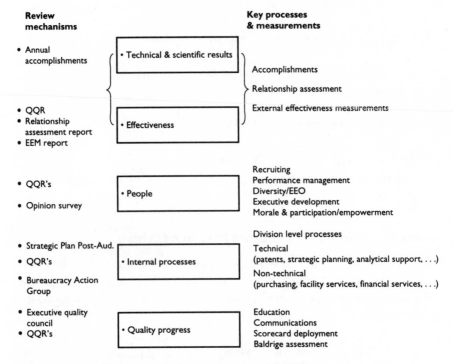

Figure 3.10 IBM's research division scorecard (1993).

nology or product development, are presented in the first quarter to the director of research. They are initially presented to and assessed by the vice president of technical plans and controls and his staff. References both inside and outside IBM (for example, for science accomplishments) are contacted to help in evaluating the accomplishments, and then they are ranked as "good," "very good," "outstanding," or "extraordinary." Nonprescriptive definitions are:

> *Extraordinary:* Major technical advances with broad product impact. Creates a revolution in the playing field.
> *Outstanding:* Significant product impact. Significant technology demonstration. Significant new materials. New phenomena. New theories. Pervasively applied instruments.

Very good: Important advance that changes direction of research for several groups/people. Products/instruments that have important business impact.

Good: Good completed piece of work. Accepted by peer groups.

A relationship assessment report card process obtains feedback from high-level manufacturing and development business unit management on their satisfaction with research division activities. In IBM terminology, these joint efforts are referred to as "joint programs," and are similar in concept to Los Alamos "programs." Joint programs are funded and head count provided by the business unit partners, based upon negotiated strategies and goals. The process uses a six-element report card format for broadly ranking research contributions to the business units. A five-point scale is used ranging from "delighted" to "dissatisfied." The elements of the relationship assessment report card are:

- *Accomplishments impact.* "These are some key accomplishments over the past year in support of your unit. We'd like your input."
- *Other impact.* "We have also made significant progress over the past year in areas which are not yet viewed as accomplishments and have assisted you in 'fire-fighting' activities. Please comment."
- *Joint program strategy.* "We have developed our joint program strategies together. How effectively have we done this, including adjusting to changes in the environment?"
- *Strategy execution.* "Having defined our strategy, how well have we executed it? Commitments and schedules met? Conflicts resolved? Understanding of complementary activities?"
- *Exploratory programs.* "We support a number of exploratory advanced technology and underlying science activities, not part of the joint program, and often with broader, generic impact. What is your reaction?"
- *People relations.* "Our people work closely together. How effectively do we work together as individuals and as teams?"

It also involves a face-to-face meeting between research and business unit executive-level management to discuss research effectiveness and action plans. . . .

The quality and impact of research accomplishments as viewed by the science and technology world external to IBM are measured broadly through the *external* effectiveness measurements. These include the following: significant external honors such as awards, prizes, medals, elections to fellowship societies, keynote and invited talks, national offices in professional organizations, and similar recognition; the number of publications in the open literature and papers at technical meetings; books and book chapters; the number of patent applications submitted and the number and quality of patents issued.

The *people* measurements are chosen to represent five very important attributes of the people resource, namely, quality of hiring, management of performance (both exceptional and poor), diversity, development of executive talent, and group morale. These attributes each have their own processes and measures and are tracked on a quarterly or annual basis. For example, an employee opinion survey, done on an annual basis, provides a measure of employee morale and participation. The division also has a policy of not promoting individuals to executive-level positions without prior management experience outside the division.

Internal support processes are, in most cases, directly amenable to process analysis, defect elimination, and continuous improvement. Progress on improving key internal support processes can have a very beneficial influence on the technical work of the laboratory by making support services more efficient and easier to use. Their improvement can also have an indirect, but very important, additional influence on the technical staff. Good results help to convince skeptics of the quality program (and R&D environments have more than their share!) that it really makes a difference. . . .

The last element of the scorecard, *quality progress,* addresses the set of measures that are used to monitor overall progress of the quality program. For example, deployment and coverage of the education and communication programs are monitored. Finally, in order to provide a comprehensive measure of overall division progress, a division-wide Baldrige self-assessment[6] is done.

Measurement Completeness: Developing Hierarchies and Linkages

Juran (1992) has stressed the importance of measurement in providing a basis for precise communication. Corresponding to the development and use of a hierarchy of financial measures for communicating and managing an organization's financial status, a hierarchy of quality measures must be developed to communicate and manage an organization's quality status. Figure 3.11 (top) is Juran's pyramid of measurement *units* used at various organizational levels. Fig-

---

[6] Chapter 4 will address Baldrige assessments in R&D organizations.

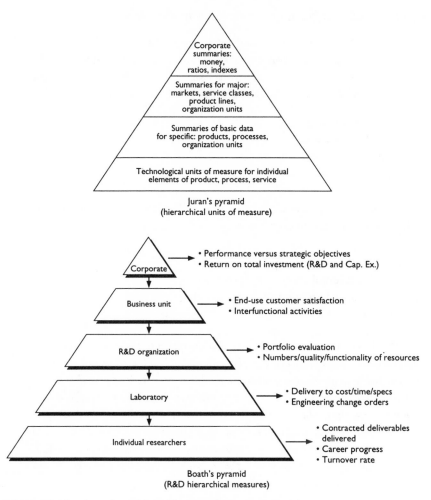

Juran's pyramid
(hierarchical units of measure)

Boath's pyramid
(R&D hierarchical measures)

Figure 3.11 Juran's and Boath's measurement pyramids.

ure 3.11 (bottom) was provided by Boath (1992) as a measurement pyramid tailored for R&D organizations.

In Chapter 2, we discussed Corning's World Class Quality (WCQ) committee's hierarchical organization developed to oversee the quality process for the technology group. Menger of Corning (1993) also discusses how the WCQ drives the development and linkages of Key Results Indicators (KRIs) for Corning's technology group (research, development, and engineering):

Linking R&D Performance Indicators at Corning

The Committee meets monthly and provides oversight and coordination for the 15 quality improvement teams within the technology group. One major responsibility of the committee is to define the measures—the KRIs—for the technology group. We identified the general areas for improvement as:

1. *Cycle time*
2. *Productivity*
3. *Customer satisfaction*
4. *Employee satisfaction*

These classifications are similar to those of Kaplan and Norton's (1992) balanced scorecard used to develop and link key measures for:

1. Customer satisfaction
2. Key internal process performance
3. Organization innovation and learning
4. Financial performance

The WCQ has worked diligently to identify appropriate methods of quantitatively assessing improvement in these areas. Each of the 15 units has likewise defined its areas of improvement and their measures. Twice a year the committee spends the better part of two days visiting each of the 15 units at their sites. We review the quality of their KRIs, consistency of unit KRIs with those of the technology group, progress made on the KRIs, and plans for improvement in cases for which little progress was measured. . . . After the units receive feedback from the WCQ committee, a sharing session is held for all the QITs so that best practices may be communicated.

Figure 3.12, from Menger's paper, depicts the KRI measurement hierarchy that Corning's technology group's World Class Quality committee uses to measure and improve progress on KRIs.

Corning's technology's group WCQ committee uses specific criteria to identify and define KRIs. KRIs must be either:

1. Related to customer deliverables
2. A process outcome
3. Customer or employee satisfaction

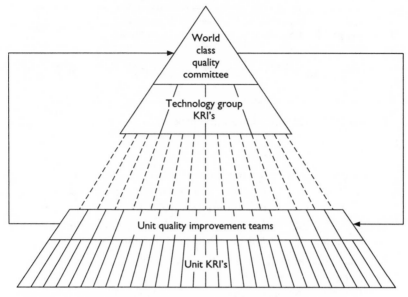

Figure 3.12 Corning's hierarchy of key results indicators (KRIs).

Menger provides helpful insights into the technology group's evolution of cycle time, productivity, and customer and employee satisfaction measures.

> Initially, we defined *cycle time* as the time it took a product to have a million dollars in sales after the project to develop that product received funding from a business area. We worked with this KRI for a while and discovered it had many shortcomings. It did not address cycle time for the substantial amount of work devoted to process development that did not result in new products with defined sales. The measure did not address the early stages of product and process development when projects were funded internally from the budget of the technology group. Finally, the "time to million-dollar sales" did not measure the cycle time of those projects that were terminated for technical or commercial reasons. We wished to compress the cycle time of these projects as well.
>
> After substantial debate, we created a different measure of cycle time, one based on our paradigm of commercialization, which we call the *innovation process* (Figure 3.13).

Build knowledge	Determine feasibility	Test practicality	Prove profitability	Commercialize
Stage I →	Stage II →	Stage III →	Stage IV →	Stage V

Figure 3.13   Corning's innovation process.

While we consider the details of our process proprietary, I can sketch it out in broad terms. The innovation process has five stages: Build knowledge, determine feasibility, test practicality, prove profitability, and commercialize. The process defines criteria that should be met before a project graduates to the next stage. Criteria include all three functions: technology, marketing, and manufacturing.

The WCQ committee gathered historical data on how long projects remained in each of the five stages for well over 100 projects. When we first analyzed the data, we found that projects showed such huge variation that we could not make sense of the data. Then we displayed the data on a grid that we use extensively—the market/technology grid (Figure 3.14).

In this format, clear trends emerged, with the durations increasing as one moved up and to the right. Having the historical norms, the WCQ committee set objectives for reducing those times. We

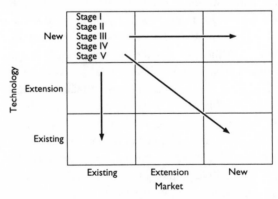

Figure 3.14   Corning's technology versus market grid.

initially decided not to compress the times in stage 1 or 2 but are now reconsidering that decision.

This is all very fine, you may say, but you may also add that this KRI is not actionable. You are right; it is not. The KRI at the technology group level is a macro-measure and cannot by its very nature be actionable. The role of the WCQ committee is to assure that units have KRIs that support ours and are actionable. We discovered, in its site reviews, that most units did not have any KRI involving cycle time, and we are remedying this inconsistency by requiring units to adopt a cycle-time measure. About half the units now have some measure of cycle time, and the others are working on it. The committee is not wise enough to tell the units in detail how to reduce their cycle time and become more efficient—we can only encourage them to do so. I will state three examples of cycle-time measures from three different units to demonstrate how widely their approaches differ:

1. $\dfrac{\text{Project elapsed time}}{\text{Agreed time with customer}} < 1$

2. Percent of promised services delivered on time $> 87\%$

3. Customer satisfaction with timeliness (from surveys) $> 90\%$

These three KRIs are measured twice annually. The goals are not arbitrary but were established by making the measurements for a year and then setting a target that entailed some stretch. Units differ as to the magnitude of challenges they are willing to assume in setting their targets. One function of the WCQ committee is to assure that all targets represent a substantial improvement over historical performance. Of the three KRIs cited above, the last is the best, in my opinion. One may meet the agreed-upon delivery time but still not meet the customers' need.

The committee is assuming that if every unit improves its timeliness, the technology group as a whole will improve its cycle time as we measure it. While this makes intuitive sense, we have not been tracking cycle time on the new basis long enough to test the validity of that assumption.

The *productivity KRI* was also subject to substantial revision. Our first stab at this KRI was based on the "million-dollar list." We tracked the ratio of new product sales to RD&E expenses.

Our original measure suffered from the shortcoming that it did not capture the major contributions made by the engineering division of RD&E to support other, ongoing businesses. In our first effort to remedy this omission, we attempted to assign dollar values to the impact statements that the engineering departments prepare every year. After much agony, we concluded this approach was not practical. There was too much overlap among projects and entanglement of engineering programs to generate credible numbers. Again, we took the macro view. We now measure the impact of engineering by tracking the gross margins of all the plants as a fraction of RD&E expense. We realize, of course, that this measure is imperfect and many factors determine the gross margins of plants. Nevertheless, we hope that the variations, year to year, will reflect the impact of our engineering advances. At the very least, the WCQ committee is sending a strong signal to the engineering units that they must continue to contribute to plant profitability. Like the cycle-time measure, we leave it to the units to define their KRIs in support of ours. The *customer and employee satisfaction KRIs* are mandated throughout the corporation. Thus, we need a mechanism to consolidate the KRIs of the 15 units. Determination of customer satisfaction is especially difficult for the technology group because we have so many sets of customers. We have top management, which sets the business direction and strategy; the ultimate customers, who buy end products; the manufacturing plants, which produce our successes; and the vice chairman, who funds the basic directed science. In our measures, we deal only with those customers internal to the company, though we listen acutely to customer satisfaction data collected by the business areas for the external (or "real") customers.

Units have created their own mechanisms for *measuring customer satisfaction.* They use a variety of approaches—surveys, focus groups, interviews, and third-party interviews. Without exception, units say they find the feedback they receive useful in improving their performance. But the issue remained as to how to boil down all this information into something we could report to the corporate office. The WCQ committee hit upon the solution of requiring all units to include one question in their customer satisfaction measurements:

What was your overall satisfaction with our performance? (0–100%)

These numbers were averaged for the 15 units, and it was the average that was reported to the corporate office. We have tracked this number for several years and, as you see in Figure 3.15 our scores are high.

But there is no increase over time, as we had expected to be the case if we were truly improving continuously. There are several possible explanations for the lack of an upward trend. Perhaps some people will not give you a rating higher than 70 percent no matter what you do. Perhaps we are not improving. Perhaps we are improving, but expectations are rising, too.

The WCQ is trying to untangle the possible reasons for the flat results. In an attempt to tease out the issue of rising expectations, we added a new question to the customer satisfaction measures:

Since our last interaction, our performance has:
__ Improved
__ Stayed the same
__ Deteriorated

While we have just added this question, our preliminary findings suggest that rising expectations on the part of our customers are at

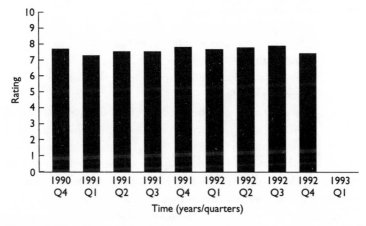

Figure 3.15 Corning's technology group (internal) customers' satisfaction.

least a part of the apparent lack of improvement. Meanwhile, we are experimenting with other approaches to gauging overall customer satisfaction. One unit is using a new measure for overall customer satisfaction: the percent of customers' suggestions for improvement that are implemented. I like that approach, but can also see problems—surely not all suggestions are valid and merit implementation.

Employee satisfaction is reported to the corporate office and, like customer satisfaction, has not been increasing. Employee satisfaction is complex and multidimensional. Our approach was first to determine the components of employee satisfaction. This we did by holding several focus groups led by external professionals. Then we were in a position to work on the constituent pieces of satisfaction. For one example, career development and the associated training are high among employees concerns. A corporate-wide goal is that an average of 5 percent of an employee's time be spent in training. Before this goal was established, the amount of training provided to employees varied greatly and was, on the average, considerably less than 5 percent. The 5 percent goal was appropriate in its time; it helped jump-start the system. But training is now an accepted part of our culture and we needed to stretch our objective.

The new goal became doubling the measured effectiveness of the training (while maintaining the 5 percent time goal). Of course, measuring the effectiveness of training is not an easy chore. The company adopted an operational definition for training effectiveness. Our climate survey now contains questions designed to measure training effectiveness such as:

1. The training I receive is linked to the business needs of my organization.
2. Before I get training, my supervisor and I discuss the reasons for attending.
3. I use the skills and knowledge gained from training on my job.

In effect, this measure of training effectiveness defines a process for getting the most out of the training. Supervisors will now have to plan training of their employees more carefully and work with their employees to assure that they get the appropriate training and actually use what they learn on the job. We believe that by focusing attention on all the components of employee satisfaction in this way, we will see the increase in employee satisfaction that we hope for and require.

Establishing Accountability and Measuring Individual Performance

In the context of the measurement pyramid, the previous materials have principally addressed measuring the following:

1. Overall R&D performance
2. Key R&D processes performance
3. Project performance

Individuals' performance was discussed by Juran (1989), who stated that individual "responsibility should be coextensive with authority." Juran's concept of *self-control* provides a means for measuring compliance with this requirement. Before *any* individual can be held responsible for their performance, they must:

1. Know the *goals* for their performance
2. Know their *actual* performance level
3. Have a means for adjusting their performance level

A properly designed and executed performance management process is therefore crucial for establishing individual accountability, self-control, and linkages among goals for the R&D organization, its key processes, and the goals established for managers and employees.

Performance Management at Olin Electronic Materials Technology

Marion (1991), director of technology for electronic materials at Olin Corporation, reported that a survey of his R&D employees revealed that they were not satisfied with their performance review and career development system. An improved performance review and career planning process was developed that incorporated Olin's TQM principles with the survey results. An additional objective for the new process was to develop stronger linkages between individual and departmental objectives. The symposium paper on page 97, excerpted from Marien (1991) will provide additional insights and examples from Olin's PMP process used within an R&D environment.

This chapter has focused on developing measures of R&D performance from the perspective of customers, processes, projects, and employees. Chapter 4 will address the development and use of processes for assessing the performance of R&D *quality system* performance. Quality system performance will be discussed from the perspectives of ISO 9000 and the Malcolm Baldrige National Quality Award.

As referenced earlier in this chapter, the R&D symposium paper beginning on page 113 provides additional insights into the benchmarking process used by the Strategic Decisions Group to identify the "best practices" in decision making for R&D portfolios.

Olin's Performance Management Process

Bruce A. Marien
Director of Technology
Olin Corporation

The four building blocks of the Performance Management Process are: its basis in Total Quality Management (TQM), its development of a dynamic job description, its congruence with departmental goals, and finally, its emphasis on professional growth. (See Figure 3.16.)

The PMP is linked to the *TQM Process* and the development of personal quality plans with the commitment that each individual will meet the agreed-upon expectations of internal and external customers all the time.

The *Job Description* may sound obvious, yet agreement upon the job description between the employee and supervisor is fundamental to successful performance. In questionnaire responses, the job description was often cited as lacking or misunderstood. Performance that is customer-driven produces a dynamic job environment—one in which job descriptions can and should reflect change as it happens.

Figure 3.16 Components of the performance management process.

Department Goals must also be addressed. Agreed-to expectations must be consistent with the goals of the organization. The goals should be clear to all as plans are developed and commitments are made.

Professional Growth is a major driving force in the research environment. Achieving the highest level of success and satisfaction in your job assignment is now a commitment that you and your supervisor, working together, will make happen.

Underpinning the PMP are three precepts. (1) Evaluate performance, and not the person, (2) employee-driven periodic review, and (3) flexibility to update expectations and objectives.

PMP's living documentation concerning performance is retained by both employee and supervisor. Objectives are written and agreed upon with significant employee input. The documentation is in the employee's possession for review and the supervisor's possession for reference. The supervisor's boss also has access to the documentation through second-level review meetings for assurance that department goals are consistent with customer expectations.

The PMP documentation is flexible as customer's expectations change in a dynamic, real-world environment. One's PMP is a living document that aids both in planning and in improving performance. PMP's documentation helps in other ways as well. Performance drives the Performance Management Process, and the results and information derived through PMP ultimately have a bearing upon decisions concerning compensation, succession planning, and professional development.

Performance Management Process Cycle

The PMP Cycle is an ongoing process that revolves around continuing sessions between employees and customers, employees and supervisors, and supervisors and their supervisors. All are involved. (See Figure 3.17.)

The Kickoff Meeting

The Kickoff Meeting is the first step in the PMP Cycle. It occurs as individual sessions between supervisors and the people who report to them from the R&D director with his staff down through the organization to the individual researchers with their supervisors. A significant task for the kickoff meeting is to identify key customers and determine who will contact each of them. Information on past performance and future expectations will be

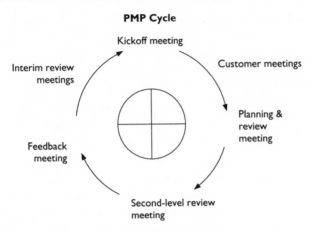

Figure 3.17 The performance management cycle.

needed from the customer for the next meeting of the cycle. The supervisor focuses primarily on past performance to customers' expectations, while the employee focuses primarily on the future expectations. The supervisor coaches the subordinate in the type of information to obtain from his customers in terms of desired products, services, and specific quality expectations. A typical researcher's customer base might include the business manager for the area, a specific marketing person responsible for the developing product, and his or her own subordinates. Additional customers may include the regulatory manager or a specific patent attorney. Basic research individuals might identify the corporate technical officer or a specific scientific society as internal and external customers respectively. As a director, my customers are the vice presidents of the various business areas associated with my research portfolio and the employees in my organization.

Customer Meetings

Between the kickoff meeting and the Planning and Review meeting a great deal of work must be done on the part of the supervisor and the employee. Each has agreed to gather critical information from customers for the next step of the process. Documentation must be developed to compare results with last year's expectations and to define the expectations for the next period. Additionally, there must be a discussion about personal quality improvements which could be included in future expectations. Finally, there must be an assessment of the degree to which the customers' expectations were met.

The Planning and Review Meeting

The Planning and Review session is the next step in which the supervisor and employee come together following their kickoff meeting. They discuss what they have discovered and documented in interviewing their customers with respect to performance and future expectations. They capture in writing the results versus expectations of the previous period. They also refer to agreed-upon individual and departmental goals for the coming cycle. If there is a key cog in the performance management process cycle, this is it. The supervisor and employee review job descriptions and go through a worksheet exercise to define key activities. (See Figure 3.18.) Once they know what must be done, they agree upon whether added knowledge or skills are required to do it, and, if so, they make concrete plans for acquiring whatever tools are necessary. A typical Planning and Review meeting will last two or three hours and it is an absolutely individual event.

The Planning and Review meeting is the key meeting in the cycle. The kickoff meeting is to prepare for it, and the results of it become the foundation for the meetings that follow.

The Second-Level Review

The second-level review meeting presents the opportunity for the supervisor to discuss the results of the planning and review meetings of all subordinates with his or her boss They meet to examine the broad departmental picture to be certain that goals reflect customer expectations and that personal quality plans and professional development plans are in agreement as well. At this point, departmental concurrence is obtained. (See Figure 3.19.)

If a conflict occurs at the second-level review between customer expectations and department goals, it is the obligation of the employee and supervisor to resolve and negotiate those differences in consultation with the customer and develop new agreed-upon customer expectations or petition their case to change the departmental goals.

Significant contributions and value added to the organization during the period are discussed. Strengths are noted as well as goals for specific areas

---

Olin Planning and Review Meeting

Space is provided for listing customer expectations during the beginning of the PMP and for listing the results at year-end. Include timing and measures of success where possible.

- Discuss results vs. expectations°
- Feedback from customer interviews
- Professional Growth needs (second-level summary)
- Skills—technical and interpersonal
- Experience—contact with other internal functions
            —contact with customers
            —team experience
- Employee Expectations

Expectations	**Results Achieved**
1.	
2.	
3.	
4.	
5.	
6.	
7.	

° EXPECTATIONS AND RESULTS MUST BE IN WRITING.

Figure 3.18 PMP planning and review worksheet.

for improvement. Major expectations are specified for the next period and commitments for resource needs and assistance requests are made. Finally, there is agreement as to the extent to which results achieved in this period met agreed-upon customer expectations. Notice that the discussion centers on future performance and growth more than establishment of a rating. Simply, either one meets customer expectations or one does not meet customer expectations. To the extent that one does not completely meet cus-

---

Second-Level Review

- Review customer expectations
- Ensure alignment of department goals/resources
- Define professional development plan

Figure 3.19 Second-level responsibilities.

tomer expectations, there is the opportunity for improvement. This becomes part of the individual's personal quality plan for the next period.

Feedback Meeting

Feedback meetings are exactly what the name implies. They occur after the second-level review meetings to enable the supervisor to keep the employee informed about such things as changes in timetables and resources and any new information that may affect priorities, goals, or objectives.

Interim Review Meetings

Interim review meetings occur between the supervisor and the employee to monitor changing customer expectations and the progress of the employee's personal quality plan. Several of these meetings occur during the course of the review period. These are especially good times to update documentation and clarify issues. We check that performance is still directed at customers' expectations and that the goals of the organization and the individual are being addressed. In the course of the cycle, the final interim review meeting is followed by the kickoff meeting for the next PMP cycle. As the cycle begins anew, the same sequence of meetings occurs.

Additional Benefits of PMP

Salary Administration

Our compensation strategy isn't complicated at all. We want to pay a competitive salary for the work performed. Our merit budget is based on surveys of the appropriate workforces in our specific environments. Merit increases are increases in salary granted to an employee to reward performance and contributions on the job. The department head evaluates the

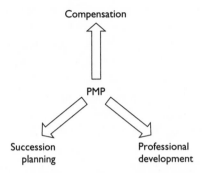

Figure 3.20 Impact of performance management process.

contributions of all employees in the work unit. We pay for performance which is documented in our performance management process. Individual merit increases are based on achievement of quality goals, that is, the extent to which one meets customers' expectations and contributes to the quality of the organization. (See Figure 3.20.)

Professional Growth

Professional growth is based on input developed in the PMP cycle. We jointly identify career objectives early and formulate specific development pathways for each employee. We plan and manage the development of individuals consistent with matching their skills and abilities with specific organizational opportunities.

Succession Planning

Succession planning is based on Quality performance and aptitudes as documented in the PMP cycle. The process, again, is employee-driven. The resolution of potential conflicts in personal aptitudes versus career expectations are part of the coaching role of the supervisor.

Conclusion

The performance is the key issue in meeting customers' expectations. PMP is designed to efficiently monitor that performance while being able to accommodate changing customer expectations. The process is not intended to be cast in concrete, but rather to be used flexibly and in ways that make sense in various environments. The result is a different philosophy of appraising performance. PMP brings with it a shared dialogue process and a positive atmosphere that is much more conducive to successful results. With PMP, two people work together in meeting and exceeding the customers' expectations. Its no longer the boss saying "let me tell you how you have been doing." Rather it is a positive partnership between employee and supervisor with each one comfortable in questioning and contributing whenever necessary. The supervisor acts as coach, mentor, and partner in achieving agreed-upon customer expectations. The employee feels more responsible for his or her own performance, professional growth, and career advancement. The communication emphasis is much more open. Documentation of goals, expectations, and performance as well as training needs, professional development, and personal growth is much clearer, much more specific.

The fundamental principles, outlined earlier, are the constants in the Performance Management Process. Workbooks and training media are simply tools to help put the principles into practice and to make them visible in the organization. Performance Management is a dynamic process which meets the needs and expectations of individuals and contributes to the success of the organization, and, most important, it works!

Today, PMP is helping us achieve our corporate vision of being a preferred supplier of innovative products and services to customers in a variety of industries. From a technology perspective, we have listened to all our customers. Our external customers expect products and services of unsurpassed quality and value. Our business managers expect us to "innovate and don't be late!" Our employees expect fair compensation, professional growth, and an atmosphere of fairness, truth telling, promise keeping, and respect for the individual. Through Total Quality Management and our Performance Management Process, we will meet these expectations.

Performance Management Process Example

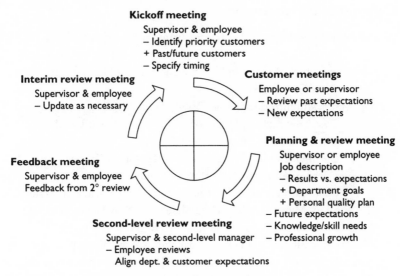

Kickoff meeting
Supervisor & employee
— Identify priority customers
+ Past/future customers
— Specify timing

Interim review meeting
Supervisor & employee
— Update as necessary

Customer meetings
Employee or supervisor
— Review past expectations
— New expectations

Feedback meeting
Supervisor & employee
Feedback from 2° review

Planning & review meeting
Supervisor or employee
Job description
— Results vs. expectations
+ Department goals
+ Personal quality plan
— Future expectations
— Knowledge/skill needs
— Professional growth

Second-level review meeting
Supervisor & second-level manager
— Employee reviews
Align dept. & customer expectations

Figure 3.21 Performance management process.

Attached: **PMP of M. W. Seal**

Kickoff Worksheet
Planning & Review Worksheet
Example Internal Customer Response
Example External Customer Response
Second-Level Review Worksheet

Employee's Name: *M. Seal*
Supervisor's Name: *B. Marien*
Date Prepared: *4/3/91*

Kickoff Meeting Worksheet

What are the agreed-upon expectations from the previous cycle?

1. Completion of updated Technician Training Manual.
   Customer: Employees, PJE and TFR
2. Successful introduction of CVD-8350 at EXCEL.
   Customer: External Customer: Kathy Brown at EXCEL.
3. Publication Goal: 4 patents, and 4 papers.
   Customer: Owners, DFW, (Chief Technical Officer).
4. Project Proposals for Government Contracts.
   Customer: External Customer: U.S. Army Capt. Phil Malone
5. Product Material Safety Data Sheets for New Products.
   Customer: Internal Customer: JHB (Safety Manager).
6. Trouble Shooting check list for Printed Wire Board plating.
   Customer: Internal Customer: CJL (Tech Service Manager).
7. Progress DOP-44 project to Pilot Plant trial stage.
   Customer: Internal Customer: T. Camp, CVD manager
8. Improve the $KMnO_4$ assay of Regen-Unit to 92–97% range.
   Customer: External Customer : P. Liu at Motorex
9. 100% professionals participate in outside technical training:
   Customer: Employees

Who are the customers to be contacted for next period?

Employee	**Supervisor**
1. Terry Camp (CVD mgr)	1. Paul Liu (Motorex)
2. Pat Evans (Employee Rep.)	2. Phil Malone (U.S. Army)
3. John Butcher (Safety)	3. Kathy Brown (Excel)

Date of Planning and Review Meeting.

May 3, 1991

Employee's Name: *M. Seal*
Supervisor's Name: *B. Marien*
Date Prepared: *4/3/91*

Planning & Review Meeting Worksheet

Space is provided for listing customer expectations during the beginning of the PMP, and for listing the results at year-end. Include timing and measures of success where possible.

- Discuss results vs. expectations (expectations and results must be in writing)
- Feedback from customer interviews
- Professional Growth needs (second-level summary)
- Skills—technical and interpersonal
- Experience—contact with other internal functions
  - —contact with customers
  - —team experience
- Employee Expectations [worksheets to follow]

Professional Development:

Ultimate career goal is to be chief technical officer of the corporation.
Next logical position: Cross training in business area.
Timing? Transfer to Electronics business group in 1994 with scheduled return in 1996–1997 timeframe as a section manager.
Training needs: Advanced Management Course at University of Maryland in October 1991 and continued work toward completion of M.B.A. (1993).

Example of Internal Customer

OLIN INTEROFFICE MEMO

TO: M. W. Seal   LOCATION Cheshire   DATE: 1/22/91

FROM: P. J. Evans   LOCATION Cheshire

SUBJECT: Performance Management Process

At our last PMP meeting, we agreed that Tim Roush and myself would represent the researchers in our group. The collective expectations were:

1. All group members would have an effective performance review by 3/31/91.
2. All group members would participate in some formalized outside training or in-house professional development course.
3. Management would issue a technician training manual for new personnel along with formalized safety introduction seminar.
4. Work with purchasing department to simplify paperwork associated with buying items below $100.
5. Promote from within at least 75% of the time.
6. Hold communication meetings on a timely basis.
7. Be visible to the organization as measured by number of personal contacts with individuals in the department.

As of March 31, 1991, the accomplishments against the above objectives are:

1. All personnel had PMPs during the first three months of 1991. A total of 35 out of 39 viewed their PMP as effective. Three individuals sought additional input from customers with emphasis on recent completion of projects. One individual was not satisfied with the system since several of his customers changed personnel during the year and it was difficult to obtain meaningful results vs. expectation information.
2. All personnel signed up for external courses during the year. A total of 24 out of 39 actually attended external seminars, courses or attended society meetings. An additional 12 people took the inter-

nal management development I course offered in June 90. Three people declined to attend scheduled training for various reasons.

3. New employee manual was completed at the end of the year. It included the Safety overview and the technician skills introduction section as agreed.

4. Grants of Authority were increased for all laboratory personnel so that items under $200.00 could be self approved.

5. In 1990 there were five promotions and no outside hires; therefore 100% of promotions were internal.

6. Communication meetings were held every two months. However, information still takes a long time to get from corporate headquarters to the troops. Increased use of the computer local area network would help.

7. Management has shown an increased presence in the laboratory. The lunchtime brown-bag meetings are a hit.

Overall, expectations were met. We should include the following items for the next period.

1. Continuation of Effective PMP objective for 1991.

2. Communication Improvement: Let's get some articles about our group into the company newsletters and TQM highlights. Target: three articles.

3. Attain 100% training opportunity for all group members. This may include attendance at national or local section society meetings.

4. Ensure that 80% of promotional opportunities are filled internally.

5. Institute an Innovation Award within the group for the most outstanding contribution during the year. Set a goal that members of the group win the R&D Innovation Award twice during the year.

Pat Evans

Example of External Customer

EXCEL Corporation
275 Winchester Ave.
New Haven, CT 06511

Dr. Bruce A. Marien
Director, Technology
Olin Corporation
350 Knotter Drive
Cheshire, CT 06410

January 30, 1991

It was a pleasure talking to you on Thursday. As we discussed, I have been impressed with the level of interaction that Olin has had with Excel on the CVD-8350 program. Mark Seal has been especially helpful in terms of getting results when we needed them. So, generally, I feel that he has met my expectations.

Specifically, we had originally agreed to review the status of the program quarterly. However, the onset of the recession brought about an accelerated timetable and we had to change to monthly meetings. Mark made the necessary changes in the schedule to accommodate the change. Mark made himself available off-hours as needed. While we never had reason to contact him at home, it was reassuring to us that we could if necessary. On the downside, Ralph Hutchinson, one of Mark's people had agreed to send statistical quality data to us on a timely basis. Several times, our people had to remind Ralph that it was due. It never became a critical issue, but some improvement in attention to detail could be beneficial here.

This year is a decision point for CVD-8350. We will need access to Mark and his people on a priority basis. I anticipate weekly conference calls on the status of the program, and I would like Mark to schedule these for Friday afternoons. I would also want to establish a linkup with your Local Area Network for on-line analytical data Hopefully, Mark can set this up for us with your information services group. Finally, I expect that Mark will assist us in a joint R&D 100 Award application on the successful CVD-8350 by the end of the year.

I hope this information is useful to you in your performance management process. If there are any questions, please don't hesitate to call me.

Sincerely
Katherine B. Brown
Principal Engineer

Employee's Name: *M. Seal*
Supervisor's Name: *B. Marien*
Date Prepared: *4/3/91*

Second-Level Review

1. Significant contributions and value added to the organization.
   a) Excellent initiative in obtaining CVD-8350 with Excel.
   b) Completed three major TQM committee projects including the video on Barriers to Innovation and survey Feedback.
   c) Progressed DOP-44 to pilot-plant stage.
   d) Obtained Government contract for chip packaging system.
   e) Completed Safety Data Sheets for all new product in area.
2. Strengths noted.
   Sound technical understanding of area.
   Good interactive and communication skills.
   Excellent support from subordinates—a real team builder.
3. Improvement opportunities.
   Understanding of area from a business perspective.
4. Major expectations for next period.
   a) Complete CVD-8350.
   b) Complete PWB equipment development.
   c) Increase the efficiency of $KMnO4$ generator by 1%.
   d) Identify two new contract opportunities in Microelectronics.
5. Resources, assistance requested:
   Continue U. of Md Advanced Management Course (Part 3 of 5)
   Continue support for completion of M.B.A. in 1993
6. Extent to which results achieved met agreed upon expectations:
   X Met expectations
   Did not meet expectations

Comments:

Mark generally meets or exceeds the expectations of his customers. We will present future challenges in job assignments to develop potential business area management opportunities and current ultimate career path to CTO position.

Ultimate career goal:
Chief technical officer of the corporation.

Next logical position:
Cross-training in business area.

Timing?
Transfer to Electronics business group in 1994 with scheduled return in 1996–1997 time frame as a section manager.

SDG's Benchmarking Study of R&D Decision Quality Provides Blueprint for Doing the Right R&D

David M. Matheson
Senior Associate
James E. Matheson
Director
Michael M. Menke
Principal
Strategic Decisions Group

Abstract

The R&D Decision Quality Benchmarking Study represents a unique attempt to bring the spirit of the quality movement to strategic R&D decision making. The results reveal a set of practices that when properly applied can significantly improve an organization's return on R&D.

Quality R&D decisions are critical for business success. In 1991, Strategic Decisions Group launched the R&D Decision Quality Benchmarking Study to learn how industry leaders make strategic R&D decisions and integrate technology with a company's strategic business objectives. The study identifies 45 decision-making practices used by the "best of the best," which represent a blueprint for doing the right R&D. Further, it presents innovative methods that enable organizations to diagnose their R&D decision making and identify those practices that, when implemented, will most improve R&D's contribution to the business.

Background

Profitable, productive R&D has always been critical for long-term business success. In today's business environment, it is even more important to manage R&D projects and resources well. In its June 28, 1993, issue, *Business Week* declared, "As the world economy limps along and competition gets tougher, nearly all companies are feeling the pressure to hold down R&D costs and at the same time speed the development of new products."

Doing more with less and getting the right products to market at the right time require exceptional R&D decision making. But how can an organization improve its R&D decision quality? Are there certain practices and procedures that separate acknowledged industry leaders from other companies with more modest records of success?

In 1991, Strategic Decisions Group (SDG) launched the R&D Decision Quality Benchmarking Study to identify the best practices for R&D decision making, with the goal of helping organizations learn how to obtain the highest value from R&D.

A Multiphased Approach

The benchmarking study was conducted in four phases over approximately one year. We started with a list of nearly 5,000 senior-level R&D and business executives representing a broad cross section of industries, eventually receiving responses from 200 of those executives.

In Phase I, we asked respondents to nominate companies that are the best at strategic R&D decision making. We also asked them to provide any objective indicators they use to judge R&D decision quality and to rate their own R&D decision making on a scale of 0–100 percent.

In Phase II, we studied how 16 specific R&D decision-making practices were used by selected organizations. Our questions focused on frequency of use, quality of execution, and potential for improving decision quality at the organizations chosen.

Phase III was a series of in-depth interviews with many of the companies that had been nominated as the best R&D decision makers in the study's initial phase. From the data we collected in these interviews, we consolidated more than 200 decision-making practices used at these premier companies into the 45 best practices for R&D decision quality.

Finally, in Phase IV, over 60 R&D executives attended forums sponsored by SDG, scrutinized and validated our conclusions, and tested and refined our proposed uses of the benchmarking results.

Several highlights from the study are worth noting. First, the companies that were singled out for their exemplary R&D decision quality came as no surprise. The list was headed by U.S. corporate leaders (non-U.S.-based companies were rarely nominated) such as 3M, Merck, Hewlett-Packard,

General Electric, AT&T, Du Pont, and Procter & Gamble. Companies that are less well known but highly regarded within their industry—such as California's Pacific Gas & Electric—also received praise. So did a handful of newer stars such as Microsoft and Intel.

Second, executives' self-assessments of decision quality showed there is a tremendous opportunity for improvement. The median score for decision quality was 56 on a scale of 100, with only a handful of companies saying their performance rated as high as 90 percent.

Third, the most pressing need for improving R&D performance was developing an improved decision process, cited by more half the respondents in the study. Learning to deal more effectively with R&D organizational or management issues and sharpening the organization's R&D vision ranked as the next highest priorities.

Blueprint for Decision Quality

The 45 best decision-making practices from Phase III of the study could be grouped naturally into nine components of decision quality that we found common to organizations making excellent strategic R&D decisions. These components form the basis of our blueprint for doing the right R&D. (See Figure 3.22.)

Near the top of the blueprint are three broad categories in which each of the nominated companies do well. The first of these is *making quality decisions,* for example, deciding whether to invest in a given program area or project, or choosing one technology over another. This part of the process can be broken into four components:

- Decision basis—Are the inputs to your R&D decisions of high quality?
- Technology strategy—Is R&D strategy in tune with business goals at the highest level?
- Portfolio management—Is your R&D portfolio and pipeline well balanced?
- Project strategy—Is each individual project being managed to its full potential?

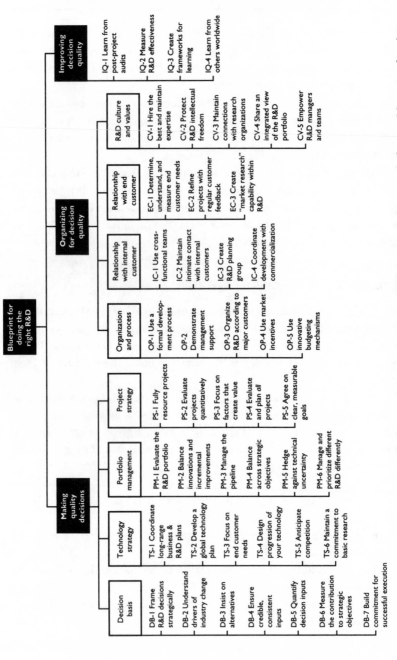

Figure 3.22 The 45 best decision-making practices from the SDG benchmarking study form a blueprint for doing the right R&D.

The second broad category is *organizing for decision quality*. The focus here is on what a company can do institutionally to maintain a high level of decision quality. This, too, is divided into four components:

- Organization and process—Does your company have a good brain? Do decision makers select the right tools and think about them well?
- R&D culture and values—Does your company have a strong heart? Does it hire the best people, train them well, and empower them to perform to their full potential?
- Relationship with internal customer—Does R&D work closely with product marketing and other internal customers?
- Relationship with end customer—Can R&D look ahead to anticipate and meet the needs and desires of the ultimate users of its results?

The final component of excellent R&D decision making is *improving decision quality*. Given that an organization is good at making strategic decisions and is organized to sustain decision quality, the "best of the best" are always trying to get better at what they do, to improve their decision-making practices and adapt to the changing business environment.

These nine components of decision quality provide a sound framework for doing the right R&D. They have much in common with the seven "best" practices by consensus identified by Ransley and Rogers.[*] Filling out this framework are the 45 best practices we identified. Although these practices are listed discretely under the various components, in our research we found that many practices support multiple components—performing a primary role in one area while making secondary contributions in others. Used properly and in the right context, any or all of these practices can contribute substantially to decision quality.

What's more, we learned that the nominated companies apply these practices *in harmony* to achieve excellence in all nine of the decision quality components. This has important implications for companies in designing and implementing change programs to meet individual requirements.

[*] Ransley, D. L. and Rogers, J. L., "A Consensus on Best R&D Practices," *Research·Technology Management,* March–April 1994.

Applying the Blueprint to Your Organization

Benchmarking has little intrinsic value. Solutions to business problems can't easily be derived by simply analyzing how other companies resolve similar problems. But if you view these benchmarks as setting a standard of excellence for strategic R&D decision making and compare *your* experience—your practices and procedures—against the best of the best, then you have the basis for meaningful change.

To help you diagnose your use of the best decision-making practices and apply the blueprint to your organization, SDG has devised three profiles. Each of these profiles plots your company's use of each practice along two dimensions. The first of these is the practice actualization profile. (See Figure 3.23.)

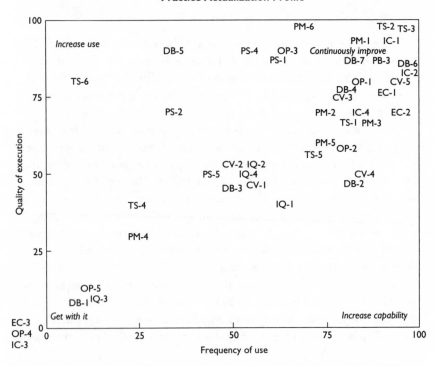

Practice Actualization Profile

Figure 3.23 The practice actualization profile identifies how well and how often decision quality practices are used.

This profile is designed to help you evaluate how often you use each decision-quality practice and how well you execute it when you do. Your objective is to have as many appropriate practices as possible fall in the upper right-hand quadrant. These are done well and often. Practices that are plotted in the upper left-hand quadrant are executed well, but are not done frequently enough. For instance, you might have a professorial type of individual in your lab who is very effective at evaluating projects quantitatively, but does not share his methods with others. Practices located in the lower right-hand quadrant are used a lot, but not done very well. These might be directives from a senior executive that have not received full acceptance. Finally, for any practices in the lower left-hand section of the grid—which are neither done well nor often—if they are important to the quality of your decision making, you'd better get with them.

The second profile is the practice screening profile. (See Figure 3.24.) Once you have determined how well you are actualizing the 45 best decision-making practices, you want to find out which ones have the greatest potential to lead to significant improvements in decision quality. Again, the target is to have as many practices as possible in the upper right-hand quadrant. These are being done well and often, and they are likely contributing to better decisions.

However, to get the most value for your effort, clearly your initial focus should be on those practices in the lower right-hand quadrant. These have just as much potential as the ones in the upper right, but they simply aren't being actualized well enough. So if you improve on the quality or frequency of your execution, you'll receive benefits.

The third and last profile is the practice prioritization profile. (See Figure 3.25.) In deciding which practices to implement, you have two alternatives. If you take the long view, you might want to prioritize on the basis of gain alone, doing those first that will contribute the most to decision quality. However, if your change program will be constrained by either time or resources, you may decide instead to start with a couple of practices found in the lower right-hand quadrant. These offer potentially excellent gains, but shouldn't require nearly as much effort to implement as those in the upper half of the grid.

The results of SDG's R&D Decision Quality Benchmarking Study demonstrate that R&D decision quality can be measured well enough to

Practice screening profile

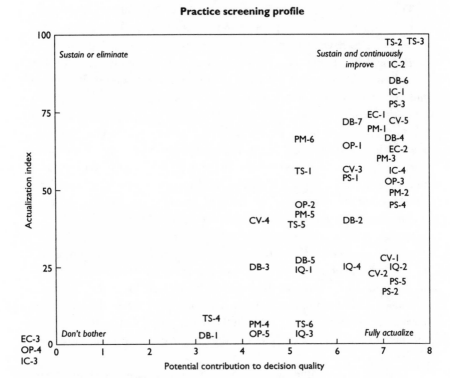

Figure 3.24 The practice screening profile highlights which practices are most worthy of your attention.

identify the best decision-making practices and to develop a solid blueprint for doing the right R&D. In addition, the study reveals that most R&D-driven organizations in the United States, by their own admission, have ample room for improvement in the quality of their strategic R&D decisions.

At SDG, we see this as only the beginning of a movement to improve R&D decision quality. The study provides an excellent platform for launching broader benchmarking studies of organizations in Europe and Asia. Already, the Industrial Research Institute—through the Quality Directors' Network (QDN)—has undertaken follow-up research that

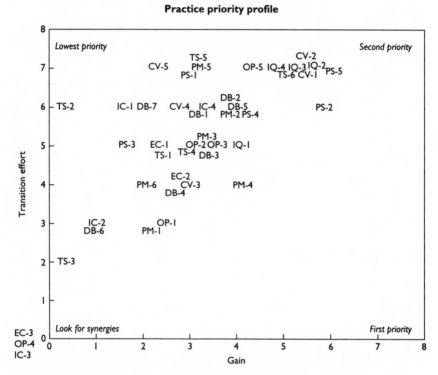

Figure 3.25 SDG's practice prioritization profile helps organizations assess the magnitude of effort required to implement the various practices.

both validates and deepens the understanding of decision quality and how to achieve it within an organization.

Perhaps the most important conclusion to be drawn from these results is that by implementing selected practices in a cohesive, well-integrated way, organizations have the potential to achieve higher productivity and greatly improve the returns from R&D.

CHAPTER 4

ASSESSING R&D QUALITY STATUS

Quality Assessment

Among the key responsibilities of quality councils discussed in Chapter 2 was the need to periodically assess quality status. Juran and Gryna (1993) have used the term *quality assessment* to mean a *broad* review of an organization's quality status for use in providing an understanding of the *size* of the quality issue and identifying the *areas* demanding attention. The recommended activities for inclusion in quality assessments are as follows:

1. Determining *performance on key product features*
2. Characterizing the current *quality culture*
3. Estimating the *costs of poor quality*
4. Defining *quality system* capability and performance

Chapter 3 provided examples of processes for identifying and measuring performance on key R&D "product" features. Chapter 3 also provided examples of the use of surveys and focus groups to obtain data on employee perceptions. The latter approach may also be used to assess quality culture.[1] This chapter will address cost-of-quality studies and the design and conduct of quality system assessments for R&D environments.

Cost of Quality

Juran and Gryna (1993) have used the term *quality costs* for those activities conducted by an organization to attain quality. Most organizations utilizing cost-of-quality studies have divided the costs into four primary categories:

---

[1] Juran and Gryna (1993) view quality culture as the "opinions, beliefs, traditions, and practices concerning quality," and they provide examples of focus group and survey questions used by various organizations.

1. *Prevention costs.* Costs associated with preventing errors in operations. Examples: requirements reviews; design reviews; supplier qualification; program audits; quality-related training (e.g., design of experiments).
2. *Internal failure costs.* Costs associated with errors found prior to delivering products to the organization's customers. Examples: redoing experiments or calculations because of incorrect or uncalibrated equipment; wrong formulas; prototype failure analysis; engineering drawing revisions necessitated by errors identified by manufacturing.
3. *External failure costs.* Costs associated with errors found after delivering products to internal and external customers. Examples: engineering support required to diagnose manufacturing problems caused by design errors; associated design changes.
4. *Appraisal costs.* Costs resulting from having to determine conformance to design requirements. Examples: inspecting prototype parts from vendors; prototype inspections; checking calculations; checking equipment setups.

Experience has demonstrated that most organizations' quality costs are concentrated in either internal or external failure costs and the appraisal costs necessitated by poorly defined or poorly controlled processes. These costs have been defined by Juran and Gryna as the *cost of poor quality.*

Identifying and Reducing Quality Costs at Corning

Cost of poor quality for Corning's technical products development group was discussed by Kozlowski (1993) who reported using a cost-of-quality task force to identify and focus on quality costs associated with core laboratory functions. Figure 4.1 (from Kozlowski) depicts the cost of quality for the technical products development department for specific process steps for seven periods. The cost of quality (COQ) data are divided into the traditional cost-of-quality categories of *prevention, detection* (appraisal), and *error correction* (internal plus external failures).

After reviewing this data the laboratory's quality council organized a corrective action team to investigate the largest cost areas. For example, one primary element of the cost of poor quality was identified as having to redo experiments. The team discovered that the primary causes of redoing experiments stemmed from one of the following:

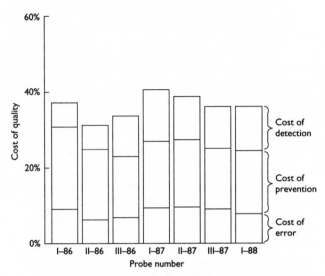

Figure 4.1 Cost of poor quality at Corning's technical products development department.

1. Poor planning of experiments
2. Poor communications with support groups
3. Wrong equipment

The experimental design issue was addressed through the development of an internal training program that covered statistical design of experiments. Poor communications issues were also addressed by training that included internal company systems, legal ramifications of technical report writing, and "shared objectives with all groups that serve us in the analytical area." The latter training "virtually eliminated the teamwork issue that was found in the cost-of-quality survey. The equipment issue was solved by instituting a department-wide electronic equipment update system that allowed maintenance and accessibility to be done more easily."

Improving R&D Quality Performance through Baldrige Assessments

In August, 1987, Public Law 100-107 was signed by President Reagan to establish a National Quality Award program named after Malcolm Baldrige, who served as secretary of commerce until his death in 1987. Among its other purposes the Award has been used to:

1. "Stimulate American companies to improve quality and productivity"
2. "Establish guidelines and criteria that can be used by business, industrial, governmental, and other organizations in evaluating their own quality efforts"

The relationships among the Award's seven-category criteria are shown in Figure 4.2. Each category is, in turn, divided into several items that guide the understanding of the intent and scope of each category. Baldrige assessments of R&D quality systems have been reported by Corning (Kozlowski 1993), Eastman Chemical (McClaskey 1992), IBM (Van der Hoeven 1993), and Los Alamos Lab-

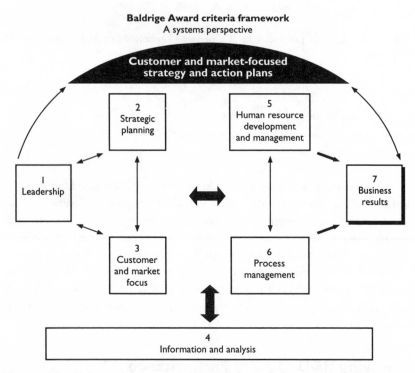

Figure 4.2 Relationships among the Baldrige Award categories. (This figure is from the *Malcolm Baldrige National Quality Award 1997 Criteria for Performance Excellence,* available from the National Institute of Standards and Technology, Gaithersburg, Maryland.)

oratory (Van der Hoeven and Whetten 1993). After prerequisite translation into the language of R&D and training, the assessments are used to develop baselines, identify gaps, and prioritize the gaps targeted for improvements.

Conducting Baldrige Assessments at IBM's Watson Research Center

Van der Hoeven (1994) has used the Baldrige criteria to help identify how IBM's Thomas J. Watson Research Center could improve its quality system's performance. Van der Hoeven provides examples on organizing the assessments, as well as interpreting and translating the Baldrige criteria for use within a research environment:

> The first, and most challenging, issue was to interpret the Baldrige questions for the IBM research environment. This was accomplished in the following manner. Each of the seven Baldrige categories was assigned to a division senior executive as follows:

Category	Responsibility
Leadership	Director of research
Data collection and analysis	VP of technical plans and controls
Strategic planning	VP of technical plans and controls
Human resources	Director of personnel
Processes	VP of systems science and tech, VP of operations
Results	Director of physical sciences, VP of operations
Customer satisfaction	VP of systems and software, VP of storage

> Key representatives of each of the principals, each with significant experience and breadth of understanding of the division, were trained in Baldrige assessment. Led by the director of quality, the group then participated in an intensive ten-hour electronic brainstorming session, developing an initial collective response to each of the seven categories and 32 subcategories. Drafts of their respective categories were written, with the participation of their executive

principals. Coordinated by the director of quality, the final draft was produced.

What was learned? First, it required a significant effort to interpret and formulate appropriate responses. For example category 7, customer satisfaction,[2] consists of the following subcategories:

7.1 Determining customer requirements and expectations
7.2 Customer relationship management
7.3 Customer service standards
7.4 Commitment to customers
7.5 Complaint resolution for quality improvement
7.6 Determining customer satisfaction
7.7 Customer satisfaction results
7.8 Customer satisfaction comparison

The division scorecard, the annual accomplishments, the relationship assessments and external effectiveness measurements are some of the ways to address customer satisfaction. But there are many other aspects of the strategic planning and operating plan processes that are used to address all of the eight subcategories. And it is in fact this very comprehensive aspect of the Baldrige assessment process that makes it so valuable, and so difficult to do.

As an example, in determining customer requirements and expectations in the research division, there is often focus on providing technology to customers where there are discontinuities, as opposed to the straight-ahead focus of development and manufacturing. These discontinuities are defined by technology opportunity or by unfilled customer needs. This requires knowing and involving the ultimate customers and the internal business unit partner who is ultimately responsible for delivering solutions to the ultimate customer. Often this requires significant effort in redirecting product strategies and may not always be "delightful" in terms of business unit customer relationships. One of the processes used in the division to maintain awareness of these opportunities is the joint program process. Another is a special customer opportunities assessment office that elicits input from external visionaries

---

[2] This category was subsequently titled "Business Results."

in selected systems application areas, and in this manner generates ideas for potential future market opportunities.

Joint programs, together with the relationship assessments, include mechanisms for managing relationships with business unit customers. On the other hand, the concept of "customer service standards" needs significant translation for research. It can be interpreted as meeting commitments, schedules, and deliverables as defined by joint program agreements. Moreover the division is committed to active participation in assisting business units in firefighting activities when called upon, which assists the business units in maintaining their own customer service standards.

Similarly, *complaint resolution* is a term that needs reinterpretation in terms of joint program review, feedback, and accomplishments review processes. The relationship assessment report card has also developed into an excellent mechanism to capture and react to this feedback.

It is this careful tailoring of responses to the Baldrige questions, in terms of existing division processes and management system, that is unique. And the assessment readily raises gaps in processes and practices to the surface.

Was it worthwhile? Absolutely. It has clearly indicated to the division where there are these gaps and has driven action plans to fill them. Absolute scores according to the Baldrige criteria probably have little meaning since it is difficult to understand with what and whom the scores should be compared. But as a comprehensive measure of a baseline for improvement, it has proved to be quite valuable. For example, the assessment indicates that there is a tendency not to close the loop on many processes—not to analyze results and then to use this analysis to improve the process in the next cycle. This recognition is driving significant change, particularly for the strategic planning process. In addition, the assessment indicated that enhancement in customer satisfaction processes and in capturing comprehensive quality data in a division-wide database were needed. Both of these actions are in progress: a strengthening of the relationship assessment measurement process and capturing division-wide data as part of the project description process. The division has now entered its second Baldrige cycle.

Revitalizing Corning's Quality Process

Menger (1993) discussed the Corning's technology group decision to utilize the Baldrige assessment criteria to revitalize its quality initiative and improve its quality systems' performance:

> *Our initial approach to quality was rather introspective; interest began to lag after several years. We needed to revitalize the process. The Baldrige Award criteria, with their intense customer focus, provided just the right stimulus. Again, training was the first step so that groups could apply the Baldrige criteria uniformly and consistently. Within the technology group, we had 15 units, roughly corresponding to departments, which undertook the assessment. Typically, the quality improvement team, or QIT, within the unit was responsible for the process. The assessments were then analyzed to determine those areas in which improvement was needed and in which improvement would have a significant impact. . . . We undertook Baldrige assessments in 1990 and 1991 and are in the process of conducting a third. The present assessment is unique because it combines the criteria of Baldrige and ISO 9000. All units must conduct the Baldrige assessment—that is the corporate paradigm. Some units support businesses that are seeking ISO accreditation, and the combined Baldrige/ISO assessment developed by Corning simplifies and streamlines their work. The present assessments are conducted internally by the units themselves. However, in our next round we plan to have independent audits conducted as well.*

Kozlowski (1993), also at Corning, discussed his lab's implementation of the Baldrige criteria to conduct an assessment of its quality system:

> *Like most quality processes, Baldrige asked where we were, gave a template of where we should be, and asked for the action plan to make up the difference. We did the assessment in two phases—the first took four months, the second took one month. . . . The Baldrige methodology added outside focus to the quality process we had developed earlier. This outside focus, specifically the emphasis on the customer, is the single biggest difference between where we started in 1985, and where we are today.*

Figure 4.3 summarizes the results of Kozlowski's lab's initial assessment scores. The numbers on the horizontal axis represent the category and the item number within the category (for example, 7.5 means the fifth item description within the customer satisfaction category 7).

Using Baldrige to Accelerate Research Performance Improvement at Eastman Chemical

In addition to using Baldrige quality system assessments to identify gaps (IBM) and revitalize TQM initiatives (Corning), Baldrige assessments can also be used to *accelerate the rate of improvement* of an R&D quality initiative. McClaskey (1992) of Eastman Chemical Company (ECC) provides the following description of how ECC uses the Baldrige criteria to accelerate ECC's quality journey.

ECC Research's Baldrige Process, 1990–1991

Research's objective in doing a Baldrige assessment is to accelerate its rate of improvement in accomplishing its mission. Research's mission is to provide new and improved product and process con-

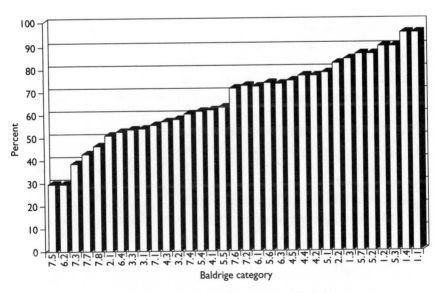

Figure 4.3 Corning's technical product development's Baldrige assessment results.

cepts. Since research's sole objective of doing annual Baldrige assessments is improvement, the Baldrige assessment process research uses is designed to maximize the probability that the Baldrige assessment would lead to improvement. To design a Baldrige assessment process that stresses using the results of the assessment to improve, item 2 in Table 4.1 became the guiding design principle.

The hints in Table 4.1 were used to modify the assessment process used by the National Institute of Standards and Technology (NIST) to select the annual Baldrige Award winners to produce the process that ECC research uses to do its annual Baldrige assessment. The process used by research is described in Table 4.2.

Notice how the steps in research's Baldrige assessment process not only take advantage of the national Baldrige criteria and assessment processes, but also consider and respond to almost every hint listed in Table 4.1 to encourage that the Baldrige assessment be

Table 4.1 Hints for Effective Use of the Baldrige Assessment for Improvement

1. Keep executives/managers involved.
2. Stress/reinforce using assessment to improve.
3. Link/align with business objectives.
4. Integrate with existing business/improvement systems and cycles.
5. Promote external comparisons to be best.
6. Use award criteria without modification.
7. Require written applications, but give several write-up options from "brief" write-ups to "full" 75-page write-ups written to Baldrige Quality Award standards.
8. Train managers/examiners/writers to understand the Baldrige criteria and assessment process.
9. Pilot.
10. Avoid the numbers game.
11. Stress cooperation and improvement.
12. Use Baldrige criteria for company quality awards. Give awards for both improvement as well as level.

Table 4.2   ECC Research's Annual Baldrige Assessment Process (1990–1991)

1. Evaluate and improve research's Baldrige assessment process based on an analysis of the effectiveness of last year's Baldrige assessment.
2. Decide which units within research will do their own Baldrige assessment in addition to research overall.
3. Set due dates for major milestones of the Baldrige assessment process.
   a. Due dates are set to integrate into the ECC improvement planning cycle.
   b. Process usually starts in April and ends in August.
4. For units that are doing their own Baldrige assessment, the management team for that unit decides which Baldrige categories each management team member will personally write up and evaluate.
5. Provide training for everyone who will write up or evaluate any of the Baldrige items.
   a. One and one-half days training initially.
   b. Two- to four-hour refresher training each year for those who had the initial training.
   c. Training teaches Baldrige Award criteria and how to assess each Baldrige item using the Baldrige assessment scoring system. *Note:* The Baldrige criteria consist of categories that are further broken down into items and areas to address.
   d. Training stresses using the assessment to improve.
6. Individual members of the management team write up their selected Baldrige categories using a brief write-up format.
   a. The brief write-up format uses brief phrases (bullets) to document the major points of each Baldrige item.
   b. Results items (Baldrige items that require data) are documented by either describing the relevant trends and levels or by showing the data in chart form.
   c. All Baldrige items and areas to address are written up (based on the current year's Baldrige criteria).

Table 4.2 *(Continued)*

7. The entire management team and the team's QM consultant review all write-ups and make suggestions on how to improve the write-ups. The management team member who originally wrote up the category makes the needed changes to the write-up.

8. Individual members of the management team personally evaluate each Baldrige item within their selected categories. In addition, the team's QM consultant evaluates all items.

   a. Evaluation includes for each item its strengths (+), areas for improvement (−), and percent (%) score.

   b. Research evaluates its Baldrige write-ups using the same evaluation and scoring system as stated in the current year's Baldrige Award criteria booklet.

9. The entire management team and the team's QM consultant review the Baldrige evaluations for each item, question the basis for the evaluation, and either accept the evaluation or suggest changes. Suggested changes are incorporated into the evaluation and the evaluation is finalized.

   a. The evaluation results and score are not conveyed outside the management team and the unit that was assessed except to pick up general strengths and areas for improvement.

   b. The management team plans how to share the Baldrige assessment with the rest of the unit that was assessed.

10. Based on the Baldrige assessment, the management team identifies the most important improvement opportunities.

    a. The vital few most important improvement opportunities are based on the "areas for improvement" identified during the Baldrige assessment.

    b. Customer and business priorities and strategic plans are strongly considered when selecting the most important improvement opportunities.

    c. Immediate actions are initiated for any area for improvement that requires immediate attention (usually rare).

Table 4.2 *(Continued)*

---

11. The identified most important improvement opportunities from the Baldrige assessment are key inputs, which are considered along with data from other sources (customer interviews, research-people interviews, process data analysis, strategic plans, etc.) in developing next year's improvement plan for research and the unit that did the Baldrige assessment.

12. Repeat the entire Baldrige assessment process next year.

---

used to improve. Table 4.3 shows a cross-referencing between the hints provided in Table 4.1 and research's Baldrige assessment process described in Table 4.2.

Two features of research's Baldrige assessment process (Table 4.2) are of special note: personal management involvement and focus on improvement. The members of the management team of the unit being assessed personally do the write-ups and the evaluation. Management team members can do a good job of Baldrige assessment with appropriate training (a 1½- to 2-day course appears sufficient). Having the management team personally do the assessment is important since it reduces the lack of acceptance that often accompanies evaluations by outsiders. It also enables the management team, who has to champion the improvements, to understand where the improvement opportunities came from and why it is important to the business to improve in the selected areas. Having the management team itself evaluate each item is also a necessity when using the brief format to write up the Baldrige assessment, since the brief format requires insider knowledge to fully understand what each short phrase or bullet means.

The emphasis that research's Baldrige assessment process puts on focusing on improvement is in recognition that the biggest danger is that the Baldrige assessment will be completed but never, or just marginally, used for improvement. Because of this danger, every step of research's Baldrige process is directed toward encouraging its use for improvement.

Table 4.3   Steps in Research's Baldrige
Process (Table 4.2) versus the Hints in Table 4.1

Steps of Research Process (Table 4.2)	Hints for Effective Use for Improvement (Table 4.1)											
	1	2	3	4	5	6	7	8	9	10	11	12*
1	X	X									X	
2	X	X							X			
3	X	X		X								
4	X	X					X				X	
5	X	X	X	X	X	X	X	X	X	X	X	
6	X	X			X	X	X					
7	X	X			X	X						
8	X	X	X		X	X					X	
9	X	X	X		X	X				X	X	
10	X	X	X		X					X	X	
11	X	X	X	X						X	X	
12	X	X								X	X	

* Not applicable since ECC does not use internal quality awards.

ECC Research's Baldrige Process, 1992

Based on continual improvement, two major changes are being made in research's 1992 Baldrige assessment process. During 1990–1991, a Baldrige assessment was only done for research overall. In 1992, each division within research will also do a Baldrige assessment. This involves, among other things, a large commitment of each lab head's time (approximately 30 hours) to take the 1½-day training course and personally do the Baldrige write-up and evaluation. Dr. Jerry D. Holmes, vice president of ECC research, stated why research expanded its Baldrige assessment to include divisions: "Annually doing the Baldrige assessment at the research division level is a key step in developing research's world-class management team as well as identifying additional opportunities to help research improve." This conclusion was based on two years' experience of the research management team personally doing Baldrige assessments at the overall research level.

The second major change involves how Baldrige results items (those that require data) will be documented in the write-up (see Table 4.2, item 6b). Previously, results items could be documented by describing the trends and levels. In 1992, the actual data in chart form must be shown.

Conclusion

ECC Research has found the Baldrige assessment to be a value-added activity and intends to continue doing Baldrige assessments annually. Research has found the Baldrige assessment process to be especially valuable in:

1. Contributing to the effectiveness of and guiding the annual research improvement plan.
2. Developing research managers (particularly in relation to developing an awareness of world-class management expectations and how ECC research compares to these expectations).
3. Promoting communication, discussion, and learning on what is required to achieve excellence in research.

Two examples of improvements that ECC research made as a result of its Baldrige assessments are:

1. Took proactive steps and set up processes to be more in touch with research's internal and external customer expectations, perceptions, and levels of satisfaction.
2. Initiated efforts to find and benchmark the world's best research practices and results for key research processes and indices.

Using ISO 9000 for R&D Quality System Assessments

Although the Baldrige criteria provide a comprehensive framework for conducting assessments of current quality systems, some R&D organizations have found it useful to utilize ISO 9000 quality system criteria for one of the following reasons:

1. They wish to establish an initial basis *from which to expand to the Baldrige criteria.*
2. Or, similarly to our discussion in Chapter 1, they wish to obtain ISO 9000 registration *as part of an organization's overall ISO quality system registration initiative.*[2]

A Brief Introduction to ISO 9000

The International Organization for Standardization (ISO) is located in Geneva, Switzerland. ISO was founded in 1946 "to develop a common set of manufacturing, trade, and communication standards." The ISO 9000 series of standards provides a growing international reference[3] for conducting assessments of quality systems. ISO 9000 actually contains five documents:

1. *ISO 9000-1: Quality management and quality assurance standards— Guidelines for selection and use.* For determining which of the quality system standards (ISO 9001, 9002, 9003) is appropriate for a particular organization.
2. *ISO 9001: Quality systems—Model for quality assurance in design/ development, production, installation and servicing.*
3. *ISO 9002: Quality systems—Model for quality assurance in production, installation and servicing.*
4. *ISO 9003: Quality systems—Model for quality assurance in final inspection and test.*
5. *ISO 9004-1: Quality management and quality system elements— Guidelines.* Contains information on interpreting the requirements of the standards as well as general information on quality concepts and systems.

Clearly, to meet either the objective of developing a basis for a comprehensive quality management system or as a requirement to be included as part of an

[2] For any organization to achieve ISO registration, it must select a quality system registrar who has been formally accredited to conduct reviews and audits of quality system documentation and practices to assess compliance with ISO requirements.

[3] A driving force for the acceptance of ISO 9000 criteria has been their acceptance by the European Community (common market) "as part of its conformity assessment plan to establish uniform systems for product certification and quality systems registration" (Peach 1994) that are recognized by all members.

organization's total registration efforts, most R&D organizations' focus should be on *ISO 9001*, which contains specific requirements for quality system elements for design/development functions.

The following papers presented by AT&T's Bell Laboratories (Fried 1993) and Duracell's Worldwide Technology Center (Gibbard and Davis 1993) provide excellent examples of processes for planning, organizing, and implementing ISO 9001 quality system initiatives and assessments tailored to R&D environments.

Implementing ISO 9001 in R&D at AT&T Transmission Systems Business Unit (TSBU)

Background

The TSBU is a strategic business unit within the network systems group of AT&T. The TSBU provides a variety of transmission products to domestic and international customers, including network multiplexers and controllers, cross-connect switches, and light-wave transmission systems. These products are manufactured at several facilities, both within and outside the United States.

The TSBU's largest manufacturing facility, Merrimack Valley Works, is located in North Andover, Massachusetts. Over 5,000 people are employed at Merrimack Valley, at which more than ten major TSBU product lines are manufactured. Research and development is performed by members of associated design organizations. R&D activities for the TSBU take place at a number of locations in Massachusetts and New Jersey. Over 1,200 people work in the TSBU's R&D organizations.

In the fall of 1991, it was determined that Merrimack Valley should pursue registration to the ISO 9001 standard for quality assurance systems. A goal was set to achieve registration by the end of 1992. With this in mind, the high-level registration schedule shown in Table 4.4 was established.

The intended scope of registration included the manufacture of all TSBU products at Merrimack Valley and all associated design organizations. The design organizations, however, got off to a late start. Their efforts did not commence until the middle of February, by which point their manufacturing counterparts were already well under way.

Table 4.4   Merrimack Valley ISO-9001 Registration Schedule

Date	Activity/milestone
12/91	Select registrar
1/92	Submit quality manual
3/92	Preassessment by registrar
3/92–7/92	Address gaps
8/92	Registration audit
8/92–11/92	Correct deficiencies
12/92	ISO 9001 registration

Constraints

A number of significant constraints were imposed upon the design organizations at the start of their compliance effort. Among the most notable were:

- *Tight schedule.*   The time frame from the start of the compliance effort to the registration audit was less than six months. At that time, it was thought that a program of that magnitude would normally require twelve to eighteen months to complete.
- *Lack of awareness of ISO 9000 standards.*   Throughout the design organizations, there was minimal awareness of the ISO 9000 standards and their implications on existing quality assurance systems.
- *Major compliance deficiencies.*   There were significant areas of noncompliance in the design organizations for several of the elements (clauses) of the ISO 9001 standard. For example, there was no program in place for internal auditing, nor was there a program for the calibration of test equipment. Moreover, the informal culture inherent in most typical design environments posed some difficulties. This was most notable in areas such as document control and quality records, which require a level of process discipline greater than that normally found in many development organizations.

- *Autonomy of design organizations.* There are distinct design organizations supporting each of the major TSBU product lines. Each of these organizations has evolved its own set of design methodologies and quality systems. Given the short time frame, this severely limited opportunities to implement common solutions across the entire TSBU design community. To a large extent, each design organization had to develop its own quality system to meet the requirements of the standard.
- *Scarcity of dedicated resources.* The amount of staff resources in the design organizations that were available to work on the compliance effort was very limited.

Organization

In light of the constraints described above, it was considered critical that an effective organization be put in place to oversee the R&D compliance effort. A team was formed that reflected a fusion of expertise—combining knowledge of the inner workings of the TSBU design organizations together with experience in dealing with the requirements of the standard.

Expertise in the standard came from members of the Quality, Engineering, Software Technology (QUEST) and Global Management and Engineering (GM&E) organizations in AT&T. QUEST and GM&E provide a variety of consulting and auditing services in ISO 9000 and other quality technologies to AT&T business units as well as organizations outside of AT&T. Team members from these organizations were responsible for:

- Overall coordination of the R&D compliance effort
- Consultation on various compliance issues
- Definition and implementation of internal auditing and calibration programs, as well as other common approaches to satisfying the requirements of the standard
- Giving awareness and coaching presentations to members of the TSBU design organizations
- Interfacing with the Merrimack Valley ISO 9000 compliance team as well as other AT&T organizations outside of the TSBU
- Working with the registrar to plan the logistics of the pre-assessment and certification audits

A representative from each TSBU product line organization was designated as "ISO coordinator." Each ISO coordinator had primary responsibility for the project management of compliance efforts within his/her organization. In addition, a manager was appointed in each major geographical location (i.e., Massachusetts and New Jersey) to oversee all of the local R&D compliance activities. The entire effort was championed by one of the directors within the TSBU design organizations.

Compliance Philosophies

In order to achieve the goal of registration by the end of 1992, the R&D compliance team worked under a set of guiding principles, which are summarized below:

- *Minimize new processes.* Wherever possible, design processes and methodologies were revised to satisfy the requirements of the standard rather than reinvented from scratch. New processes were developed only for those areas where nothing was in place.
- *Be pragmatic.* At times, there was the temptation to implement solutions that went well beyond the minimum requirements of the standard. This desire had to be balanced, however, against the realities of a very ambitious compliance schedule. Wherever possible, compliance initiatives that exceeded the minimum requirements were deferred until after registration.
- *Encourage information sharing.* Despite the aforementioned autonomy of the design organizations, particular focus was placed on sharing effective solutions to common problems. Information sharing took a number of forms. For example, nonbinding advisories were developed to suggest solutions to a number of requirements, including document control and training.
- *Manage the effort like a development project.* Due to the magnitude of effort that had to be completed in a relatively short time frame, it was clear that activities and progress needed to be monitored closely as in any large-scale development project.

Compliance Activities

The compliance effort began in earnest after the preassessment, and continued until the registration audit. The major activities that made up this effort are described below.

Analysis of ISO 9001 elements. In order to put the upcoming work into better focus, the 20 elements of the standard were analyzed from two standpoints. The first was to identify those elements that are generally applicable to R&D organizations. Each element identified as applicable to R&D was then evaluated to determine whether it could be most effectively addressed by a solution common to multiple organizations, or on an individual basis by the local design organization. Those elements addressed globally generally had distinct solutions in Massachusetts and New Jersey. The primary reason for this was that the Massachusetts design organizations had access to a number of services of the Merrimack Valley facility due to its location. Most notable among these were in the areas of internal auditing and calibration. Certain elements were addressed both globally and locally. The results of this analysis are shown in Table 4.5.

Self-assessments, compliance plans, and project meetings for each applicable element. The ISO coordinators performed an assessment of their organization's compliance to the standard. The gaps identified by the self-assessments drove the creation of project plans to achieve compliance in time for the audit. By the end of this exercise, a compliance plan existed for each of the design organizations covered by the scope of registration. Progress against these plans was tracked at weekly project meetings. To ensure that the R&D and manufacturing compliance efforts were synchronized, the R&D compliance team coordinators also participated in weekly project meetings of the manufacturing compliance team.

Staff presentations. During the course of the compliance effort, a series of presentations was given to members of the TSBU design organizations. These presentations covered a variety of topics:

- Awareness sessions provided an overview of the standard as it applied to the design organizations as well as the high-level plans for achieving compliance.

Table 4.5 R&D Analysis of ISO 9001 Elements

ISO 9001 Element	Applicable?	Global/Local
Management responsibility	Yes	Both
Quality system	Yes	Both
Contract review	No	
Design control	Yes	Local
Document control	Yes	Local
Purchasing	Yes	Local
Purchaser supplied product	No	
Product identification and traceability	No	
Process control	No	
Inspection and testing	No	
Inspection, measuring, and test equipment	Yes	Global
Inspection and test status	No	
Control of nonconforming product	No	
Corrective action	Yes	Local
Handling, storage, packaging, and delivery	Yes	Local
Quality records	Yes	Local
Internal quality audits	Yes	Global
Training	Yes	Local
Servicing	No	
Statistical techniques	No	

- Quality system rollout sessions were conducted to ensure that all staff were made aware of changes to local procedures resulting from the compliance effort
- Shortly before the registration audit, coaching sessions were conducted to give an overview of the audit process and to advise the staff of appropriate behaviors during an audit situation.

Audit Results

The registration audit was held in August 1992 and resulted in a recommendation for registration. Merrimack Valley Works and associated TSBU design organizations were granted ISO 9001 registration in September, three months ahead of schedule.

Lessons Learned

Many lessons were learned from the R&D compliance experience:

- *Don't accept conventional wisdom.* The target date for ISO registration was considered to be unachievable by some observers, given the short time frame. The end result was in large part due to the success-oriented attitude adopted by the compliance team.
- *Management commitment is critical.* In an environment where resources are limited, management's commitment to ISO registration must be made clear. Otherwise, the compliance activities will always be given lower priority than development commitments. Moreover, it is important to engage the entire organization as early as possible in the compliance program.
- *Registrar preassessment is valuable.* The preassessment performed by the registrar helped the ISO coordinators identify compliance gaps in their respective organizations. Another unanticipated benefit resulting from the preassessment was that it served as a quick, compelling introduction for many people to the requirements of the standard and to the dynamics of the auditing process.
- *Schedule internal audits early.* As with the preassessment, internal audits tended to bring the issues pertaining to ISO 9000 compliance into focus for many people. Those organizations that underwent an internal audit early in the process appeared to be the best prepared for the registration audit.
- *Project-manage the compliance effort.* Due to the activities and dependencies inherent in a compliance effort of this magnitude, it is essential that the progress be monitored closely on a regular basis.
- *Teamwork is essential.* The TSBU's compliance program would not have been successful without an extraordinary level of teamwork and cooperation. In this case, teamwork took several dimensions—between the various design organizations, between the ISO 9000 consultants and members of the design organizations, and between the design and manufacturing communities.

ISO 9001 Implementation at Duracell's Worldwide Technology Center

As a part of Duracell's commitment to quality improvement, announced officially in 1990, the New Products and Technology Division decided to implement a quality management system based on the ISO 9000 series. The first facility to be registered was the Duracell Worldwide Technology Center, which did not have a formal quality system in place. The scientists and research engineers of this RD&E center were concerned that imposition of a quality management system would stifle creativity in a mass of red tape. Leadership from upper management was required to initiate a top-down effort to meet the registration schedule and objectives. Numerous benefits were derived from the process of obtaining registration to ISO 9001. These include greater appreciation of the importance of teamwork and training, and the establishment of a foundation for continuous improvement of quality.

Background

Toward the end of the 1980s the concept of adopting total quality as a way of life was gathering momentum within Duracell. This culminated in the announcement of the company's commitment to quality improvement under the banner "XCells" in May 1990. As a part of the push for quality, a proposal was made in November 1989 to the senior vice president of New Products and Technology that the Duracell Worldwide Technology Center (DWTC) be registered to ISO 9001. For a global company with a substantial business in Europe, several benefits accrue to companies registered to ISO standards. These include the following:

- Meeting legal requirements and reducing the probability of product liability problems
- Meeting contractual requirements prior to receiving purchase orders
- Meeting requirements of prime contractors that their subcontractors be registered
- Reduction of assessments for multiple audits

These advantages for companies registered to ISO standards were not the only driving forces for registration of DWTC, and perhaps they were not even the most important ones. Early registration provides a method for organizations to distinguish themselves from the competition, but even more important, ISO registration provided DWTC the foundation of a quality management system on which a program for quality improvement could be built. Before the rapid push for total quality in the United States, whether a company's RD&E center had a quality management system often depended on the amount of business the company did with the federal government. Most companies that bid on contracts with the Department of Defense were required to be certified to the military quality standard MIL-Q-9858A, for example. Organizations that already have a quality system in place are at a distinct advantage in gaining ISO 9001 registration; as the R&D arm of a consumer-products company, DWTC had no formal quality management system.

Another initial barrier to ISO registration was the fact that our technical staff, like the majority of scientists and development engineers in R&D centers of nonmilitary businesses, tended to consider systems for management of quality unnecessary and irrelevant. They felt that the requirements for documentation would stifle creativity. Not until well into the process of registration, and in some cases well after it had been completed, were the advantages of ISO 9001 fully perceived by the staff and some of the management.

Process of Registration

The process of ISO 9001 registration was regarded at the outset as fairly simple, following the flowchart in Figure 4.4. In fact, down to the point where we began to conduct internal audits, the process ran quite smoothly according to the planned schedule. At that point, as is discussed below, we began to realize that the organizational problems of the process, and the degree of commitment to its implementation required of management and staff at all levels, had been rather badly underestimated.

First, documents describing the ISO 9000 series of quality standards were obtained from the Geneva-based International Organization for Standardization. In April 1990, a British consulting firm with international experience in gaining ISO registration was

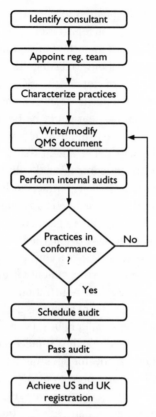

Figure 4.4 Flowchart for ISO 9001 registration process.

retained for advice on the registration process. The first decision that faced management was the choice of the ISO standard to which DWTC was to be registered. Since the "product" supplied by DWTC includes advanced battery (technology relating to materials, design, processes, and equipment) as well as the provision of analytical and testing services, the decision was made to obtain registration to ISO 9001, the most comprehensive of the ISO conformance standards.

Toward the end of April, 1990, a detailed internal audit was conducted to characterize the practices already in place in DWTC. The staff had the apprehension that ISO standards would impose a large number of specific practices on laboratory procedures and processes. It came as a considerable surprise that the primary purpose of the quality management system was to describe the practices in place within the organization, and then to make sure that those ISO-approved practices were systematically followed and documented. At the end of the first internal audit, a schedule was written for the registration effort, with the goal of conducting the registration audit in July, 1991. Also at this time the important choice of a registrar to conduct the registration audit was made.

In 1991 the choice of a registrar was relatively simple, since only a few firms offered this service in the United States. The increasing number of firms that offer ISO registration services makes this choice considerably more difficult today. Some of the factors that should be considered (according to the *ISO 9000 Registered Company Directory*) are the following:

- The market or industry served by the organization seeking registration
- Possible conflicts of interest of firms offering both consulting and registration services
- Costs of registration and ongoing follow-up audits
- Backlog of the registering firm and its ability to meet the planned registration schedule
- Details of the assessment and registration process
- Auditor qualifications
- Policy with regard to quality system suspension, withdrawal, or cancellation

The issue of possible conflicts of interest is significant. According to Weightman (in the *ISO 9000 Registered Company Directory*), "European customer(s) may perceive a conflict of interest if a registrar offers and performs both consulting and registration services." ISO/IEC Guide 48, "Guidelines for third-party assessment and registration of a supplier's quality system," states in part:

> "... an organization that, directly or through the agency of subcontractors, advises a company how to set up its quality system, or writes its quality documentation, should not provide assessment services to that company, unless strict separation is achieved to ensure that there is no conflict of interest."

DWTC avoided any appearance of a conflict of interest by choosing a consulting firm with no direct connection with the registering firm, but this strategy could have its pitfalls, in the light of a comment that one of the registration audit team members made to DWTC staff after the completion of our first, and successful, registration audit. The comment was that, in the experience of this specific registrar, only 5 percent of all firms that had not employed the consulting services of the registrar for a preregistration audit passed the registration audit the first time. Taken in combination with ISO/IEC Guide 48, this appears to be a sort of catch-22, the avoidance of which the prospective applicant for ISO registration may wish to consider carefully in its choice of consulting and registering firms.

In June 1990, the leader of the ISO 9001 implementation team had been selected, and a first version was drafted of the Quality Policy of the New Products and Technology Division of Duracell, of which DWTC is a part. Eventually this Quality Policy became the Level 1 document of the three-level documented quality management system. The three levels of documentation selected to control the quality system used by the New Product and Technology Division of Duracell are described below:

> *Level 1: quality assurance manual.* This manual describes the New Products and Technology Division's quality assurance policy, the manner in which the quality system is controlled and monitored through related documentation, and the overall organization for the division. This document, and any change thereto, is approved by the senior vice president of New Products and Technology and is an integral part of the site's documented quality system.
>
> *Level 2: quality assurance procedures.* These procedures contain the organization, responsibilities, and details that define the way in which the New Products and Technology Division's operations will implement the quality policy. These procedures are the interface between the quality assurance manual and the drawings and specification level of documents. These documents are authorized and controlled as defined by site procedures.
>
> *Level 3: specifications and drawings.* This documentation defines in detail the operations and processes that are per-

formed at each operating site. These documents are authorized and controlled as defined by site procedures.

The ISO registration team consisted of the team leader, Carl Davis, and two staff members from the standards, performance, and quality department in Bethel, Connecticut, Frank Ciliberti and Ed Sczepanski. Beginning in March 1991, they issued preliminary versions of the quality system documents and began training the DWTC staff on ISO and conducting internal audits of actual practices against the documented ones. The strategy to reach the goal of ISO 9001 registration was to address four major areas:

1. *Commitment of the staff.* The team and the consultant repeatedly stressed that they were as concerned about red tape as the research scientists and design engineers. They emphasized that the audits were necessary to achieve ISO registration and were not intended to place an unreasonable burden on the staff. This was not an easy sell.

2. *Documentation control.* The Level 1 and Level 2 documents were distributed in hard-copy form to all department managers. It became clear that the logistics of maintaining revision control, an essential requirement of ISO 9001, would be very difficult with so many hard copies of the documents in so many hands. Eventually distribution of, and access to, the documents was made through the personal computer network that connects all of the professional staff of DWTC. The documents can be read on the computer monitor but cannot be copied. In this way, all problems associated with collecting and eliminating out-of-date documents were eliminated.

3. *Design control.* Specifications, drawings, and methods are critical to the design process. Project leaders and team members were frequently audited to verify the revision currency of product drawings, specifications, and test methods.

4. *Instrument calibration.* As a lead center for providing technical services to Duracell's worldwide operations, DWTC has hundreds of test and evaluation instruments, all of which were inventoried. Nearly two-thirds were iden-

tified as critical and entered into a calibration database. A schedule for calibration was constructed, and a process was instituted to ensure that the schedule was followed.

In March 1991, the preparations for the registration audit appeared to be going well, and the team notified the registrar that we were ready. The date for the registration audit was set for July 1991. By April, however, serious problems had surfaced. The ISO team began to feel frustrated because some of the staff were treating them as a low-priority nuisance. The number of noncompliances in successive internal audits was not decreasing with time in all departments. Some of the directors questioned DWTC's ability to be ready for the July registration audit and recommended postponing the date. When advised that rescheduling could add six months to the registration effort, the vice president refused to consider that option and insisted that the original schedule be held. He decided to intervene personally in the ISO registration effort and selected benchmarking as the most efficient method of accelerating progress.

The criteria chosen for selecting companies to benchmark were that they had recently achieved ISO 9001 registration, so that their memory of the process would be fresh; that they be close to DWTC; and that their business is completely noncompetitive with Duracell's, so that they would feel free to speak openly. In May 1991, the authors selected and visited The Foxboro Company in nearby Foxboro, Massachusetts. The manager of corporate quality assurance, Hasam Rizvi, and a member of his staff, Richard Anderson, were extremely cooperative and spent several hours openly discussing their quality management system and their recent push for ISO registration. Many topics that they discussed were useful, but one turned out to be critical. This was simply that *ISO registration must be a top-down effort.*

Reflection on the Foxboro discussions showed the authors that too much of the responsibility for ISO registration had been given to the three-man team rather than the DWTC management and staff. We had not accepted the axiom that everyone is responsible for quality. This was the turning point in the ISO registration process. The day after the Foxboro visit, the vice president informed the directors that passing the registration audit was priority number one, that they were each responsible for making that happen, and that they were to pass this message directly to each of their subordinates, who would do the same with theirs.

Within days a noticeable change had occurred in the behavior of the staff who mattered most in the implementation of the formal quality system—the bench-level scientists, engineers, and technicians and first-line supervisors. They immediately began to seek out the members of the staff who by training or by inclination had always kept good records and followed laboratory procedures. These individuals were a previously underutilized and highly valuable resource for training. Spontaneously, with no further intervention from upper management, these "select few" initiated seminars and training sessions which were voluntarily attended by those who needed quality management skills. Members of the staff who had been avoiding contact with the registration team now avidly sought out the team members as well as those already skilled in quality management for mock audits of their departments. Within two weeks the registration team began to have confidence that the laboratory would be ready for the registration audit. In June the British consultant and the ISO registration team conducted a full-scale preassessment audit to determine the readiness of the fledgling quality management system to withstand intense outside scrutiny. Based on prior experience, the consultant confidently predicted that DWTC would pass. The last push to correct the deficiencies found during the readiness audit required very little prompting from management. By now the staff were all integrated into a team effort, and no one wanted his or her department to be one that would let the team down.

In July the registrar sent a three-person team to spend three days examining DWTC's quality management system and the degree to which actual practices adhered to that system. They found no show-stoppers; their audit generated only 21 relatively minor action requests requiring corrective action. Within a few weeks the corrective actions had been taken, and this fact was communicated to the registrar. In September, DWTC received a certificate as an organization registered to ISO 9001, for the goods and services described as follows:

> "The research, development and design of batteries, relevant technologies and the provision of technical support services for Duracell's worldwide operations."

Maintenance of ISO 9001 Registration

Attaining ISO 9001 registration on the first assessment audit, beginning with no formal quality management system and adhering to a tight schedule, provided a great sense of satisfaction to the staff. But it was by no means the end of the quest for quality at DWTC; rather, it was the beginning. The registration team continues to hold monthly internal audits of the practices of departments against the quality management documentation. A numerical system for scoring identified nonconformities provided one of the first metrics for continuous improvement of DWTC's quality. Routine external surveillance audits are conducted every six months by the registrar, and the registration is reissued annually. As the vice president said in his message of congratulations to the staff after registration was assured, "ISO 9001 is forever."

Benefits of Registration

In retrospect it is difficult to sort out the benefits that DWTC received from the process of ISO registration and those derived from the XCells corporate quality program, since our involvement with both was and is contemporaneous. Yet there were some things that the establishment of a formal quality system forced us to do for the first time in a systematic way, and which yielded benefits to many of our operations.

The first thing, and perhaps the most important, is that it forced us to identify precisely who our customers were. For all projects carried out in our center, the first step in our quality management system (see Figure 4.5 for a flowchart of the design/control process) is the completion of a document called a *project initiation request*. On this form the customer for whom the project is to be carried out must be identified. Completion of the process requires that the customer's precise specifications be documented. None of this was done systematically before our ISO registration, and yet all of it is key to any program of quality improvement. XCells, Duracell's company-wide initiative for quality improvement, mandates working together in teams. The first major success of DWTC directly attributable to teamwork was ISO 9001 registration. It was clear that neither management nor the registration team nor both taken together could have achieved what the entire staff accomplished by effective teamwork. This was the second important lesson learned

Design/control

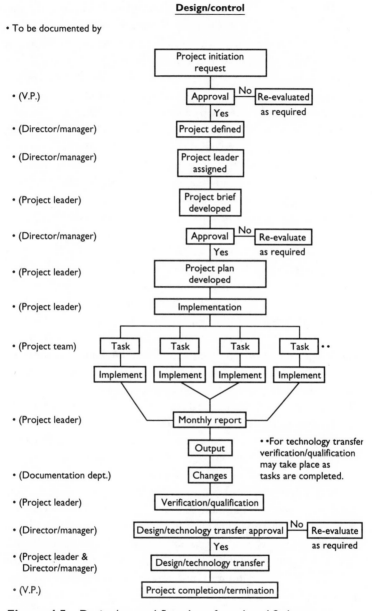

Figure 4.5 Design/control flowchart from Level 2 document.

by DWTC in the ISO registration effort. The momentum of this accomplishment has not diminished, for it set us on the road to adoption of working in teams as a standard practice, as is recognized in the DWTC vision that the staff prepared and adopted as an expression of deeply held values. Before ISO, not all departments and managers were careful to set out goals and milestones against which performance on every project could be measured.

Development of the project plan (Figure 4.5) mandates this detailed planning and provides the basis for systematic performance improvement through the development of performance metrics. The keeping of records and documents in the way described by the quality management system is absolutely essential to pass the periodic audits, but it also prevents rework whenever a project is temporarily shelved. In retrospect, what ISO forced DWTC to do was to concentrate on processes, and this is exactly the sine qua non of cycle-time reduction leading to continuous improvement of quality.

The calibration of instruments caused us more work than any other single issue. There are hundreds of instruments and devices in DWTC that can be calibrated; the question was, which ones must be? It was clear that any instrument used in qualification of a design had to be in a good state of calibration, and that had been our practice for many years. ISO registration forced us to define and enforce a calibration policy that we were prepared to live with. Eventually it was decided to create a new calibration center, with the projected results that calibration costs will decrease, that all instruments requiring calibration are calibrated in a timely manner, and that the integrity of all information requiring the use of calibrated instruments will be enhanced. Interestingly, the work on calibration policy did not end with the achievement of ISO 9001 registration. The initial policy that was implemented was unwieldy and poorly understood. An XCells project team was formed to improve the calibration policy, and when their recommendations were adopted, the quality management system documentation was revised to describe the changes. The important point here is that the quality management system is a living document subject to revision as practices change.

Preparing our quality management system's documentation forced us to consider systematically for the first time not only when and how a new project begins, but when and how one ends. It was decided that each project must be reviewed at least annually, with a view to its continuation, modification, or termination. The first year, this review was combined with third-generation R&D concepts (Roussel 1991), in which strategic priorities are decided cooperatively among R&D, marketing, and upper management, approximately 25 percent of all projects on the books were canceled. This clearing of the decks has promoted a tight focus of RD&E resources on agreed-upon, strategic priorities.

Finally, initiation of our ISO 9001 quality management system forced us to consider training in a systematic way. This led to systematic completion of the section of the annual performance review form dealing with training requirements. In this way the training needs of every employee are considered at least yearly, which is essential for the improvement of quality and competitiveness.

A summary of the benefits that accrued to our ISO 9001 registration effort shows how important this has been to launching our total-quality quest:

- Customers identified
- Customers' specifications understood
- Project planning: clear goals, milestones defined
- Documentation: rework prevented
- Calibration standards defined and enforced
- Project implementation and termination procedures defined
- Teamwork enhanced by the registration effort
- Basis for defining metrics and reducing cycle time provided by process emphasis
- Training schedule completed as a part of the annual performance review

Lessons Learned

We conclude this paper with some comments on those things we learned during and after the ISO 9001 registration effort which may be helpful to other organizations which are considering following the same path.

1. *Choose a good consultant.* Particularly for an organization that does not have an existing quality management system on which

to build, the selection of an experienced consultant is critical. The consultant should have a good track record in helping organizations, ideally ones very similar to the applicant, in attaining ISO registration.

2. *Benchmark.* Identify individuals in organizations that have recently achieved registration and ask them to meet to discuss their experiences. We have found that firms that have embarked on a quest for quality will want to share their knowledge with noncompeting organizations. This willingness to share experience related to quality improvement is an extremely healthy sign of the return of American industry to global competitiveness, in which we have been pleased to participate.

3. *Build on your strengths.* In every organization there are individuals who keep good records, either because they have been trained to do so or because this behavior comes naturally to them. These people are a great asset. Their departments are models of traceability, a virtue valued above all others by registration audit teams. Generally, they are pleased to work with the registration team in documenting current practices; and they are enthusiastic about sharing their knowledge with their colleagues in training sessions. Identifying and recruiting these internal assets early in the registration process is a major step forward for the registration team.

4. *Make it a top-down effort.* Registration to ISO standards requires a very serious commitment of time and money, and it takes both early commitment and ongoing attention from upper management. But upper management cannot do the job alone; they must obtain commitments from successive levels of management all down the line. In our experience, the most important group to recruit is mid-level managers, the project leaders on whom much of the burden of preparing for ISO audits will fall. In hindsight, we did not adequately persuade the scientists and research engineers who are the backbone of our organization that the discipline of living with ISO 9001 would not stifle creativity and add unnecessary paperwork. The one way in which we could have simplified our ISO registration effort more than any other was early recruitment of this group of key bench scientists, managers, and supervisors by training

them in the benefits that an ISO-registered quality management system would bring. In our case, this training would have been best presented in the context of how an ISO-registered quality management system is an integral part of our total quality improvement initiative, XCells.

5. *Concentrate on processes.*   Preparation for ISO registration forces concentration on how work is initiated, how it gets done, and when it is finished. It is in the understanding of the organization's processes that the opportunities for quality improvement come. A tip we received from Foxboro: Include process flowcharts in the documentation of the quality management system—the reviewers love them. Our final word on the process of obtaining ISO 9001 registration: "Document what you do, and then be sure that you do what you documented."

CHAPTER 5

INTELLECTUAL PROPERTY MANAGEMENT PROCESS IMPROVEMENT

Dimensions of Intellectual Property Management

The concepts, processes, and tools of the previous chapters can be, and have been, successfully used by organizations to improve the effectiveness of their principal internal R&D processes. In addition to improving strictly *internal* R&D activities, organizations can also benefit from improving processes that are used to accomplish the following:

1. Explore and develop research *partnerships* with academia, government, and research consortia.
2. Ensure that intellectual property is successfully *transferred* into new processes and products for global manufacturing and distribution.
3. Maximize returns on R&D investments through *intellectual property management* (e.g., through improving the patent process and monitoring or enforcement of licensing agreements).

This chapter provides examples of how organizations such as AT&T, Duracell, General Motors, and Motorola have used concepts and processes from quality management to help meet these objectives.

Alliance Development and Management

In an environment of increasing resource restrictions, one external pathway for addressing the need to conduct research in multiple potentially promising areas is to explore the development of partnerships with academe, government, or research consortia. General Motors' R&D center has recognized the "growing impossibility of internally creating all innovation required for corporate competitiveness." Anderson and Zimmerman (1995) have presented insights on the processes GM uses to identify, assess, coordinate, and couple government, university, and industrial science and technology competencies with GM's R&D center's priorities and capabilities.

Developing a Virtual Global Laboratory for General Motors

The Research Portfolio

As we work to effectively globalize research and development activity through satellite labs and collaborations, three key ingredients to success are identified. First, we must coordinate the scientific and technical competencies of diverse government, university, and industrial laboratories and development centers to complement our internal competencies and gain synergy. Second, this requires that we develop objective (and sometimes subjective) metrics for assessing the core competencies of a potential collaborator in relation to our strategic objectives. Finally, once opportunities and capable potential collaborators are identified, it is necessary to balance the leveraging of internal and external resources and opportunities to optimize (nearly) the return on investment.

Difficult though it may be to form successful partnerships, the driving forces to succeed are very strong. Global leveraging, particularly with national laboratories or other companies who can also invest resources, reduces the risk to each individual participant for projects with potentially high payoff and a high degree of uncertainty. Collaboration substantially increases access to resources, including capital equipment and highly specialized facilities, people, and shared funding. Through carefully chosen industrial partnerships for both research and commercialization it becomes possible in many cases to establish much broader markets for a technology by addressing opportunities in other industries. This may serve to substantially accelerate technology commercialization.

There are many significant challenges and hurdles to overcome in the path of becoming a global virtual laboratory, however. Although easing somewhat, issues of intellectual property protection and export control compliance continue to affect certain technologies. There is also substantial diversity not only in culture, but in business practice, legal systems, and regulatory climate between countries. Consequently, the difficult challenges of communication, trust building, and technology interchange can become particularly formidable when cultural differences are also added to the mix. Nevertheless, we are finding that with careful selection of the partner, identification and discussion of all issues ranging from technical to intellectual property ownership and protection, a clear definition of project responsibilities and linkage of projects to the strategically driven corporate R&D portfolio, these and other challenges can be overcome. A key to GM's business and technical process is the R&D portfolio (Figure 5.1).

This portfolio is a mix of near-, mid-, and long-term projects, with a planned 80 percent applied to identified business strategic needs as agreed to by the operating units of the company. Exploratory research with very long term commitments and high risk of failure from technical challenges comprises the remaining 20 percent. The selection of exploratory projects is the responsibility of the R&D center strategic management team, since the relationship of any particular project to short-term specific business objectives may be uncertain, and the probability of success is equally uncertain. As the portfolio of projects is defined in dialogue with our internal cus-

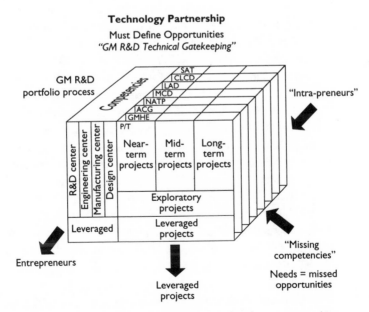

Figure 5.1 GM's R&D portfolio and technology partnerships.

tomers, the scientific and technical competencies required to achieve the objectives of the projects in the portfolio are assessed.

As a result, our R&D portfolio is balanced for customer pull and technology push and is aligned with corporate strategic directions that address specific consumer value. The balance of pull to push is coordinated by the portfolio management team using a list of strategy- and technology-oriented criteria within a *dialogue decision process* (DDP) analysis including corporate customers. For the purpose of this discussion, we will focus on criteria used for resourcing and leveraging decisions. The DDP addresses the specific business situation and strategic needs by incorporating the following topic areas:

1. *Criteria for deciding R&D funding.* Propose an overall strategic funding level for R&D in selected research focus areas (e.g., energy, environment) as a first approximation. These funding levels are influenced by strategic priorities, historical patterns, and budget constraints.

2. *Metrics for deciding balance of funding across the focus areas.* Create metrics to estimate the value of research projects to the company and the customer. These metrics become the drivers for analysis, and the process requires a dialogue with the affected parties to the benefits (the internal customer community). This dialogue may be the most important and influential factor for success of collaborative projects and programs. Our experience shows that the level of shared understanding between consumer, technologist, and implementor, when developed around a common process, is a major step forward in successfully managing industrial R&D and transferring innovation from research to product.

3. *Continually improve and monitor allocation of funds.* Establish criteria to adjust the first approximation allocation of funding to each research focus area as a function of strategic alignment to national goals, value or benefit to society, and so forth. Some level of exploratory research must be preserved to support long-term technical and business-related corporate initiatives—we reserve 20 percent of our internal budget for this purpose.

4. *Develop a process to coordinate internal and external R&D.* This is GM's *virtual global laboratory* initiative, which focuses specifically on the leveraging of internal and external resources, including government funding, industrial partnerships and licensing, and academic contracts and satellite laboratories. Key to success is an understanding of internal and external technical competencies and facilities.

Opportunities for leveraging that would provide additional intellectual resources and technical competencies, provide access to required essential capital equipment, or speed commercialization of key deliverables are identified. (As these leveraging needs and opportunities are identified, the requirements of particular projects can be assessed against the characteristics of available partnering mechanisms.) These mechanisms include academic, industrial, and government national laboratory partnerships, each with specific terms and conditions and specific advantages and disadvantages. This discussion focuses on academic and industrial partnerships as an approach to global technology sourcing and research collaboration.

The Virtual Global Lab

The virtual global laboratory is made "real" by a systematic process for establishing and monitoring partnerships. The process begins by first determining if the prospective partner would, indeed, like to collaborate in the specific research focus area and share the expectations. Then it is necessary to raise four questions internally: (1) Is the partnership good for the (corporate) customer? (2) Will the partnership develop a better (or more timely) solution to the technology need than the single entities could produce? (3) Is there a critical element supplied by the partner that either makes the research project possible or speeds completion of the deliverable in a meaningful way? (4) Does the partnership save the company money, including considerations of time and capital investment? If the answer to each of these four questions is yes, then it is probably wise, both legally and financially, to establish a partnership. The term *partner* can represent either an internal or external entity, and it can also represent a supplier and/or a customer group. In terms of the R&D portfolio the *customer* is internal to GM (e.g., one of GM's component groups or one of the other centers within the technical center). On the other hand, because of GM's vertical integration the *supplier* can be either internal or external. Therefore, when the term *leverage* is used it must be explained from the viewpoint of the customer and/or the supplier, as well as from an internal or external viewpoint. This lends itself to a more thorough explanation of the term *leverage*. The term *leverage* has been used throughout this document from various viewpoints. In terms of *leveraging* projects within the R&D portfolio, we begin by assessing the needs of the internal projects in terms of additional resources, head count, facilities, etc., and then determine which sector (academic, industrial, governmental) can best satisfy these needs. It may be a combination of all the above.

If we specifically look at partnering with the academic sector, GM begins by assessing the areas of academic and technical expertise of university programs *worldwide* in relation to our strategic priorities and internal competencies. These strategically selected university programs are then linked to the business and operating needs of the corporation as represented in the R&D portfolio. This process/mission is maintained by (1) identifying basic automotive science and engineering expertise and research competencies at universities; (2) matching expertise areas to the needs of the R&D portfolio; (3) leveraging *basic* science and research potentials to allow GM to focus on *applied/product-related* R&D; (4) establishing a global "visiting scholar" program to support technology transfer; and (5) using comprehensive (common) legal and financial templates.

The single most important factor in establishing an effective partnership with the academic sector is the monitoring of technology being transferred through the respective researchers. GM maintains this part of the process through a visiting scholar program, which places GM scientists in university laboratories to conduct research, as well as providing opportunities for faculty and students to work in GM laboratories. This visiting scholar interchange forms the cornerstone of GM's satellite laboratories. Satellite laboratories are simply the consolidation of key strategic projects established at selected universities. These projects are nurtured and eventually, over five to ten years, developed into research programs. During the five to ten years, projects are monitored for effectiveness of technology being transferred. The metrics for measuring the technology transferred are determined using the same DDP tool that is used to evaluate our internal R&D portfolio. Therefore, if the technology has been successfully transferred from the academic institution into GM, then it will materialize, either directly or indirectly, into one of our future products.

To establish a mutually beneficial industrial partnership it is essential to consider the business case for the external partner in addition to all of the aspects considered for academic partnerships. The steps to an industrial partnership for research or commercialization are illustrated in Figure 5.2.

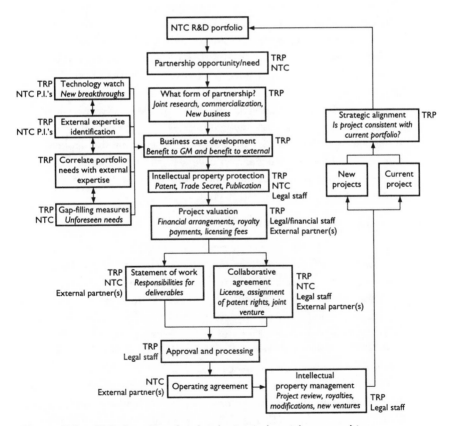

Figure 5.2 GM's flowchart for developing industrial partnerships.

Just as for an academic partnership, the internal and external competencies must be evaluated and compared for synergy. In addition, the partner's business sector and share of the relevant market may be an important consideration, especially for partnerships whose aim is technology commercialization. In certain rare instances, the joint development agreement may include some advance purchase agreement, provided certain functional requirements are met within the established pricing schedule. Typically, the partnership makes sense simply on the basis of technical expertise and the knowledge that the potential innovation has a real market within GM. If combined with the head start afforded by cooperative development, then investment by the external partner is warranted.

Issues of intellectual property are key and must be resolved early, although specific royalty rates can be negotiated later in good faith once the commercial value has been established and the relative contributions of each of the partners defined. Our strong preference is to request a short-term (three-year) exclusive access for automotive applications and to negotiate a license to the partner to develop nonautomotive applications. This provides GM with a competitive advantage and possibly license revenue; the partner gains immediate access to the GM market and to nonautomotive applications and only somewhat delayed access to the broad automotive market. It therefore becomes incumbent on GM to efficiently implement the technology and to continue to innovate.

Conclusions

Since the early 1990s, industry has experienced a paradigm shift and an evolution that has driven General Motors to become aligned with and support the globalization of technology sourcing for our products and manufacturing processes. General Motors' R&D center has responded to this by establishing a directorate for research technology partnerships, which focuses on complementing our internal technical competencies through leveraging with external competencies to support our strategically developed portfolio of R&D research projects. The vehicle for executing the partnership activity is embedded in the virtual laboratory concept and the business joint-venture process (Figure 5.3). The virtual lab executes the transfer of technology by utilizing the visiting scholar program and

The Virtual Lab Is Also *REAL*:

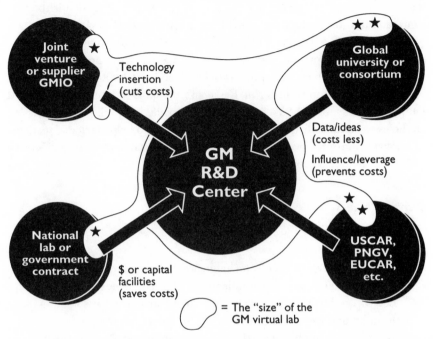

Figure 5.3 Virtual global laboratory of shared resources.

the satellite laboratory concept while the business process commercializes.

We believe it is impossible to achieve internally all the innovation necessary to successfully compete in our industry. Through global research and technology collaborations it becomes possible to leverage the accelerating pace of worldwide scientific and engineering discovery to develop key competitive advantages for General Motors today and into the twenty-first century.

Technology Transfer Success Rates and Organizational Performance

The ability to successfully transfer technology from research to manufacturing is a leading indicator of an organization's long-term success in the "white water" of domestic and international competition. Similarly, Boath (1994) has stated that "the ultimate measure of success for any research organization is the percentage of new technology that actually ends up in products."[1]

Holmes and McClaskey (1994) at Eastman Chemical Company have discussed the development and use of the metric "net present value of new/improved products and processes commercialized with major research input" to drive improvements in Eastman's technology transfer process. At Duracell, Kelsey and Milewski (1994) have provided the following discussion on the use of Duracell's quality management system to help facilitate "seamless technology transfers" by integrating research, development, and engineering with cross-divisional product development teams.

Duracell's Lessons Learned from International Technology Transfer

In the late 1980s Duracell's technology expertise was dispersed both geographically and organizationally. The company's ability to develop and transfer new technology to manufacturing was nonuniform around the world for a product that was marketed under the same name. Inefficiencies in communication and strategic focus arose because there was a great degree of independence of implementation, depending on local management. The corporate research center, referred to henceforth as DWTC (Duracell worldwide technology center), was at times not linked to manufacturing engineering and operations groups, making the diffusion of new technology all the more difficult.

In 1988, research, development, and advanced engineering functions were consolidated within DWTC and ultimately under a single vice president. That change poised the company for a reengineered product development and transfer process. This paper describes that process, using an example of a product development program from the core business—alkaline manganese primary batteries.

---

[1] See checklist at the end of this chapter. The list can be used in planning, reviewing, and identifying improvement opportunities for an organization's technology transfer process.

Technology Transfer: The Vision

Before describing the dynamic process that has evolved within Duracell for new product development and product improvement, a brief description of our ideal technology transfer concept will be attempted.

To consistently achieve a high-quality, timely product of the collective efforts of the company, its business goals at the highest level must be clearly understood and enthusiastically shared by all employees. These keys to success become the playing field for all projects, whether technical or administrative. Strategic objectives provide the road map across that field for achieving the goals. The identification of projects for development of technology arises from a customer focus, first external (the ultimate customer, in this case the consumer), then internal. The internal customers are the teammates who share the responsibility of accomplishing the strategic objectives. For DWTC, the ideal is to so understand the internal customers' needs that a mutual desire to see it carried through permeates the team. The development process becomes a natural evolution, with the final product emerging without fanfare, almost without the customer realizing that it happened. This ideal can only be realized in the absence of interfaces or barriers.

Traditional technology transfer implies the movement of the product-in-process across organizational or functional interfaces. The way these hurdles are avoided is by having these intermediate customers be part of the work team from beginning to end (Figure 5.4).

The net results are that even tall organizations can act "flat" and that the customers benefit from more robust products, processes, and follow-up support.

This flowchart depicts the continuous nature of the technology transfer process from problem definition to follow-up support. Interactions among the subteams (inner circles) generate the various steps in the development and transfer process (outer circle).

Now that the ideal process characteristics have been defined, an example of how Duracell has embodied them will be presented.

Technology Transfer: An Example

Within Duracell, corporate strategy is dictated by the "nine great investments," which are contained in the CEO's strategic proclamation. The nine great investments are superior batteries, high-power products, consumer value added, a great consumer brand franchise,

The Transfer Process

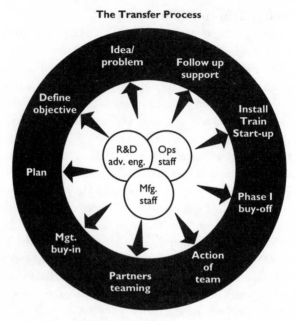

Figure 5.4 The transfer process.

adaptive alliances, geographic expansion, manufacturing infrastructure, environmental responsibility, and the leadership organization. This particular project met the goal of the first great investment— "superior batteries," providing the best service life, quality, and cost. Duracell's goal is to market a best-in-class alkaline product, and to this end, like many companies, we benchmark our competition, as well as ourselves, and have been doing so for many years. The tools used include a worldwide quality audit system, customer and consumer feedback, engineering analysis, and others. Criteria include product performance, appearance, seal integrity, age at retail, and packaging quality.

From DWTC's perspective, technology transfer starts this early in a program since linkage to corporate goals is critical to obtaining buy-in from all our customers and team members.

The Project: Initial Definition

DWTC is charged with providing Duracell with quantum leaps in technology, whether for current or new products. The incremental move forward of 1 to 2 percent is not acceptable in our organization, although it is welcomed by our manufacturing organizations and, indeed, it is shared.

The assessment of the above-mentioned benchmark data by DWTC identifies areas of opportunity to improve our core alkaline product. One such opportunity is the subject of this paper.

The opportunity identified was to design, develop, and implement a sealing technology to eliminate cell leakage once and for all at, or preferably below, current costs. Ongoing competitive benchmarking identified this category of alkaline battery quality as one without a clear world-class performer. This objective has linkages to manufacturing, marketing, and finance, as well as to the nine great investments.

This project proposed a radical change in approach to sealing compared to what had been used very successfully over many years and in billions of Duracell batteries.

The Key Steps to Achieve the Goals

At this point, we did the obvious; we put a plan together and did all the things that you have heard about and, indeed, have probably done yourselves: project planning, skills identification, budgeting, resource phasing, tracking.

However, we at DWTC believe that we did some things a little differently that made technology transfer part of the natural evolution of the project, and we will review those items as we step through this process.

Objective

The objective was clearly defined by a core team with membership from RD&E. This initial team developed design criteria, set quality standards, established a development timetable, outlined product qualification goals, and set cost targets. Clear short- and long-term targets were set. Then they initiated *design feasibility studies*.

They also defined a strategy to get management buy-in. Buy-in was required from DWTC staff and senior management from our divisional new products and technology staff and Duracell management worldwide. This was achieved by a step-by-step presentation of a strong, aggressive plan, with impact on the business defined and linkage to other programs shown, as well as presenting *show-me samples of the product from the initial feasibility study.*

While this was going on, the core team, not yet including our major customers, was gathering information from and sharing the design concepts and initial results with their Duracell engineering, manufacturing quality, and marketing sources worldwide. They asked for *feedback and feed forward* about the leakage issue and initial design concepts and began the first phase of *exciting your customer.* During this sales phase, Duracell's IDM (International Development Markets) expressed interest in the design concept. They specifically saw an *opportunity* to implement it in their Mexico City manufacturing operations during their next phase of manufacturing scale-up and product performance improvement. They were prepared to be a Beta site for this project.

This initiative appealed to the team and appeared to be a significant opportunity to bring this product improvement forward to a division that had not always had the benefit of being first with new technology, and if (the new technology were) introduced into their business, the ability to measure success would be easier. The customers were also excited, as they perceived an opportunity to participate in technical leadership that would delight both their internal and external customers. However, this Beta siting in Mexico City also presented risk. The IDM group was concerned that we might overdo the technology, and DWTC was concerned with their lack of new technology experience. But it was also clear to DWTC that the old adage, *KISS* (keep it simple, stupid!), was even more important and that the design and build of the assembly technology needed to be *compatible with the operations in the plant.*

We believe that an opportunity to leap forward in quality, an excited customer, and a willingness to develop assembly technology compatible with the needs of the customer established common respect and a foundation for the team to achieve the project goals. As a result, a proposal was made that Mexico would be our Beta site for the rollout of this project. Why Mexico?

- Opportunity for significant improvement in quality.
- A chance to be first in introducing a new technology.

- Could be done on a smaller scale than in the United States or Europe.
- A chance for DWTC to show that new technology was robust and did not require a higher level of technical skills in manufacturing.
- In addition, the technology would also prove that it could be adapted to high-speed manufacturing.

Customer Is On Board: The World Was Watching

What were our customers' needs? Did we understand them? Was our perception of what they wanted correct?

A team was assembled that encompassed senior management of both organizations, a technical team that incorporated DWTC, IDM, and plant engineers, quality, manufacturing, purchasing, accounting, and other personnel.

Respect for each other's abilities, cultural differences, and values allowed a shared vision and commitment to achieving the planned project. The project evolved through early and ongoing project meetings. Out of those came a redefined plan of action that met not just product objectives, but local plant needs and longer-term objectives of IDM.

The following are examples of some key actions that flowed from the plans:

- We established supplier relationships in the host country (Mexico). We did not want to create another set of supplier relationships that would add to cost and management complexity.
- We shared technology skills and knowledge with suppliers.
- We defined the interface of new and old technology and supplied linkage to recognize the then-current technical limitations of the plant.
- We recognized that to be successful we needed to have the whole team, including a number of key plant technicians and operators, buy in prior to plant installation.
- We brought plant technicians and operators in to train on and help debug equipment prior to shipment to the plant.

Their feedback was used to make changes, resulting in operational improvements.

By asking the manufacturing personnel what additional tools, gauges, test equipment, and computers they needed to successfully start up manufacturing the advanced product, the ability to maintain long-term quality was enhanced.

Implementation: The Actual Technology Transfer

As stated earlier, the transfer of technology within an idealized process should be part of a natural evolution, almost without the customer realizing that it has happened. To try to achieve this, the team executed a number of important actions that would make the integration of this new product and assembly technology into the plant as smooth as possible.

The critical steps in the actual transfer of the product, process, and equipment included the following:

- A commitment was made by the DWTC team to be members of the manufacturing operation team.
- The joint establishment of systems to measure quality, equipment operating parameters, etc., ensured a level playing field during the start-up and evaluation of the product and operations.

Early on-site preparation of the manufacturing area with detailed planning of new work flows drew in plant industrial engineers early on, facilitating the installation by the team and plant resources later.

Formalized training was an understood necessity. On-the-job as well as classroom training helped make all the plant employees aware of the project objectives, goals, and benefits. The training included the use of quality tools, equipment operation, and maintenance, and was extended to personnel working on all shifts.

Improvement areas identified by staff and employees as manufacturing experience grew were addressed at operations reviews after implementation. A level of continued but diminishing support was thus provided.

All of these specific actions were equally important and played a major role in successful introduction of the product improvement and manufacturing technology. A key point is that while the customer, in this case IDM, was excited and indeed pleased, the other customers, mechanics, material handlers, and so on were equally pleased by the process of introduction, which enhanced their knowledge and skills.

Was This the End? No

Another item that ensures the success of technology transfer from our perspective is like that of our advertisement, "We never stop." We do not walk away; we do not disappear; we follow up. Follow-up is critical from two perspectives. First, the immediate issues dealing with the just-introduced product technology have to be addressed. Second, it demonstrates to this customer and future ones that the RD&E group (DWTC) does provide an ongoing service, formal and informal, to support company programs. Customers are as critical to us as they are for the product the company makes.

Examples of some of the follow-up services are audits of product, process and equipment technical and quality support, off-site testing, and scale-up support.

Lessons Learned to Enable Technology Transfer
General
> *Show-me* prototypes made management buy-in easier.
> *Input from global company resources* assured technical buy-in and robust product design.
> *Team approach* is critical.
> *Pick Beta site* as early as possible.
> *Build relationship* with suppliers.

Research, development, and engineering–specific
> *Understand the customers* and their specific needs.
> *Hands-on* capability is a must.
> *Follow-up* support is critical.
> *Share credit* for success.
> *Exceed* the customer's expectations.

While this project had its share of trials by fire, and, indeed, not everything done and how it was done could be defined as a success, the lessons learned have had a major impact on new projects.

This project provided a benchmark for future projects involving the transfer of technology from R&D. Measures developed in the course of the work allow a semiquantitative evaluation of effectiveness and efficiency of execution. Specifically, the early signing on of customers, with clearly defined and measurable objectives, is now required at the time of initiation. The agreed-upon performance targets include timing as well as technical milestones. The use of project planning and tracking through review meetings at the subteam level will permit assessment of team efficiency for complex projects. And finally, there will be a formal customer satisfaction audit upon project completion.

Next Steps: Nothing Succeeds Like Success

When the new product had time in the marketplace, the worldwide quality audit team evaluated it for leakage under the new, more strenuous criteria established by the project team during its development. The results were that it lived up to its design expectations in the real world. The plant manufacturing data showed that the cost projections were also being satisfied such that operations became a happy customer.

So successful was the product (and project) technically that the CEO recognized the possibility of having like quality worldwide, and proceeded to launch a global product unification team. This, with other global quality initiatives (like ISO certification), has allowed the technical community to reengineer the way it does business.

Intellectual Property Management

Improving Motorola's Patent Filing Process

Once an organization has succeeded in developing and internally transferring technology, it must ensure that the results of its R&D are protected through an effective patent process. Rauner (1990) presented the following discussion of the process and results associated with introducing quality concepts and tools at Motorola's Intellectual Property Department.

Background

When Motorola adopted total customer satisfaction as its overriding objective and suggested a process analysis as an aid to customer satisfaction through ever improving quality, we in the Intellectual Property Department were asked to be pioneers in applying the approach in the office environment. Officers of the company had all attended classes on reducing cycle time and pursuing defect-free product, but most of us felt that this was a program to get manufacturing yields up and rejects down in products shipped. At first, we certainly did not think that documents written by lawyers could be improved using the company's approach to quality. Now we know otherwise.

Basically, the process calls for defining a product to be delivered to a customer to be satisfied. In the work effort to do this there are certain steps and actions, and there are inputs or needs that the people have—for example, information from others, perhaps from a different department. Once the steps in the work process are mapped in detail, we look for places to eliminate waste or where errors, especially fatal ones, most likely occur. Then we go about eliminating steps or redesigning the activities, simplifying, using work aids, training people, teaching people the jobs of the others they work with, and so on. Finally, we try to devise follow-up measurements and give attention to the fatal and critical points in the process, all the while expecting to continue to refine and reuse the analysis as improvements are made.

Early Mapping

As our first trial, we selected the preparation of patent applications as the subject for quality improvement. We have dozens of attorneys preparing hundreds of applications per year, which represents a major effort for us. Of course, the patents are significant in the business to protect investment in technology, which runs around 8 percent of sales as a cost of engineering. We mapped the activity in the Intellectual Property Department, initially starting with the receipt of an invention disclosure, then an optional search of the prior art, next the start of the patent drafting job, then obtaining the patent drawings, getting further information from the inventor, finalizing the documents, getting inventor signatures, and finally filing the documents in the U.S. Patent and Trademark Office. We looked at the times involved in these various steps and the particular steps where quality improvement would be significant. Then the thinking began to expand, and the real issues became clearer.

First, we saw that the entire process from start to finish must be mapped. The starting point really is the conception of the idea by the engineer, then his initial record making, his testing of the idea or experimentation, and the decision to pursue or not to pursue for patent—all of which must occur before the project even reaches our department. After we file the patent application, there is, of course, prosecution or arguing with the Patent Office examiner, usually followed by patent issuance, all before the real test is even encountered. The final proof of the pudding is whether the patent stands up in infringement negotiations or in a court action.

Second, in our preliminary analysis, we noted the times for the various steps and the fact that such times were unnecessarily and harmfully long in many cases. Third, the "customer" situation was apparent. One customer is the inventor, and the patent write-up must satisfy him. Another customer is the Patent Office examiner, who must be satisfied or the patent will never issue. Finally, an infringer must accept, and not find defects in, the patent or it will not be protecting technology. If litigation is necessary, the judge must not find defects, either.

Map Value Revealed

Having such a comprehensive map, starting with the inventor's conception of the idea through the enforcement of the patent, the value of the improvements became clear. We, of course, knew these individual steps, but placing them in a continuous flowchart was key to seeing improvements.

Reducing cycle time from conception of the invention to patent filing would solve a growing problem for us. Our competitors were increasingly filing on the same inventions we were, but sometimes with an earlier patent-filing date. Under the laws of most countries of the world (not the United States), the one with the earliest filing date is entitled to the patent, and a later filer on the same invention is out of luck. Perhaps he will not be able to use the invention or perhaps he must pay royalties to the one filing first. Therefore, driving down the time for these steps of the map could make a difference between owning the technology or maybe being shut out of it altogether.

Also, a study of the process map suggested places and ways to raise the quality. For example, some aspects of patent preparation can be standardized due to the commonality of certain laws and rules. Other actions in the preparation may need experience and skillful analytical ability. Some believe that it is an art to draw good patent claims. There are still other parts of the process that rely heavily on information from others—the inventor, for example— and quality improvement is readily suggested here, too.

In using the company quality approach, we learned that there is a gradation in types of mistakes, from the fatal through critical and major errors down to the lesser ones of the type that should be avoided but are not so critical. As our staff considered the patenting process, we noted such mistake types as a guide for the improvement plans.

Quality Steps Taken

In raising the quality of the patent document, we made choices of the steps to work on. For example, at this time we have not yet focused on the activities after filing of the patent. We recognize there is review by the government patent examiner and there are, of course, sales techniques in negotiating with infringers or trying lawsuits to enforce the patent. These actions do not fit a formula. They are ad hoc activities that take the skill and experience of the attorney and his judgment in working out the best definition of the invention possible in view of limiting prior art or in convincing an infringer that his design is within the patent.

However, there is a part of the process that is more subject to standardization and measure. Therefore we developed a template of a patent application format that will generally fit the rules of the U.S. Patent Office as well as those of many European and Asian government patent offices. Using this reduces the basis for examiner objection on formal matters (i.e., other than the patent claim breadth), so that the patent as originally submitted should avoid these rather mechanical and binary kinds of errors. The template has a number of guide statements under the various sections, so it is self-administering as a checklist and can further be used in occasional spot checking in a peer review of drafted patent applications. We have a number of beginners who are training in the department, so having this type of template is a great help for them.

By standardizing the format and the manner of writing up the application document, time can be saved and there is greater confidence that the document will be acceptable with a minimum of modification in most countries. This then allows better focus and more time for the difficult part of the preparation, which is the drafting of claims and analyzing an optimum definition of the invention. In many cases this is quite difficult, and this is where the expertise or "art" of the patent attorney comes into play. We cannot be sure that one knows all of the prior inventions, because some may come to light years later. Furthermore, we do not know how someone may vary a product later to escape the patent if the wording of the claims is not prepared carefully enough. So more time today is valuable for the attorney to establish claim wording to fit these unknown situations of the future. Failure in proper claim wording can render the patent worthless, so a mistake at this point may indeed be fatal.

At first, we counted defects that were found by the patent examiner, but review of that suggested that these were correctable, and there is more value in extra effort in areas other than counting the relatively few errors of formality that the Patent Office was finding.

Cycle Time Is Vital

As previously noted, the competition to invent and patent means that being first to file on a given invention can be critical. In studying the process maps and identifying the persons responsible for the steps and listing the times taken for such steps, we really saw there were weeks and months from conception of an invention to deciding whether to file—and equally long times while a file lay on an attorney's desk after the decision and before he managed to get the patent filed. We adopted a process of computerized tracking to give a focus and to manage these times.

Each attorney has a computerized list of each of his invention disclosures with the date of conception of the invention and the date of the decision to pursue that one for a patent. The computer program subtracts these dates to list the number of days between them, and then the program averages these. We also produce a monthly graph of the average numbers. Similarly, the computer program provides the number of days between the date of the decision to file and the first of the month, which is the date of the report for the attorney. These aging days are also averaged in a graph. Managers work with their people in groups of three or four to drive down the curves of the input times and the aging times. These attorney groups make monthly plans from the charts. We even found cases of friendly competition between attorney groups. Our overall aging cycle time went down 74 percent over one year, and the overall input cycle times went down about 30 percent over a year and are still going down. (See Figures 5.5 and 5.6.)

Merely counting days, of course, does not in itself cause times to go down. It does provide a focus on the problem. We could see that the attorneys were making better monthly work plans, were managing their personal time better, were adopting new techniques such as our template of standardized document format, were picking up a file and continuing to work on it until completed, were more quickly seeking help from others if there were a question, and so forth. All of these, and other actions like them, seem to build a greater psychological satisfaction in achieving a good job and to engender a pride in the work accomplished.

Summary
We believe that the process map gave us visibility of the areas to work on, that is, our timing and the artful part of patent drafting. Managing these areas has the greatest impact on making the patent valuable in the business. It also means that our people see the importance of their efforts in working on quality, so there is a pull-

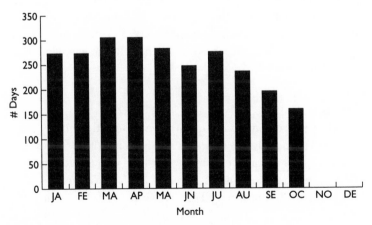

Figure 5.5 Disclosure input average time.

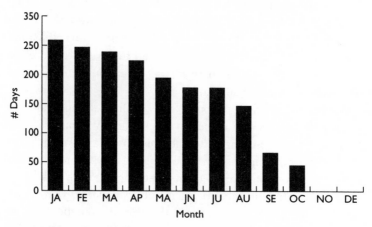

Figure 5.6   Disclosure aging IP department.

through effect that makes them more aware of quality in other parts of their work as well. Overall, we see good progress and an excellent path to continue following along the quality journey.

Optimizing Returns from Intellectual Property at AT&T

Once patents are obtained, the processes used to protect and license the technology contained in the patents must be effective. Increasing the effectiveness of these processes will ensure that the patent holder gains the maximum return on its investment. The following material on AT&T's Intellectual Property Division's quality journey was presented by Michael R. Greene, vice president of Intellectual Property.

Introduction

AT&T is fully committed to quality. We believe that quality principles are key to achieving customer satisfaction. Within the last three years, three of our major business units have won a Baldrige Award: Consumer Communications Services, AT&T Network Systems–Transmission Systems, and AT&T Universal Card. These three business units have set a standard of excellence that the corporation and all of our business units and divisions are now striving to achieve.

We illustrate AT&T's broad commitment to quality by focusing on the quality journey of a single AT&T division, the Intellectual Property Division. AT&T's Intellectual Property Division (IPD) is a corporate headquarters division charged with the management of AT&T's portfolio of approximately 25,000 active patents. Our overall conclusion is that aggressive application of quality principles in a corporate headquarters division setting can yield dramatic improvements, even though headquarters divisions typically face shifting stakeholder expectations and budgetary uncertainties. Furthermore, IPD now believes that quality principles can yield substantial results improvement, even in a context where a significant measure of success is already being achieved.

IPD's quality journey begins with a brief look at the history of how AT&T's management of its patent portfolio has evolved since the 1984 breakup of the Bell system. As a direct consequence of this breakup, IPD has experienced several shifts in the nature of its relationship with other AT&T business units and divisions and their expectations of IPD. While these shifts reflect some unique internal AT&T considerations, we believe that frequent shifts in the expectations of internal company stakeholders is a common dilemma faced by many corporate headquarters divisions.

Despite frequent shifts, IPD has managed to deliver significant increases in patent royalties to the corporation in the last five years. Nevertheless, by late 1993, IPD and many of its business unit and division stakeholders believed that IPD's processes and results could be significantly improved by the aggressive application of quality principles. These beliefs led to the formation, in 1994, of an Intellectual Property Process Quality Improvement Team (IP-QIT). The IP-QIT was chartered to conduct a comprehensive review of AT&T's IP-related processes and whether these processes were maximizing the value of the corporation's patent and technology assets.

Intellectual Property at AT&T after Divestiture

Table 5.1 briefly summarizes the policy changes that have defined the strategic role that patent assets have played at AT&T, particularly from the 1984 Bell system breakup to today. In each of the periods shown in Table 5.1, IPD responded to the challenge of frequent shifts in the nature of intellectual property service support

Table 5.1   AT&T Postdivestiture
Patent Management Policies

Dates	Policy
1994	IP-QIT and new AT&T patent management policy
1991–1994	Business units set licensing policy
1988–1991	Broad cross-licensing
1984–1987	Postdivestiture, no licensing
1956–1984	Consent decree era: license all companies at reasonable terms

required by corporate headquarters and the various AT&T business units.

During the 1984–1987 transition period, AT&T was adjusting to the free-market competitiveness faced by its various businesses. For example, the former Western Electric equipment and component manufacturing division faced external market competitors after decades of life as an internal captive supplier.

In this postdivestiture period, the managers of the Equipment Manufacturing Division had little time to devote to patent management policy issues. As a result, IPD's primary internal AT&T customer was corporate headquarters.

IPD's challenge from 1988 to 1991 was to implement a patent management policy that called for broad licensing of our patents, for both royalty returns and reciprocal rights to the patents of others. Reciprocal rights were valued in this period because our product designers wanted the freedom to be as innovative as possible and to design without inadvertently infringing on the intellectual property of other companies. Royalties continued to be important to corporate headquarters during this period.

In the 1991 to 1994 interval, AT&T business units, now fully responsible for their individual financial objectives, demanded and received the right to participate in the creation of patent licensing policies and to share in the received royalties, based on licensing decisions. In this environment, the business units were the customers of IPD. In turn, IPD became the licensing agent for the individual AT&T business units, while retaining the requirement to satisfy corporate headquarters with enhanced returns from licensing technologies and patents. During the 1991 to 1994 period, IPD's management of the internal process to communicate and resolve cross–business unit licensing strategy differences became especially critical because of a sharp increase in the variety of licensing strategies that business units wished to pursue.

While experiencing these dynamic changes in its stakeholder environment since 1984, IPD achieved significant financial returns. The division returned steadily increasing royalty income to the corporation. Over the past three years, total patent royalty returns rose by more than 30 percent.

Despite this strong record of financial success, other U.S. companies were achieving greater royalties by aggressively licensing their patent portfolios for royalty income. The question arose as to whether AT&T could gain much greater business value from its intellectual property assets if it comprehensively and aggressively applied quality principles to the management of those assets. Thus, in 1994, the IP-QIT was chartered by the senior vice presidents of Law and Corporate Strategy and Development to investigate how quality principles should be applied to the management of intellectual property in the context of AT&T's highly competitive, highly innovative, and globalized business environment.

The IP-QIT Recommendations and the New Patent Policy IP-QIT Methods
The IP-QIT was chartered to examine AT&T's intellectual property management processes to determine if efficiencies in the delivery of intellectual property services can be achieved and to review or establish processes and metrics to obtain optimal value from AT&T's intellectual property on a global basis.

The IP-QIT was guided by Senior Vice President Jim Kilpatric, whose leadership drew upon prior experience guiding a total law quality implementation process. Kilpatric charged the team with finding answers to what appeared to be inefficiencies and unacceptable delays in IP-related decision making and the attainment of economic returns on AT&T IP assets that were less than fair market value. Kilpatric's coaching also included a commitment to the IP-QIT team that their solution recommendations would receive full consideration by the senior executives of the corporation.

In implementing its task, the IP-QIT benchmarked the intellectual property management practices of four leading technology-oriented companies whose global business focus and intellectual property asset strengths are similar to AT&T's. The purpose of this benchmarking was to compare the value AT&T receives from its intellectual property assets with the value received by similar companies and to evaluate the specific processes these companies use to obtain economic value. The IP-QIT also conducted extensive interviews of senior business unit, IPD, and IP-Law representatives within the AT&T IP community, along with their appropriately designated subordinates, to develop a comprehensive evaluation of the IP processes that were used within AT&T.

To develop its overall recommendations, the IP-QIT asked each team member to separately evaluate the internal and external data that had been collected and to draft his or her own individual set of recommendations. These individual recommendations reflected broad areas of agreement and disagreement. The IP-QIT then worked collectively to synthesize the individual member recommendations into a single set of final recommendations.

IP-QIT Findings

The IP-QIT concluded that AT&T does not have effective processes to validate fair market value achievement from its IP assets. Also, according to the IP-QIT, processes required better integration. As an example, in mid-1994, when the IP-QIT recommendations were issued, IPD and IP-Law, the AT&T organization that creates and maintains IP assets, provided overlapping intellectual property services. These groups came together organizationally only at the level of the AT&T chairman.

While both IPD and IP-Law were seeking to advance business unit and AT&T goals and to optimize the value derived from AT&T's intellectual property on a global basis, each organization looked to the business units as customers and often operated as competitors in situations where the responsibility for specific intellectual property functions was not clearly delineated. As a result, many functions and process were performed by both IPD and IP-Law, and sometimes by the business unit customers as well. For example, both IPD and IP-Law recognize the importance of processes to create and deliver intellectual property awareness training to the business units. Yet the IP-QIT found that the educational activities of both organizations were ad hoc and rarely coordinated.

In the area of patent licensing, where close cooperation and teaming between managers and attorneys is often critical to success, the IP-QIT determined that the competitive environment between IPD and IP-Law often led to situations where patent license negotiations could take years and yield less than fair market value for the IP assets involved. Furthermore, it was found that license agreements that were completed often employed complex payment formulas, making contract compliance difficult to administer.

The IP-QIT also found deficiencies in the critical Intellectual Property Review Board (IPRB) process. This process communicated business unit and IPD intentions to license intellectual property throughout the company and resolve cross–business unit differences that frequently arise as a result of such licensing proposals. The IP-QIT findings were that the IPRB process operated restrictively and permitted one business unit to block a licensing proposal without documenting an economic justification. These process deficiencies contributed to excessive license negotiation intervals and to an inadequate realization of economic value on AT&T's intellectual property assets. The corrective steps taken to improve the quality of this particular process are discussed in detail under "Implementation."

Finally, and most important, the IP-QIT concluded that AT&T was achieving significantly less economic return than other world-class companies gained on intellectual property assets. This finding was obtained by benchmarking information exchanges with the intellectual property management organizations in companies whose intellectual property asset base and business environment were similar to AT&T's. The IP-QIT estimated that AT&T could earn more than five times the economic return on its intellectual property assets than was being achieved. While the absolute amount of the economic return target identified by the IP-QIT is not material, the identification of a specific growth objective does represent a substantial challenge that required substantial process and productivity improvement efforts. The identified targets with greatest impact are processes that overlapped organizational boundaries.

IP-QIT Quality Improvement Recommendations

The IP-QIT made a number of specific recommendations that are being implemented aggressively. Additionally, the recommendations provided a significant impetus to AT&T's issuance of a new Patent Management Policy on October 10, 1994. The next section summarizes the new AT&T Patent Management Policy.

As a result of its findings regarding interorganizational competition, reduced value capture, and excessive intervals, the IP-QIT first recommended that AT&T manage its intellectual property under an organizational structure that brings IPD and the IP lawyers responsible for intellectual property contract negotiations together under a single vice president. The purpose of this structure is to minimize the interorganizational competition between IPD and IP-Law. The author is the first vice president, Intellectual Property, with both management and law responsibilities. I currently report to both the AT&T senior vice president, Corporate Strategy, and senior vice president, Law.

Having IPD and IP lawyers report to a single vice president will significantly speed up license negotiations because alternative business negotiation positions can be interpreted and crafted into suitable contractual language in real time. It will also improve negotiation team effectiveness by having a business analyst and legal analyst working in close cooperation as negotiations proceed.

A second important IP-QIT recommendation advocates the creation of business unit/IPD/IP-Law teams, called IP teams, whose functions are to establish patent portfolios and support their development and to provide guidelines on patent licensing negotiation objectives within specific areas of AT&T technology. These teams will also contribute significantly to the minimization of the interorganizational competition, negotiation delays, and suboptimal value-capture characteristic of the pre-1995 environment.

The IP-QIT recommended that each business unit prepare an annual intellectual property plan. These plans are integrated by IPD with the plans of other business units to form an overall AT&T IP business plan. The AT&T IP business plan establishes specific economic objectives that are jointly shared by the business units and IPD. Going forward, the sum of the economic objectives of the individual business units and IPD will constitute a total AT&T financial objective that is consistent with the economic return on intellectual property assets of similar companies.

The IP-QIT established a number of additional improvement recommendations for specific intellectual property management processes. These include patent portfolio development, patent assertion planning, licensing, collections, and information systems. The IP-QIT made quality improvement recommendations that span all areas of AT&T's intellectual property creation and management efforts. These recommendations led to a new patent management policy, issued by the chairman.

The New Patent Management Policy

On October 10, 1994, Robert Allen, AT&T chairman, issued a policy letter that endorsed the findings of the IP-QIT and articulated guidelines implementing many of the IP-QIT recommendations. Central to the chairman's new policy was the directive that a single organization is charged with the responsibility of implementing all of AT&T's licensing objectives. The policy named the IPD as the appropriate place for this responsibility to reside. In practical terms, the chairman's endorsement fully empowering a single licensing organization responds directly to two key IP-QIT recommendations, namely, that competition among licensing organizations should be eliminated and that the economic return that AT&T earns on AT&T's intellectual property should be substantially increased.

The chairman's policy letter did not dictate specific implementation methods to increase the economic return on intellectual property assets. Under the new policy, AT&T business units are free to pursue other forms of economic return on intellectual property assets, such as increased product profits that may be available through limited licensing or cross-licensing. The important difference from the pre-IP-QIT–policy letter era is that business units that oppose licensing have to provide a full economic justification for such strategies to AT&T. The chairman's Patent Management Policy also reinforced the IP-QIT's recommendation to improve communication among the business units through an IP board of advisors.

Implementation

Achieving the top-to-bottom quality improvement goals that are called for in the recommendations of the IP-QIT and the new AT&T

policy has been a massive and successful, year-long undertaking that reflects AT&T's and IPD's total commitment to quality. What makes the totality of this commitment clear is the comprehensiveness of the changes involved and the commitment of scores of volunteers who carried this quality improvement program forward while still meeting and frequently exceeding all the goals and objectives that were assigned to them prior to the IP-QIT implementation effort.

The first phase of the implementation occurred in late summer 1994. In this phase an overall implementation blueprint was established and seven specific Process Quality Improvement teams were chartered and staffed with volunteers from all functional departments. Table 5.2 lists the seven Process Quality Improvement teams and an abbreviated activity description for each.

The process QITs listed in Table 5.2 had the dual goal of setting and implementing improvements in their respective process areas and assuring that their recommendations were mutually reinforcing rather than conflicting. To ensure the latter objective, the project management of the whole implementation effort was coordinated by IPD Vice President Gene Partlow. Each process QIT reported on progress against current action items to this director and the other QITs in bimonthly meetings. Cross–QIT issues were addressed at these meetings and in numerous informal communications that took place between progress review meetings.

The seven process improvement QITs jointly issued their final process improvement recommendations on January 25, 1995, and the complex process documentation, reorganization, and retraining implementation steps necessary to put these recommendations in place began immediately after this joint report was issued. To more clearly articulate the implementation steps, the implementation history for one process, the creation of the Intellectual Property Board of Advisors (IPBA) and its processes will serve to illustrate the scope of this implementation effort. The IPBA process communicates licensing proposals to the AT&T business units and resolves cross–business unit issues that are frequently associated with such proposals.

Case Example: The IPBA Process

AT&T's process for communicating licensing plans to the business units, allowing them to comment and reach a cross–business unit

Table 5.2 Implementation Process QITs

Process QIT	Activity Description
IP teams	Create and define mission for AT&T teams regarding technology-specific patent portfolio development and licensing strategies.
Intellectual Property Board of Advisors processes	Draft and implement revisions to cross–business unit communication and issues resolution process.
Patent portfolio development	Define the patent portfolio development process to be utilized by IP teams.
Patent assertion	Define the process for identifying patent users and enforcing AT&T patent rights.
Licensing process	Define licensing process improvements to guide IP teams and IPD in licensing efforts.
Collection process	Monitor and ensure compliance with existing intellectual property agreements.
Information systems	Harmonize databases used within AT&T.

consensus on what is ultimately to be licensed was called the Intellectual Property Review Board (IPRB). The IP-QIT's findings regarding the IPRB's effectiveness were that licensing proposals submitted to it for cross–business unit approval frequently experienced lengthy delays.

Under the IPRB's processes, any business unit or division that wished to license patents or transfer technology was obligated to bring its proposal to the IPRB members representing each business unit. Upon receipt of such proposals, any other business unit had the right to object to the proposal if it deemed its business interests harmed. However, even one such "harm" objection, if unresolved through cross–business unit negotiation, could force a withdrawal of the proposal—even though the objecting business unit was under no obligation to document the nature or magnitude of the economic or strategic harm it alleged. In sum, any one of 20-plus business units could hold another business unit's licensing proposal hostage, and the intervals required to reach consensus on individual proposals was frequently unsatisfactory.

Even before the IP-QIT review of the IPRB process, IPD (the process owner) was continually striving to make, and did make, significant process quality improvements. For example, a significant quality metric is the average of the interval that proposals remain in the IPRB process queue. This interval was nearly halved to just over four weeks from 1993 to 1994. Such interval reductions were the direct result of IPD process innovations such as a full conversion from a fax- and phone-dominated process to an e-mail-dominated process and more aggressive expediting of cross–business unit dispute resolutions. Furthermore, IPD created and implemented a weekly status report process in 1994. This process provided all IPRB representatives with an up-to-date profile of the views of all business units on every open proposal. However, despite these improvements, the IP-QIT recommended that even further and more fundamental process quality improvements be made to the IPRB process.

The IP-QIT was chartered to examine comprehensively all processes impacting the value that AT&T achieves from its intellectual property assets. From this perspective, the IP-QIT was positioned to question the fundamental rationale for processes such as the IPBA and to consider whether the roles of these processes were properly chartered. In contrast, individual organizations like IPD, even though process owners, were not generally positioned to effect such multistakeholder processes. Thus, while IPD's process quality improvements to the IPRB were acknowledged, the IP-QIT's recommendation was to recharter the process completely.

Both the IP-QIT and the chairman's new Patent Management Policy strongly endorsed the effective functioning of a cross–business unit communication and conflict-resolution process concerned with IP issues. However, the IP-QIT challenged the basic roles the business unit participants play in the processes and recommended that these be altered.

To address these findings, AT&T disbanded the IPRB and created a new Intellectual Property Board of Advisors (IPBA). Like the

IPRB, the IPBA includes representatives of all the major business units and technology-focused AT&T divisions, such as Bell Labs. However, under the IPBA, the criteria business units can use to object to another business unit's licensing proposal has been changed fundamentally. Today, any business unit that wishes to object to a licensing proposal must be prepared to make an economic justification for its objection. Furthermore, if such objections are not resolved between proposer and objector within a three-week interval, both parties must bring an economic analysis for their position before a formal meeting of the IPBA members. These members will then review both positions and vote to recommend the position that benefits AT&T shareholders the most. Effectively, the new process procedures now make it impossible for a single business unit to table indefinitely licensing proposals they did not favor.

Implementation of the IP-QIT's recommendations with respect to the IPBA process occurred during the first quarter of 1995, and we have not had sufficient time as yet to measure the results of the changes that were made. However, we are confident that the changes to the IPBA process that were made will result in dramatic improvements in two fundamental areas: the increase of economic return on AT&T's intellectual property assets and reduction in the fundamental IPBA process metric of average interval.

The IPBA process changes and improvements just described are a single process example of the changes that were undertaken on in all of the processes listed in Table 5.2. When combined, these changes constitute a fundamental departure for AT&T's organizations, particularly IPD, involved in intellectual property matters.

Conclusions and Recommendations

The overall conclusion our experience suggests regarding the application of quality principles to situations confronted by internal corporate divisions is that unless and until quality principles are applied in a comprehensive, coordinated, and fully empowered way, the results achieved are likely to be suboptimal. To be successful, process reviews should span all the significant corporate-wide activities that impact the specific corporate goals ascribed to the internal division under consideration.

Internal divisions acting on their own can apply quality principles and achieve some improvements in stakeholder satisfaction. Since our case is typical, it suggests that a high-level and multiorganization process quality review is required to achieve order-of-magnitude improvements. Our confidence is high that we are about to experience significant improvement gains in a whole cluster of interrelated processes that focus on AT&T's intellectual property asset utilization.

Full involvement of senior management in this comprehensive quality improvement effort is essential. Until AT&T's senior management got intellectual property fully on its radar screen, apparently satisfactory, yet suboptimal results (as seen in hindsight) were the norm. In AT&T's case, the visibility of the IP-QIT was high enough to succeed on its own. However, its effectiveness was significantly reinforced by an endorsing policy letter from the chairman.

An important corollary to the last point is that, absent the corporate application of quality principles, it is very easy for internal divisions and their stakeholders to be satisfied with performance that is suboptimal. Thus, to ensure that functions performed by internal divisions are as productive and effective as possible, a comprehensive application of quality principles represents a solution to optimize division operations.

Checklist for Technology Transfer Process Improvement

Section I. Checklist for Innovators

	Strongly Disagree			Strongly Agree	
	1	2	3	4	5

Innovator

- The technology has been adequately marketed within the organization. ❑ ❑ ❑ ❑ ❑
- The researchers have an understanding of the needs of the organization. ❑ ❑ ❑ ❑ ❑
- There are adequate resources to do the transfer. ❑ ❑ ❑ ❑ ❑

Technology

- The costs and risks associated with developing this technology are known and quantified. ❑ ❑ ❑ ❑ ❑
- The technology promise and how it relates to the strategy is known and agreed upon. ❑ ❑ ❑ ❑ ❑
- The technology is familiar to the recipient. ❑ ❑ ❑ ❑ ❑
- The technology is important to the recipient's business. ❑ ❑ ❑ ❑ ❑

Channel

- A plan for the technology proper hand-off has been developed. ❑ ❑ ❑ ❑ ❑
- The responsibilities have been mutually delineated and accepted. ❑ ❑ ❑ ❑ ❑

Recipient

- There is adequate technical expertise to develop the technology. ❑ ❑ ❑ ❑ ❑

	Strongly Disagree				Strongly Agree
	1	2	3	4	5
■ There is training that can be provided to the recipient to ease the transfer.	❑	❑	❑	❑	❑
■ Management in the receiving organization is committed to the technology.	❑	❑	❑	❑	❑

TOTAL ____

Section II. Checklist for Recipients

	Strongly Disagree				Strongly Agree
	1	2	3	4	5

Innovator

	1	2	3	4	5
■ The recipient has done an adequate job of sharing market strategies and opportunities with the research organization.	❑	❑	❑	❑	❑
■ The innovator has an understanding of the timing and needs of the receiving organization.	❑	❑	❑	❑	❑
■ The innovator's organization is willing to dedicate resources to the transfer.	❑	❑	❑	❑	❑

Technology

	1	2	3	4	5
■ The impact that the technology can offer the business has been evaluated.	❑	❑	❑	❑	❑
■ The costs and risks associated with developing this technology are known and quantified.	❑	❑	❑	❑	❑
■ The technology is important to the business.	❑	❑	❑	❑	❑
■ The technology is familiar to the recipient.	❑	❑	❑	❑	❑

	Strongly Disagree				Strongly Agree
	1	2	3	4	5

Channel

- There has been agreement on what constitutes a demonstration of technical feasibility. ☐ ☐ ☐ ☐ ☐
- The relationship between the two organizations has been productive in the past. ☐ ☐ ☐ ☐ ☐

Recipient

- There is a plan to receive the technology. ☐ ☐ ☐ ☐ ☐
- There are adequate technical resources to accept and develop the technology. ☐ ☐ ☐ ☐ ☐
- There is a product champion available. ☐ ☐ ☐ ☐ ☐

TOTAL _____

Section III. Scoring

The maximum score obtainable is 60. If you received:

12–24: Your organization is likely experiencing difficulty in its technology transfer.

25–36: Your organization realizes the value of efficient technology transfer and is starting down the road to more effective transfers.

37–48: Your organization is likely realizing significant benefit from its technology transfer efforts.

49–60: Keep up the good work!! You have a top-performing technology transfer organization.

Provided by Boath (1994) and adapted from Ounjian and Carne (1987).

CHAPTER 6

IMPLEMENTING QUALITY IN RESEARCH: A CASE EXAMPLE

This chapter provides a case example of implementing a quality process within a research organization. The case is intended to demonstrate the use of many of the concepts and processes discussed in the previous chapters. The case was also designed to demonstrate additional insights into the real-world challenges faced by senior research managers and quality professionals in implementing a comprehensive approach to managing for quality.[1]

Implementing TQM in Research at Eastman Chemical Company

ECC: General Background

Eastman Chemical Company (ECC) was founded in 1920 in Kingsport, Tennessee. Its initial primary mission was to make methyl alcohol for the photography business. Since that time, many other sites and products have been added. Eastman sells its products to other industries that use them to provide a wide variety of consumer products. Today, ECC is a $4 billion diversified, global, and highly integrated chemical company that markets and manufactures over 400 chemicals, fibers, and plastics to 7,000 customers around the world. ECC employs approximately 17,750 people. Eastman's employees are divided into three major types:

[1] This case was designed and developed by Dr. Al Endres, Director, Center for Quality at the University of Tampa. Dr. Endres was assisted in case development by his graduate assistant Mr. Pedro Rodriguez. The case was partially funded by a grant from the American Society for Quality Control's Education Board Research Fellowship Program. Generous contributions of information and review time were made by Dr. Jerry Holmes, (then) VP R&D, and Mr. David McClaskey, Quality Management Coordinator, at Eastman. Dr. Frank M. Gryna, Distinguished Professor, Management, at the University of Tampa, also provided valuable comments for case development.

business and technical, business and technical support, and operations. Eastman is highly respected in the industry as a leader in product quality, manufacturing capability, reliability of supply, technical service to customers, environmental protection, and ethical business conduct. In 1993, Eastman Chemical Company, received the Malcolm Baldrige National Quality Award.

Products and Key Quality Characteristics

Eastman's facilities are large, complex, and highly instrumented, with long operating lines. Maintenance costs are significant. Chemically, all of Eastman's products are organic compounds that require the use of both unipurpose and multipurpose equipment in both batch processes and large continuous processes.

Examples of consumer products that contain Eastman products are 2-liter drink bottles, toothbrushes, photographic films, artificial sweeteners, chewing gum, foods, vitamin E, highlighter pen tips, tape, coatings for flooring materials, Christmas decorations, hand lotions, sunscreens, photographic developers, household fabrics, computer diskettes, steering wheels, plastic cups, videotapes, and disposable diapers.

Among key product quality requirements are uniformity, purity, chemical stability, and appearance. Specific parameters vary in importance by product type. These chemicals, fibers, and plastics are sold in various sizes and types of containers, including bales, large boxes, drums, tanks, and trucks.

Organization

Eastman's mission is to create superior value for five stakeholders: customers, employees, investors, suppliers, and the public. To accomplish this effectively, Eastman's business is managed in four matrixed dimensions (Figure 6.1):

- Functions
- Geographies
- Core competencies
- Business organizations

Core Competencies

The core competencies are deeply embedded strengths in Eastman's business. Eastman has eight core competencies, which are divided into *technology core*

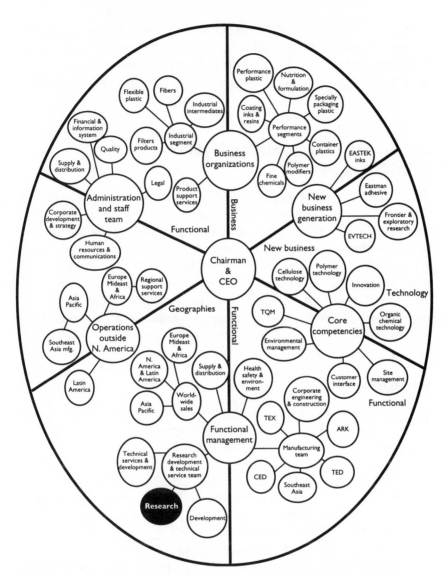

Figure 6.1 Eastman Chemical Company organizational chart—January 1, 1995.

competencies and *functional core competencies*. Technology core competencies are polymer technology, cellulose technology, organic chemical synthesis technology, and innovation. Functional core competencies are site management, environmental management, customer interface, and Total Quality Management.

Drivers for Implementing Total Quality in ECC Research

From founding leader George Eastman to the executives of today, Eastman Chemical Company's leadership has been dedicated to quality excellence. Each generation of leaders has left a profound legacy of attention to customers' needs, concern for employees as individuals, and commitment to the highest product quality. Beginning with Eastman President Earnie Davenport, the entire senior management team has created a vision that promotes customer focus through the values captured in the foundation documents of "Strategic Intent" and "Quality Policy." The senior management team is personally and actively involved in guiding the company toward its vision.

Strategic Intent

The *strategic intent* of an organization is determined by senior Management through a process that internalizes the appropriate information, factual and opinion-based, on what the future may look like.[2]

Vision:	To be the world's preferred chemical company
Mission:	To create superior value for customer, employees, investors, suppliers and publics
Guided by:	Company directions
Driven by:	Quality Policy and the Eastman Way[3]
Focusing on:	Exceeding customer's expectations while achieving our major improvement opportunities

---

[2] Definition by Suzanne Graves and John Moran, "Developing an Organization's Strategic Intent and Operational Plan," *The Quality Management Forum,* spring 1995.

[3] ECC's set of values and principles.

Quality Policy

Goal:	To be the leader in quality and value of products and services
Operational policy:	Focus on reduction of variability around the customer's target
Principles:	Customer satisfaction, continual improvement, innovation, process emphasis, management leadership, empowerment, statistical methods, employee development, partnerships, and assessment.

ECC's Strategic Planning Process

Eastman's Strategic Planning Process is used to achieve its vision, fulfill its mission, and implement its quality policy. The process begins by defining and deploying major improvement opportunities (MIOs), and overall direction (Strategic Intent) to all business, functional, geographic, and core competency organizations. These organizations then develop strategic alternatives that link with and support the Strategic Intent.

Critical planning inputs used by the organizations for developing strategic alternatives include customer requirements, competitive comparisons and benchmarking, evaluation of risks and uncertainties, company capabilities, and suppliers' capabilities. As part of its Strategic Intent, Eastman leaders have established MIOs, which are company-wide areas of emphasis for improvement. The MIOs begin with a focus on exceeding customer expectations while achieving the following:

- Rapid globalization
- Superior return on assets
- Aggressive sales revenue

ECC's TQM Initiative: The Beginning

In 1987, Eastman started its company-wide quality management effort. As in many organizations, Eastman's quality process first focused on improving its manufacturing processes. Eastman then began to focus on administrative and support functions and processes. For example, measures tied to customers'

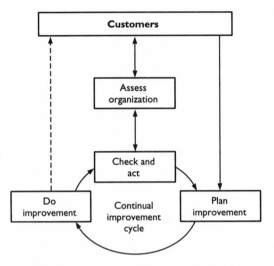

Figure 6.2 ECC's quality management process (QMP).

needs and expectations (quality, cost, timeliness, and effectiveness) were established to benchmark and improve human resource processes.

Eastman introduced its quality management process (QMP) as an ongoing improvement approach throughout the company. This approach is based on the *Plan-Do-Check-Act* continuous improvement cycle (Figure 6.2).

At all levels, interlocking teams enable employees to develop objectives and measures that are aligned with company and organization goals generated and defined by the Strategic Planning Process.

Research as a Business Unit

ECC has eight business organizations each containing a number of business units (BUs). The projects are selected by the BUs. The BUs are led by the management team, whose primary role is managing particular segments of the business. For example, in the research business unit, the management team is led by the research director and, in general, by people from the research unit.

Research for design and introduction of new products is accomplished through Eastman's innovation process (Figure 6.3), a multifunctional and companywide process managed by the executive team.[4] Multifunctional teams are

---

[4] A team comprised of ECC's senior and middle-level management.

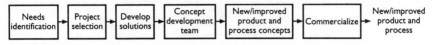

Figure 6.3 Eastman's innovation process.

used in the innovation process to coordinate and integrate the subprocesses. Customer requirements and market needs are considered in each subprocess. The owner of the innovation process is the management team working in the process; however, the ultimate owner is the senior vice president for Technology Management.

Eastman's Research Organization (1987)

In 1987 Eastman research was comprised of 660 people; of these, 300 were professionals, including scientists and engineers. Eastman research provides new and improved product and process concepts for all of Eastman's business units. In 1987 Eastman research was divided into six divisions (Figure 6.4): Chemicals Research, Polymers Research, Physical and Analytical Chemistry Research, Fibers Research, Engineering Research, and Administration.

Initial Activities for Incorporating TQM into Research

In 1987, Dr. Jerry Holmes was selected to lead the research unit. Holmes saw TQM as a potential means of driving the changes he thought were necessary to realize the unit's full potential. Initial TQM activities began by Holmes and his research directors agreeing to develop measurement criteria for establishing relative project priorities. Two fundamental criteria were chosen for use in evaluating each *current* and *potential* project:

1. The project's objectives were relevant to Eastman's current key business goals or strategies.
2. Technically, the project had a high probability of meeting its objectives.

These two criteria were then used to reduce the size of the research portfolio and focus the research organization's resources on the remaining vital few projects.

The ultimate measure for judging the research's effectiveness was that the new product and process *concepts* must be accepted into the next phase of ECC's

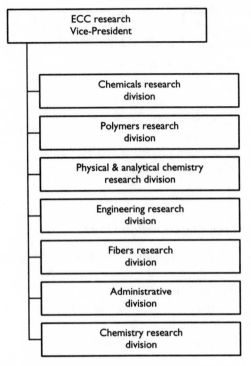

Figure 6.4 Eastman's research organizational chart (1987).

innovation process, *concept development* (Figure 6.3). The criteria used by ECC to evaluate potential development projects are the criteria related to commercialization. If the product or process concept can be commercialized,[5] then the project would be developed; otherwise, the project would be stopped. Research reviewing and focusing on the projects that meet the organization's criteria for commercialization were key in improving the portfolio management process.

In 1989, ECC's quality management effort was expanded to include all research people on teams. There were 650 people involved in 50 research teams. By the end of 1989, everyone was on teams, measures had been developed, and processes were studied and flowcharted. Designed experiments and statistical process control were being used to improve process knowledge.

---

[5] The product must be profitable in no longer than seven years. ECC must have both expertise and access to the raw material to meet ECC's definition of *commercialization*.

Reviewing and Reflecting on Results

As a "check" step for assessing progress, the company conducted an employee survey designed to measure employees' opinions on research's effectiveness at developing and supporting new products and processes. The survey results were 15 percent *positive* and 85 percent *negative*. Furthermore, a trend chart of research's main output (Figure 6.5) showed that research was getting very small, if any, value-added results from its considerable initial TQM effort. Interviews of research personnel, conducted as part of a check step, confirmed that little value was being obtained from research's TQM efforts even after three years of intensive effort. The same survey also revealed the following TQM process problems:

- The TQM process had been designed but not really fully implemented.
- Measures had been developed but not used.
- Emphasis had been on means and activities rather than results.
- People in research were unclear as to research's main output.

As a result of the late-1989 check, it became apparent that the main reason the research's TQM effort was not producing significant results was that the TQM effort had become too activity-oriented. The *means* of doing the activities, such as teams, measures, flowcharting processes, had in most cases become the *end* rather than a way to improve research's value-added outputs. This activ-

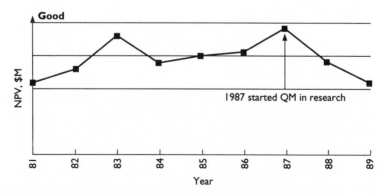

Figure 6.5 Estimated value of new/improved product and process concepts accepted with major research input (NPV/$M, 1981–1989).

ity focus, without sufficient attention to key research processes' results, had prevented TQM activities from yielding substantial value-added results. Compounding this problem was the fact that there was a lot of confusion among research people on what research's main output was or *should be*.

Improving and Institutionalizing Research's TQM Process

The results of the survey necessitated a major refocusing of research's TQM initiative. After reviewing and reflecting on the results, Holmes and his directors, with David McClaskey, their recently assigned quality coordinator, decided that research's implementation strategy needed to be main-output-focused. In January 1990, the research management team began to define and focus on the key research processes that would increase the value of new process and product concepts.

As a result of this shift from tools and training effort to improving research's "products," Holmes and his directors truly became the champions and leaders of using TQM to achieve their objectives. Analogously to Eastman's Strategic Planning Process, research's TQM effort became integrated into the way research was *managed*.

Personal top-management leadership actions were as follows:

- The vice president of research personally championed the effort.
- The research directors personally lead efforts to improve critical research processes.
- Research top management integrated TQM principles into the way they routinely managed research.
- The research management team focused on the company's competencies and provided the resources required to maintain and improve them.

Senior research managers were actively involved in focusing, communicating, reinforcing, and using quality values in the following ways:

- Role-modeling process improvement. Senior management led the executive team that meets five or more hours each week to review important processes and projects. This team also performs checks on quality, financial, business, and strategic issues. Improvement projects are championed by individual management team members.

- Regularly visiting with internal and external customers to discuss their expectations and current priorities for research projects.
- Making presentations on strategic intent, the Quality Policy, the Eastman Way, and Responsible Care®.
- Setting an example for continually learning by seeking the counsel of renowned quality professionals, such as Drs. W. E. Deming and J. M. Juran.
- Scheduling regular visits within Eastman to discuss quality and how quality values link to MIOs.
- Defining and managing major company wide processes.

Research management personally reviewed with each project manager what went right and what could be improved. This person-to-person communication means that there is both an emotional as well as a technical impact of the message. (Learning experts have determined that true learning occurs when both are present in the message.)

Success of the TQM effort was measured by the improvement in the net present value (NPV) of new/improved product and process concepts accepted for commercialization by research's primary customers: Eastman's business units. In 1992 the focus was expanded to include improving the value of *commercialized* products and processes, the next step in the innovation process (Figure 6.3). Research management personally led the effort to identify the vital few improvement opportunities to improve the Eastman innovation process, as well as to select the improvement project teams formed to address these opportunities. Fulfilling these nondelegable leadership responsibilities caused a previously ineffective TQM effort to achieve breakthrough results.

Another result of the output focus of the innovation process was the development of a set of indicators for Eastman's innovation process. These indicators helped to improve and control ECC's total innovation process. (See indicators in Figure 6.6.)

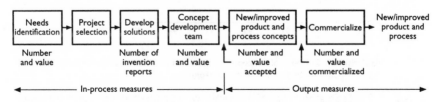

Figure 6.6 Eastman innovation process with indicators/measures.

Results and Critical Success Factors

The net result of improvements to Eastman research's key processes has been to double its productivity in five years (Figure 6.7).

The improved results were obtained by using a management-led, output-focused TQM effort. When properly used, TQM resulted in more than just incremental results. TQM created a significant *breakthrough* in results. The main factors that led to the improved results were as follows:

- Research's management *led* output-focused TQM effort.
- Improved linkages to business organizations.
- Improved resource allocation and needs processes.
- Improved concept development processes.
- Improved project management.
- Increased the amount of research resources and focus devoted to commercializing new products/processes.
- Used TQM principles to *manage* research (customer focus, continual improvement, manage with facts and data, organizational learning, improving key processes, and respect for people).

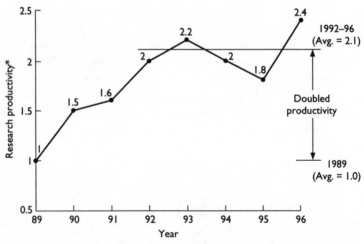

*As a ratio of 1989 NPV of concepts accepted and commercialized with major research input divided by total research expenditures.

Figure 6.7 Estimated value of new/improved product and process concepts accepted with major research input (NPV/$M, 1981–1996).

- Focused on the major outputs that provide customers with value.
- Developed overall measures and goals for the innovation process.
- Improved the processes that drive the major outputs.
- Recognized and reinforced the right behaviors, actions, and results.

Internally, ECC research's TQM process has contributed to improved manufacturing process efficiencies. ECC has been able to produce more at lower costs. ECC's *external* customers have also received benefits from research's successful TQM implementation. ECC was able to take customers' requests for new products and/or revisions to existing products and turn them into products that provided greater value. Simultaneously, ECC doubled the number of products and processes offered to the market. ECC's customers are therefore receiving more (and quicker) incremental value-added improvements from existing product lines, as well as more new products that can help them be more competitive.

Future Plans for Using TQM to Improve ECC Research Performance

Future opportunities identified and targeted for improvement via TQM activities are as follows:

- Portfolio analysis
- Technology strategy implications in business plans and strategies
- Cross-business research planning
- Cross-organizational learning
- Flexibility of internal resources
- Linking of frontier (radical) research to business objectives
- Spreading good project management skills to all project managers

CHAPTER 7

VIEWS AND LESSONS LEARNED AT THE TOP

Introduction

The previous chapters have provided the necessary concepts and processes to prioritize, design, and develop quality systems for R&D environments. However, without knowledgeable and active senior-management leadership, these concepts, processes, and tools are likely to become the relics of another failed program. Juran (1993) stated that among the primary reasons for the success of the Japanese quality revolution, "The senior executives of Japanese companies took *personal charge* of managing for quality." Juran (1988) also stated that he is unaware of *any* organization that has been successful in implementing and sustaining a quality process without the active participation of its senior management. The purpose of this chapter is to provide some key perspectives, deeds, and lessons learned from a senior R&D manager's perspective, as well as from the perspective of the Juran Institute's chairman, who has observed and facilitated multiple R&D organizations' quality journeys. The first TQM perspective is that of Dr. John Mayo (1994), reporting as the president of AT&T's Bell Laboratories.

Total Quality Management at AT&T Bell Laboratories

Our implementation of total quality management, the major lessons we learned, and the key challenges in this process should have broad applicability beyond AT&T Bell Laboratories.

Quality methodology certainly has broad application at AT&T. Over the past decade, we have reengineered our corporation—going back to the breakup of the Bell system and to our renewed focus on quality.

During this period, when I spoke at the Juran Institute I stressed that "our traditional definition of quality would no longer be appropriate to the new era." I added that "future product and systems development [would] have to reflect quality as defined, and redefined, by continually changing expectations in the marketplace."

To meet these changing expectations, AT&T took the momentous step of reengineering itself into a decentralized structure with some 20 nimble, customer-focused business units. (*Reengineering*, as you know, refers to radical or discontinuous process improvement.) The goal of AT&T's reengineering was to become the world's best at delivering the benefits of information technology to customers. And the method was to empower employees and align the business units directly with customers. At the heart of the reengineering were related commitments to striving for customer satisfaction and to using quality methodology to ensure that satisfaction by continuously improving responsiveness to customers.

The reengineering was combined with traditional continuous process improvement to redesign virtually all of our business, R&D, and manufacturing processes. The aim was to achieve dramatic improvements in the major dimensions of product and service quality: in their cost, timeliness, and performance, and, most important, in customer satisfaction. These quality dimensions are, of course, critical to global competitiveness.

AT&T's global competitiveness got a major boost beginning in 1989, when the corporation adopted the Malcolm Baldrige National Quality Award criteria and established a Chairman's Quality Award process to evaluate its progress toward customer focus and continuous improvement. The Chairman's Quality Award provided a disciplined and rigorous process for ensuring a full and regular so-called Plan-Do-Check-Act cycle. It drove improvement, reduced self-delusion, and pointed to where improvements were needed. Bell Laboratories built on the discipline of the Chairman's Quality Award by establishing a President's Quality Award—with Baldrige-based criteria—to encourage and reward progress specifically within R&D.

We have compelling evidence that we are on the right track. Our quality journey so far, as you may know, has led to two AT&T units winning Malcolm Baldrige National Quality Awards in 1991.

The same marketplace pressures and customer commitment that were driving the reengineering of AT&T were also impacting

AT&T's R&D community at Bell Laboratories. In 1988, the leaders of Bell Labs signed a landmark document outlining the role of R&D in implementing the AT&T commitment to customers and to quality. The document was called simply "Implementation of AT&T Quality Policy at Bell Laboratories," and it contained the important customer-oriented definition of quality that has become so widely familiar throughout AT&T: "Quality is the degree to which a product or service meets evolving customer expectations. Quality includes cost, performance, and timely availability" (as mentioned earlier). The document stresses the importance of "continuous improvement in quality"—for both reducing intervals and costs and increasing customer satisfaction.

Key principles in the Quality Policy document were that "all organizations and functions have customers" and that "all organizations must continuously improve the quality of the products and services they deliver to their customers." And, importantly, the document stressed that "quality improvement comes from process improvement" and that "quality improvement is everyone's responsibility."

It was one thing to articulate a quality policy; it was quite another to implement it. We recognized that implementation would require a dramatic reengineering, that it would require measures and goals, and, above all, that it would require an ongoing commitment to total quality management.

Thus, Bell Laboratories undertook the arduous task of reengineering and redefining itself—in large part to become more responsive to the needs of AT&T's customer-aligned business units. Out of this effort, among other changes, came the alignment of Bell Labs' development organizations with the AT&T business units they support with the technologies for today and into the future. That structural arrangement enhances both our understanding of customer needs and our responsiveness to those needs in the form of customer-focused innovations. These aligned development organizations are closely coupled to a group of Bell Labs core functions—including product, service, and network architecture, enabling technologies, software technology, and research. Such broad changes not only affect organizational structure and operating style, they also affect personal lives, professional skills, and expertise. We therefore examined the human-resources side of quality—in this case, the impact on people of our reengineering and redefinition. In order to measure that human impact, we conducted a survey to determine those attributes that have made Bell Labs the world's premier R&D organization. Overall, we found that the people of Bell Labs feel increasingly satisfied about the jobs they're doing to team with and serve their business-unit customers, and they say redefinition is working. For example, the highest-rated attributes were "creates AT&T opportunities" and "lays a foundation for AT&T's technology future."

But there were also some ongoing challenges for Bell Labs leadership, and they are challenges characteristic of corporate America. The challenges stem from cost and schedule pressures infringing on areas such as continuing education and intergroup learning, career mobility and opportunities for advancement, and job security. We intend to continue to reengineer our processes in order to better meet these challenges and resolve potential conflicts to the fullest extent possible—given the pressures of global competition and today's business climate. We would like to lead our industry into new solutions for the conflicts that sometimes arise today between personal goals and corporate goals.

As an important part of our reengineering, we made progress in establishing measures for our results. We defined an R&D *effectiveness measure,* which consists of new product revenues in a given year divided by total R&D costs in that year. New products are defined as products and/or services introduced in the last three years. We also defined an R&D *quality measure,* which consists of total customer-found faults in new products in a given year divided by the total number of new products. Again, new products are defined as products and/or services introduced in the last three years. And we defined an R&D *innovation measure,* which consists of new product revenue in a given year divided by total revenue in the given year—with the same definition of new products as in the other two measures.

In addition to these specific R&D measures, Bell Laboratories is committed to key AT&T measurement initiatives. For example, AT&T recently adopted a new measure—*customer-value-added*—that tracks AT&T's "worth-what-it-costs" relative to competitors. Customers' perceptions of worth-what-it-costs are based on their perceptions of relative worth and relative price—two areas that are critically impacted by R&D contributions such as product and/or service intervals and costs.

Those, then, are some of the initiatives toward quality methodology and total quality management that grew out of the reengineering of our corporation over the past decade. And over the next decade, we at AT&T and Bell Laboratories will be participating in a much larger task. We and others must reengineer our industry. This will be an extremely difficult and complicated transition. The need for industry reengineering is being driven, in large part, by the powerful force of information technology, which is propelling the digital thrust that's transforming the way we work and play. That information technology—together with the user demands it is driving—is bringing about the redefinition of numerous industries.

This redefinition has already begun with the merging of telecommunications, computing, consumer electronics, and entertainment. What's emerging from these combined industries is true multimedia communications that are highly customer-focused. And this includes multimedia products and services that are connected over telecommunications and information networks. To the consumer, it ultimately means voice, data, and images, in any combination, anytime, anywhere. And consumers will be connected to content providers through hosting services—now a missing industry.

As Bell Laboratories and the other AT&T units enter the difficult and complex transition to a reengineered industry, our application of the same quality principles and methodologies that helped us reengineer our corporation over the past decade will help us to successfully navigate the sea of change in the decade ahead. Importantly, Total Quality Management, or TQM, including reengineering, is an enduring management process for all of us—along with its focus on customers, on process improvement, and on intergroup learning and best current practices.

Total Quality Management, as we have learned, is the modern methodology for managing the creative and innovative R&D process as well as other corporate functions. It's the ideal methodology for managing this process in a global competitive environment, because it knows no geographical bounds. The worldwide goal, as you know, is full satisfaction of customers. Although TQM is not by itself a guarantee of business success, it is absolutely critical for creating an environment where such success is possible in the ever changing global competitive marketplace.

Consider a few brief examples of how Total Quality Management, including reengineering, enhances innovation:

- From 1991 to 1993, software development intervals for AT&T's international 5ESS® local telephone switching system were cut in half for large, medium, and small software releases. Initially, from 1988 to 1992, faults found by customers were reduced tenfold. (Successful fault reduction spurred the simultaneous reduction of intervals.)
- From 1992 to 1993, customer problem-resolution time decreased from 100 days to 30 days for a new software release for a key/PBX system. Customer service costs were reduced, while service was improved.
- A 30-fold improvement in field quality performance was achieved in less than two years for cellular software development.

Now let's review our goals in reengineering the processes for realizing new products and services. The first goal of the reengineering was to achieve a greater customer focus, including a global focus. The second goal was faster time-to-market—to be achieved largely by shortening what we call the front-end process as well as the development and manufacturing intervals. The third goal was to increase an already high rate of innovation. And the fourth goal was to significantly lower both the cost of the product or service and the cost of the R&D producing it.

As I've just implied, closeness to customers is at the heart of competitiveness. As AT&T ceased to be a monopoly, we quickly saw that allegiance to customers is more important than allegiance to function. We could no longer be satisfied with doing just a superb R&D job. We could be satisfied only when the customer was totally satisfied. So we had to align R&D, manufacturing, and business management into small, highly focused, nimble teams. At the same time, we had to find ways to maintain and enhance functional excellence in each area of expertise.

Virtually no other process is more critical to accelerating the conversion of emerging technologies into new products and services than the process for discerning and capturing the needs of customers, both domestic and international. That is a very difficult process, and I expect in the third millennium developers of technology will still be seeking better ways to ascertain customer needs. Corporate organization and alignments are at best only a partial answer to the challenge. Nevertheless, they are a powerful driver for a customer-oriented culture.

Perhaps the most powerful driver for customer satisfaction remains the pervasive application of quality principles through total quality management, as I've just emphasized. And that complements the organizational approach to customer focus. Our quality program is instrumental in our striving for customer satisfaction, because we have learned to define and measure quality in terms of such satisfaction, as I noted earlier. In fact, quality must ultimately be defined and measured by the customer, both domestic and global. So, across our industry, quality includes the features the customer wants, the timeliness the customer wants, and a price the customer is willing to pay. Doing the quality job well is the ultimate source of global competitiveness.

These organizational and quality thrusts drive Bell Labs' alignment with both customer needs and business needs. These alignments extend through development—and, for an entirely new product or service, extend all the way back to research or exploratory development. And the alignments are vital to the critical process of technology conversion, of moving emerging technologies to the marketplace in the form of new products and services. Technology sitting on a shelf or in a research lab is virtually useless. In the arena of global competition, the key is *how fast* technology can be moved to the marketplace.

In addition to these alignments, the prowess of an R&D organization is closely tied to its mechanisms for intergroup or organizational learning—and especially for on-the-job learning in groups of more than critical mass that contain many stimulating coworkers. While basically occurring inside an organization, intergroup learning can also be supported across companies—by benchmarking, publication, and professional societies. Conferences, too, play an important role in this learning.

The organization or, indeed, the nation that learns the fastest should eventually win. For if you can't apply it competitively, you haven't learned it. It is not easy to learn in a distributed environment such as we have at AT&T, however, so we have to work very hard at it—and we are still inventing new mechanisms for dealing with intergroup learning across small customer-focused teams scattered around the globe.

One highly effective way to capture that learning has been through *best current practices,* or BCPs. They are key to shortening development intervals, lowering development costs, and improving performance. As such, they represent a vital process for enhanced creativity and innovation. BCPs attempt to promote tried and proven approaches that are deemed to be "best in class" by people inside and outside AT&T. They supplement the creative and innovative processes so central to an R&D community. Importantly, they are broad, flexible guidelines, not rigid commandments. And that, of course, is because intergroup learning should be enabled, not legislated.

In addition to the vital need for intergroup learning, there is a critical need for opportunities for self-development, and especially for continuous education. One key reason for this need is the rapid pace of technological progress and change—the same forces that require continuous renewal of innovation. In fact, the vast majority of engineering jobs deal with subjects that inevitably change and disappear. There is no question that the engineer who does not continuously renew his or her learning will eventually become a nonengineer. It's impossible to overemphasize the importance of lifelong education in the engineering profession. The methods by which we learn shift from grade school to high school to university to self-motivated and industry-assisted learning.

Now let's turn to applying quality principles to improving and optimizing the creative and innovative R&D process within and among companies—or, indeed, within and among nations—because this process is absolutely central to the successful management of R&D, as well as to the successful transfer of technology.

As part of improving the creative and innovative process at Bell Laboratories, we have organized our research efforts around a series of key competencies that include fundamentals, photonics, electronics, computing, software engineering, networking, and speech and image processing. Fundamentals is a collection of various activities and a spawning ground for new competencies. Our processes continually groom this list, and effort shifts among elements on the list. And we keep in focus the fact that we cannot research everything. We look to outside competencies as well as to our own for the ideas that fuel our business.

Accelerating technology conversion within these competencies often involves concurrent development—that is, no serial handoffs. But that is just a part of our reengineering of product and service realization processes in order to shorten time-to-market. We avoid handoffs and shorten intervals by liberal use of concurrent development. A very important part of our concurrent development initiative is our many applied research projects, where research, development, and manufacturing people are brought together in tightly knit teams to speed ideas to market. This also focuses our research with increasing effectiveness. In fact, over 40 percent of research personnel are teamed in joint programs with developers who are aligned with AT&T business units. And they are doing good research as they solve real-world problems. In fact, a major key to good basic research is finding important, critical, real-world problems to solve.

This focus on real problems does not lessen our commitment to research. It simply means that good research and good development are often done concurrently. Research is still managed centrally and holistically. The Bell Labs' vice president of research and the president of Bell Labs have the responsibility to set the research program and to align it with AT&T's strategic intent and the long-term technology needs of the AT&T business units. We have not reduced our commitment to basic research.

In fact, contrary to some public perceptions, many of Bell Laboratories' most significant inventions came from focused projects with definite goals. The transistor, for example, was invented to meet the express need for a reliable, low-power amplifier for long-distance communications. The solid-state laser was invented to meet the need for a small, stable source of coherent light.

Over the past decade, we have enhanced our focus on architecture. Moreover, we have learned to pay as much attention to process architectures as we do to product and service architectures. A world-class innovation system requires a coherent, unifying family of core processes to identify customer needs, translate those needs into product and service specifications, and then produce designs that are manufacturable at competitive costs and intervals. Such an innovation system yields the best competitive advantage. In fact, we have been doing more and more development even with the same resource level. We can do so because our process improvements are so powerful. Consider a few examples:

- According to a survey conducted by Dillon, Read & Company of 51 senior telephone-company decision makers, AT&T Network Systems' 1993 product ratings led all competitors in almost every category. AT&T's margin of leadership widened in current-switching and transmission products. And AT&T's new responsiveness in pricing, service, and product delivery was frequently cited and praised by customers. The analyst who covers AT&T for Dillon characterized the performance as an "extraordinarily successful 1992–93 resurgence."
- The most recent data from the Federal Communications Commission shows that the 5ESS® local switching system was over three times more reliable than that of our nearest competitor for the first half of 1993—due largely to process reengineering and superior software design.
- A working prototype of a new, small private branch exchange was developed in 13 days—through reuse of software, circuit packs, and power supply. And the project went from requirements to controlled introduction in 26 weeks, with no changes required. (The usual interval was 38 to 60 weeks.)

As my last example clearly illustrates, an important aspect of these successful developments is the reuse of previously developed assets, such as previously developed and tested software modules and hardware platforms. Asset reuse also is a powerful facilitator of technology transfer and the underlying R&D management process.

Let me illustrate the importance of asset reuse. A decade ago, we designed just a few products and used them in large numbers in our own network. Today, we supply a large number of products to networks around the world. So it is no longer practicable to design all systems down to the component or element level. More and more of our R&D assembles systems at the circuit-pack, code-block, or equipment-frame level. In so doing, we try to build a storehouse of assets to be used across many designs. In many software systems, for example, we find about 80 percent of code can come directly from the storehouse. Of the remaining 20 percent to be written at the line-of-code level, three-fourths can go into the storehouse and be reused in follow-on designs.

It's important to stress that intelligent digital systems have much in common. Widely different systems can still draw heavily on a common asset pool. This pool must be managed around standards of quality and operability, and we still have a way to go in that regard. But even with a loosely controlled asset pool of in-house and out-of-house elements, we already see enormous benefit. An example of this is our current work on so-called asynchronous transfer mode, or ATM, communications, where we are able to use common elements for both premises solutions such as PBXs and central office solutions in a way that was never before possible in the history of our company.

The most important message I can give you is just that: The most powerful mechanism we have for improving R&D quality and productivity under the quality banner is the creation of high-quality, reusable assets—and the creation of processes that enable projects to draw from those and all other assets from around the world in order to meet customer needs at very low costs and with very short intervals. In short, well-managed reusable assets are increasingly key to innovation that gives the best competitive advantage. I would go so far as to say that there is the opportunity for an order-of-magnitude improvement in R&D productivity through the full utilization of the reusable-assets concept. With that improvement come development costs and development intervals that utterly delight customers.

In summary, we at Bell Laboratories have learned that we can increase the global competitiveness of AT&T's innovation by applying quality methodology and Total Quality Management to our R&D. This effort includes the broad pursuit of both continuous process improvement and periodic process reengineering. It also includes critical focus on the fastest rate of intergroup learning, on self-development, and on lifelong education. And, importantly, it includes the measurement of results. This methodology is already increasing AT&T's global competitiveness—by increasing our number of innovations, by more rapidly converting emerging technologies into desirable new products and services, and by substantially increasing our level of customer satisfaction.

But looking to the twenty-first century, we are barely started. We have reengineered our corporation. Now we must help reinvent and reengineer our industry. We must collectively bring the telecommunications, computing, consumer electronics, and entertainment industries into integrated, customer-focused solutions— solutions that will be multimedia communications flexibly tied to people, machines, databases, and video servers. That, in turn, will free people from many of today's limitations—free them for more productive work and for more enjoyable play. There is much yet to do, and I assure you Bell Laboratories remains committed to leading the way.

The following materials were contributed by Dr. A. Blanton Godfrey, a former executive with Bell Laboratories Quality Assurance Center, and who is currently chariman and CEO of the Juran Institute. Dr. Godfrey, like Dr. Mayo, has both observed and practiced the implementation of quality in R&D organizations.

R&D Quality: Views and Lessons Learned

Introduction

In the past few years quality management activities have become commonplace in R&D organizations. At first many R&D professionals felt that quality was an important concern of the production or service functions, but that it really did not apply to R&D. This changed rather quickly as R&D departments began to make numerous quality improvements and began to see concrete results.

Quality in R&D started in a fashion similar to the way quality started in other functions. The early efforts concentrated on improving the tasks researchers and developers already did. People first started looking for areas where they could reduce defects. By concentrating on the visible wastes, people were able to make substantial improvements in the costs of R&D activities, to reduce the times different phases of the development cycle took, and to improve overall efficiencies.

The second major effort was in reducing cycle times. In many industries, development cycle times are critical success factors. The pressure in the automotive, electronics, and consumer products industries to reduce design and development cycle times has been intense. For many companies, developing a new product faster than your competitors means the difference between a profit and a loss on the entire effort.

A third effort in this early phase of quality activity was in improving the quality of the output of the R&D efforts. This was slowed down by lack of good measurements for R&D quality and by long discussions about what R&D quality actually is.

The second phase of managing for R&D quality began when R&D functions began to understand their interdependence with other functions in the organization. Companies throughout the world had built up strong barriers to cross-functional work, and those barriers created enormous wastes and delays and often suboptimization of organizational resources. At first, people concentrated on building cross-functional information systems to provide the right information to R&D organizations. Without knowing field failures, production inefficiencies, customer preferences, and other information available only from other areas of the company, R&D personnel had made only semieducated guesses about critical design features.

Soon people realized that just having comprehensive databases was not enough. They also needed to build strong relationships between R&D people and the rest of the organization. This horizontal and vertical integration of R&D with other areas of the company began to produce results. New tools such as quality function deployment (QFD) were developed and were widely used in well-structured quality planning processes to go from the voice of the customer to the final delivered product.

The third phase of quality in R&D began with the realization of the strong role the customer should play in the design and development process. Companies started creating strong project managers to head the development team from start to finish. These new development teams included personnel from all over the company and incorporated frequent customer contact into the entire process of design. This was quickly followed by some organizations moving R&D people into customer premises and building true customer/supplier partnerships. Now many R&D organizations are redefining their entire roles—becoming "design-process designers" and creating tools for customers to use to do the design themselves.

In the following section, I'll explore each of these phases and cite some notable examples of these changes in the practice of R&D quality management.

Improving Current Practices

As in most other functions, quality in R&D in many organizations started with the simple activity of removing defects within the R&D process itself. People started looking at any possible source of rework, waste, and avoidable delays and started looking for ways to reduce these problems. The quality improvement process, basically the scientific method, reduced to a structured step-by-step approach to problem solving, was readily accepted by R&D personnel. With a little thought, R&D people were able to come up with long lists of things they wished to improve. One R&D organization took three groups of 50 people off-site for brainstorming sessions about quality improvement. They came back with 2,500 ideas. The problem quickly became setting priorities rather than finding something to improve.

Reducing Wastes

As in any work process, R&D work is full of defects and other wastes. Reports must be rewritten; tests are redone; lab reports are lost; lab equipment breaks down; samples are contaminated; designs must be changed; needed materials are not available; bureaucratic procedures add days or weeks or even months to "necessary" approvals or decisions; and much work is done that is never used.

Examples of the types of opportunities in R&D organizations include reducing high testing costs, improving the transfer of repaired equipment from maintenance to operations, improving the design review process, and reducing process air valve failures (Yoest 1991).

Other organizations (e.g., Jensen and Morgan 1990, at Shell) use more systematic means to analyze processes and products to discover bottlenecks, delays, inconsistencies, and other deficiencies. Their goals are to find opportunities to improve product quality, reduce cycle times, remove bureaucracy, and develop more cost-effective products, services, and processes.

AlliedSignal Research & Technology Laboratories focused on improving their services from their customers' viewpoints. They quickly identified dissatisfaction with overhead charges, time cycles to commercialize products, and general charges for work performed (Ferm, Hacker, Izod, Smith, and Israelow 1993). Los Alamos National Laboratory quickly achieved significant results by focusing on some key processes within the labs. They revised the laboratory rearrangement work order process to reduce turnaround times for filling customer requests from an average of over two months to less than two weeks. They reduced production of chemical wastes by 80 percent in photochemicals and improved system availability by 300 percent. The publications ordering process was improved to complete order fulfillments in two days rather than the previous six weeks. The ordering of PC hardware and software was simplified to remove multiple levels of signatures and handoffs (van der Hoeven and Whetten, 1993).

Software quality is one of the hardest challenges in many R&D organizations. Lo Presti and Mucha (1995) report on research conducted at Battelle Pacific

Northwest Laboratories and give many examples of how they have defined defects in software. Faulty software causes reruns, retractions, dead ends, and crunches. Incorrect input data causes the same.

Lack of programming expertise by scientists often causes clumsy solutions, inadequate error checks, design flaws, and inadequate software process. Inadequate software inspection (reviews) causes undiscovered errors, which are then more expensive to fix. Inadequate design documentation causes other errors. Inadequate system testing leaves many undiscovered errors.

As discussed by Mayo (1994) earlier in this chapter, software defects were also one of the areas of focus early in AT&T's quality efforts in R&D. From 1988 to 1992, faults found by customers of AT&T Bell Laboratories' software releases were reduced tenfold. They also were able to make a 30-fold improvement in field quality performance in less than two years for cellular software development.

Reducing Cycle Times

Almost every R&D organization focuses on cycle times early in its quality management activities. Delays are common and have significant impacts on corporate profitability and the organization's ability to reach critical targets. Some R&D organizations start quickly, looking at the entire product development process and the time to launch the new product or service. Others make a more modest start, looking at internal cycle times for important parts of the overall process.

Some of the early quality improvement projects in the Shell Development Company included developing a sophisticated protocol for requirements that reduced the product development cycle time by 12 months, reducing the time required for generating one type of document by a secretarial team from 4 months to 2 weeks, and improving response times on material tests (Jensen and Morgan 1990).

At Corning Incorporated, researchers identified early in their efforts cycle time as a key results indicator (KRI). For them, time-to-market is a competitive weapon. Initially they defined *cycle time* as the total time it took a product to have $1 million in sales after the project to develop that product received funding from a business area (Menger 1993). This initial definition helped them get started, but it had many shortcomings. It did not address those process development activities that did not result in new products. It did not address the early stages of product and process development. And it did not address those projects that were terminated for technical or commercial reasons.

Later, Corning developed and deployed a more sophisticated model of cycle time measurement that measured their innovation process in five stages: building knowledge, determining product feasibility, testing practicality, proving profitability, and commercializing. The World Class Quality Committee gathered historical data on the time projects remained in each of these five stages for over 100 different projects. Their analyses yielded new knowledge about time cycles and showed clear trends. This enabled them to start setting objectives on reducing cycle times (Menger 1993).

Other key results indicators relating to product cycle times are also used at Corning. These include project elapsed time as agreed to with the customer, percent of promised services delivered on time, and customer satisfaction with timeliness.

As discussed by Mayo earlier in this chapter, cycle time reductions have also been a major effort at AT&T. From 1991 to 1993 they were able to reduce software development intervals for the internationally marketed local switching system by half. From 1992 to 1993 they reduced customer problem-resolution times from 100 days to 30 days for new software releases for a key PBX system. One of their more spectacular results was developing a working prototype of a new, small private branch exchange in 13 days through reuse of software, circuit packs, and power supply (Mayo 1994).

Improving Quality of Output

The third, and perhaps the most important, area of improving what we do is improving the quality of the output. The output of R&D organizations is often thought of as knowledge or technology (see Chapter 1). This output is used to create products (goods and services) that in turn create value for the organization. How to measure the quality of this output is one of the most difficult questions in managing R&D quality. In Chapter 3, the difficulties of R&D quality measurement are acknowledged, and many examples of what leading R&D organizations are doing to get past this hurdle are given.

Jensen and Morgan (1990) see this extension of R&D quality management to the improvement of the product as a natural "next level of sophistication in work improvement . . ." They saw problems in generating new ideas for the business unit customers where idea after idea was being discarded by the customer. By using standard quality tools and methods, the teams were able to generate ideas focused on business unit missions and requirements, and within 12 months their ideas were hitting targets and becoming part of the business programs.

In the earlier discussion by Dr. John S. Mayo, we see some of the measures AT&T Bell Laboratories is using to start to get at this question of R&D output quality. Their R&D effectiveness measure consists of new product revenues in a given year divided by total R&D costs in that year. They further define *new products* as products (goods and services) introduced in the past three years. They also use an R&D quality measure that consists of total customer-found faults in a given year divided by the total number of new products. They have a third measure, R&D innovation measure, which consists of new product revenue in a given year divided by total revenue in the given year—with the same definition of new products as in the other two measures.

Alcoa has developed similar objectives to guide their improvement in the output of R&D. The Alcoa Technical Center has implemented three basic measures: customer satisfaction, cost reduction/system simplification, and time-to-commercialization. For the quality of their output, they measure the percentage of deliverables actually delivered and the customers' satisfaction with the deliverables. In four years they have improved their results from 46 percent to 76 percent at the business unit level and from 53 percent to 64 percent at the corporate level (Wasson 1995).

Other efforts at improving the quality of the output are just as impressive. The U.S. Army Tank–Automotive RD&E Center has used virtual-reality simulations to create interactive phenomenology models to gather unprecedented customer input during the entire development process. From these realistic prototypes, soldiers actually use the tank to fight on the Army's virtual-reality battlefields. By observing the soldiers' choices of display designs they are able to make major gains in product performance before the first item has been built. Using these methods has reduced time to complete missions by 42 percent, reduced fuel consumed in executing missions by 35 percent, and reduced time to plan combat orders by 60 percent (Sarna 1994). These results led, in 1995, to the RD&E Center being awarded the government's highest level of recognition for quality achievements available to a government agency: the President's Award.

Breaking Down the Barriers

One of the major problems facing most organizations when they undertake a Total Quality Management approach is the numerous barriers that exist in the organization. Internal departments and functions have often erected serious barriers to cross-function work and even created internal rivalries. Necessary information is often not shared, communication is frequently through memos and reports, and few people have any understanding of the entire process.

Information Flows across the Company

For many organizations one of the first steps in developing a strong quality effort in R&D starts with building the necessary information flows. Some years ago Electrolux AB, the giant Swedish appliance manufacturer, set ambitious goals to reduce the field failures of all products by half within three years. It soon became apparent that this was going to be a difficult task. The R&D organization had no knowledge at all about what failed in the field due to design errors. Manufacturing had almost no knowledge about the production defects that caused field failures. Purchasing had no data about failures of purchased components. The field service organization had extensive records of repairs and parts used, but these service reports had never been shared with other functions.

Until the data system was revamped and redeployed there was little that design, manufacturing, and purchasing could do to contribute to the goal of cutting the failures in half. Many organizations have faced the same challenge. They had no comprehensive database of field failures and the root causes. The R&D organization had to run special studies if they wanted to identify and remove design defects. Many organizations even found that their data flows from manufacturing to R&D were lacking. The designers were likely to produce new designs with the same manufacturability problems as the previous designs, since they had no information to lead them to do otherwise.

Developing a Strong Research and Development Process

One of the first steps in solving this problem, beyond just making the data easily available, is to develop a structured process management approach to the entire research and development process. One of the best examples was given by Edward A. Brown, chief of the Program Support Office, U.S. Army Research Laboratory (Brown 1993). Brown describes how the Army Research Laboratory identified eight business macroprocesses: acquisition of matériel, specifications, and standards; contracting from request for proposal through government acceptance; logistical support and maintenance; technology generation; control of funding, planning, budgeting, and execution; management of personnel; control of infrastructure; and provision of all information.

Each macroprocess was assigned to a member of the senior staff, who acted as a process owner. These owners formed process action teams to define the processes, define the constituent processes and subprocesses, and identify all customers, suppliers, inputs, and outputs. They then instituted improvement projects to gain new efficiencies. One specific result of this new approach was an effort to improve communications with their users and to generate ideas more efficiently. At their first Technology Opportunities Conference they brought together 500 of their 2,000 scientists and engineers with 100 of their customers to spend an entire week discussing users' requirements and suggested solutions (Brown 1993). There were over 300 innovations proposed during this week-long conference.

A similar process was carried out by Lederle-Praxis Biologicals, a division of American Cyanamid. They identified 15 subprocesses, which they then organized into six major process groups (Hildreth 1993). They assigned a process owner to each major process and charged the owner with improving customer satisfaction, increasing cost-efficiency of average product R&D, decreasing average product R&D time, and improving the awareness and external recognition for scientific/technical excellence. The processes they identified as major were prototype discovery research, candidate development research, GMP vaccine production, clinical research, product transfer into manufacturing, and R&D regulatory.

As in many such efforts, they focused not just on understanding the process and improving its performance, but on redefining the needs of customers and suppliers and developing measurement plans and control plans, which led to both improved current process and redesign of large process segments.

Companies are now tackling an even harder problem: integrating different processes and different parts of the company. Hewlett-Packard recently brought together three different but related divisions: the makers of the automotive electronics that are in the car, the makers of electronic test sets for service bays at dealers, and the makers of automation and testing electronics used by the automotive manufacturers. These three divisions brought in their customers to plan an entirely new approach for developing these equipments. These diverse groups came up with a new strategic plan for this key part of Hewlett-Packard, as well as suggesting many new products.

A Structured Process for Quality Planning

Many R&D organizations are now adopting a more structured approach for quality planning. As described earlier in this book, quality planning is a step-by-step, structured approach, which starts with the customers and collects valuable information to develop both the product and the process for producing goods and services. One of the best tools available to be used in the quality planning process is *quality function deployment* (QFD). QFD is a tool used to determine and analyze product performance requirements.

The Alcoa Technical Center has used QFD to determine what was important to the customers of the research, development, and engineering organization. Although they were not designing a product, they chose this tool as a process/framework for organizing customer requirements and linking them to the Center's "product" requirements. They were able to identify customer requirements, map the desired performance, develop performance measures, and create a way for negotiating specific project outputs with the business unit customers. From this process they were able to create a clear measure of customer satisfaction based on percentage of required deliverables actually delivered and a measure of performance based on shortening the time-to-commercialization (Hersh et al. 1993).

When faced with a critical product design, many R&D organizations are today using structured design processes. Florida Power & Light (FPL) faced the need for one of these critical products when they decided to design and implement a voice response unit (VRU). FPL receives over 8 million telephone calls a year from customers, so any failures in the design of the VRU could cause many repeat calls, increase call-handling times, and cause customer dissatisfaction. In order to identify customer problems, needs, and opportunities with respect to the VRU, they used focus groups to gather a rich level of detailed wants and needs. They simulated conversations using tape-recorded conversations between employees and customers.

By using the structured approach of QFD, FPL was able to rank 20 design features for the VRU and focus on the most important features for the design of the system. This structured process allowed them to design the VRU based on what the customer wanted, not on what they *thought* the customer wanted. The reactions to the deployed VRU were overwhelmingly positive; a high percentage (88 percent) of the customers were "very" or "mostly" satisfied.

Building a Strong Customer Focus

One of the strongest trends we have noticed in reviewing the lessons learned in R&D quality management over the past ten years is the movement to bring customers into the design process. Organizations that were plagued only a few years ago with numerous handoffs across multiple departments and functional barriers now have strong project teams with the entire cast of characters of internal customers, and often external customers, represented.

Boeing (Black 1995) has made customer focus an integral part of its corporate strategy. Two years before the Boeing board of directors approved offering the next-generation 737 for sale, researchers from Boeing were going out to airlines with blank sheets of paper asking, "What are your needs in a 100- to 200-seat airplane?"

These researchers talked with airlines' engineering, marketing, operations, maintenance, and finance functions to understand their key issues and perspectives on the basics of airplane requirements. They created formal airline working groups to look at propulsion systems, interiors, and maintainability for the airplane. There were ten airlines represented in each working group (Black 1995). All this effort was done even before approval was received to develop the new airplane!

The Strong Project Team

As companies develop strong customer focus and build new infrastructures for R&D, they began to employ what many writers have called the "strong project team." Ford's Team Mustang is a perfect example of this approach. When Ford felt it was time to develop a new version of its much loved Mustang, they decided it was time to "break the current car development paradigm and attack the issue from a new perspective" (Coletti 1994).

Ford put together a skunk-works team with representatives from all the key stakeholder organizations within the company. These groups included vehicle planning, vehicle engineering, vehicle design, manufacturing and assembly, body engineering, power-train engineering, finance, sales and marketing, and purchasing. The team's members operated as a team of peers reporting directly to a senior-management steering committee that streamlined communication and accelerated the decision-making process.

The strong project team as implemented by Ford has some other striking characteristics. The team is totally dedicated to the project, is collocated at an off-site location, has a high level of autonomy, has unique disciplines, has central prototype control, and is run by a heavyweight program manager. The team focused its efforts on four major areas: design the car to meet customer needs and wants; manage the program to deliver quality events and results; build a car to be defect-free repeatedly; and "surprise and delight" the customer.

The results of Team Mustang were striking. The car was designed in 25 percent less time with 30 percent less capital investment and 40 percent less staffing—and with a significant improvement in quality (Coletti 1994).

Customer Supplier/Partnerships

When developing new products (goods or services) many leading organizations are now involving both suppliers and customers from the very beginning. As Boeing started developing the 777, they executed a handwritten agreement between the executives of United Airlines and the executives of Boeing. This agreement included a series of mutual pledges about *trust, cooperation, teamwork, listening, responsiveness,* and *quality.*

"The 777 was not just designed with the customer in *mind*—it was designed with the customer *in the room.*" (Black 1995) Boeing brought the customer right into the design/build teams, right into the buildings and factories, right into the process of designing and building the 777. Four 777 customers have offices and staffs on-site at Boeing and are considered an integral part of the 777 team. The suppliers were brought into the processes as well and are regularly included in team meetings, addressing potential supply problems *before* they happen.

But just as important as bringing customers and suppliers into the process, Boeing has carefully integrated the different functions within Boeing into the design teams. By bringing engineering and manufacturing together at the start, many substantial problems and costs have been avoided. Black cites numerous examples of problems avoided by engineers and manufacturers working together, designs being radically altered when customers explained significant costs and changes they would have to undergo if the design were to go forward as initially planned, and maintenance activities that would take unnecessary hours if changes were not made.

One of the best examples of customer/supplier partnerships in R&D was given by Sanford and Tsiakals (1991). Baxter Healthcare Corporation has been creating partners with leading U.S. corporations who use their established product and service strengths to serve the special needs of hospitals. Baxter's own customers then benefit from the experience and skill made available from these partners. An example Sanford and Tsiakals give is food service, which typically comprises about 10 percent of a hospital's operating budget.

By working closely with the industry leader Kraft Foodservice, Baxter is able to offer a complete line of refrigerated and frozen foods, produce, and dry goods, enabling hospitals to consolidate most of their food purchases under one vendor. One hospital reduced its number of food-service invoices from 252 to 56 a month, saving over $200,000 a year in administrative costs and achieving a 30 percent reduction in the average cost of a meal.

Another example from Sanford and Tsiakals shows how creative companies can be in designing and providing new valued services by establishing strong customer/supplier partnerships. Hospitals in the United States generate 480,000 tons of infectious waste each year. Working closely with Waste Management, Incorporated, a leader in handling, transporting, and disposing of waste, Baxter/Waste Management is able to provide hospitals a wide range of essential services. These services include waste-reduction consulting, materials recovery and recycling, waste-collection systems design, transportation, and safe disposal. In one year, one hospital saved over $500,000 through waste reduction, recycling, and employee training programs. Another hospital reduced employee injuries by one-third by focusing on needle-stick injuries related to medical waste.

Baxter has extended these services to include designing custom packs for surgeries, with significant results. Although the custom packs cost more than individual items purchased separately, the savings in labor, handling, sterilization, and inventory far outweigh the incremental costs. One hospital was able to save 5.2 percent on supply costs in surgery, 2.3 percent in labor costs, and reduce infections by 22 percent. Fewer people were able to perform 16.3 percent more surgeries (Sanford and Tsiakals 1991).

Customer Design

One of the most exciting trends in R&D in recent years has been the move toward customer design. Levi's recently made a major gain in market share in women's jeans by having customers "custom-fitted" in the showrooms; the dimensions are sent by computer to the factory for custom-made jeans. Another company, Custom Foot, uses computer measurements to send data to Italy for handmade shoes to be delivered in two weeks. But these are examples of "mass customization," not true customer design.

Other companies are taking these ideas even further. Federal Express has designed a system where customers can make inquiries about packages over the Internet, a job that FedEx used to spend millions of dollars doing for the customers. Almost all the major U.S. airlines are now distributing software so customers can make their own travel arrangements—bypassing travel agents and reservation clerks. Other companies are placing CAD tools in customer locations so that the customer's own designers can create the chip they want produced. Hallmark is placing computers in shops for customers to design their own cards.

There may come a time when R&D organizations are spending more time making design tools for their customers than actually designing products themselves. Already, major changes are taking place in the publishing and printing businesses.

Summary

In a very short time, organizations have gone beyond reducing their R&D process defects and cycle times and improving the quality of the process output. They now build truly cross-functional teams that include all members of the development spiral as well as customers and suppliers. They have created new means to focus on customers and value-generating activities with new measurements that have yielded impressive results. But implementing these tried-and-true quality methods and tools in R&D is only part of the story. We need to move beyond just supporting the organization's vision and goals to creating a new R&D strategic vision.

Inn Hee Lee of 3M (1995) argues that the first element of R&D strategy must be a strategic vision. Since one of the missions of R&D is to provide a new direction for corporate and business vision, R&D leadership is critical for the development of a strategic vision for research and development as well as for business development. The second element of the R&D strategy must be alignment to business units. All R&D efforts must be focused on core strategies and corporate and business unit visions and missions.

The R&D effort must also include technology leveraging and technology building. This must include the management of innovation-nurturing embryonic technologies for future business ventures and successes.

REFERENCES

Chapter I

Altland, H. W. (1995), "Robust Technology Development Process for Imaging Materials At Eastman Kodak Company," *Proceedings of Symposium on Managing for Quality in Research and Development,* Juran Institute, Wilton, Conn.

Ascarelli, S. (March 15, 1996), "European Telecom R&D Labs Adjusting," *Wall Street Journal,* Dow Jones & Company, New York, N.Y.

Boath, David, D. (1993), "Reengineering the Product Development Process," *Proceedings of Symposium on Managing for Quality in Research and Development,* Juran Institute, Wilton, Conn.

Cole, R. M. (1990), "Quality in the Management of Research and Development," *Proceedings of Symposium on Managing for Quality in Research and Development,* Juran Institute, Wilton, Conn.

Darby, R. A. (1990), "R&D Quality in a Diversified Company," *Proceedings of Symposium on Managing for Quality in Research and Development,* Juran Institute, Wilton, Conn.

Endres A. C. (1996), "Research and Development," draft of section in the fifth edition of the *Quality Control Handbook,* to be published by McGraw-Hill, New York, N.Y.

Endres A. C. (1992), "Results and Conclusions from Applying TQM to Research," *Proceedings of American Society for Quality Control's Quality Congress Transactions—Nashville,* Milwaukee, Wis.

Garfinkel, M. (1990), "Quality in R&D," *Proceedings of Symposium on Managing for Quality in Research and Development,* Juran Institute, Wilton, Conn.

Godfrey, A. B. (1991), "Information Quality: A Key Challenge for the 1990s," *The Best on Quality,* vol. 4, Hanser Publishers, Munich, Germany.

Hall, Earl (1996), *R&D Organization and Management Practices in U.S. High Technology Firms,* Published by Hall and Associates, Los Altos, Calif.

REFERENCES

Hammer, M. and Champy, J. (1993), *Reengineering the Corporation*, Harper-Collins, New York, N.Y.

Holmes, J. D. and McClaskey, D. J. (1992), "Improving Research Using Total Quality Management," *Proceedings of Symposium on Managing for Quality in Research and Development*, Juran Institute, Wilton, Conn.

Holmes, J. D. and McClaskey, D. J. (1994), "Doubling Research's Output Using TQM," *Proceedings of Symposium on Managing for Quality in Research and Development*, Juran Institute, Wilton, Conn.

Hooper, J. (1990), "Quality Improvement in Research & Development," *Proceedings of Symposium on Managing for Quality in Research and Development*, Juran Institute, Wilton, Conn.

Industrial Research Institute (July 1996), *Industrial Research and Development Facts*, Industrial Research Institute, Washington, D.C.

Juran, J. M. (1974), editor in chief, *Quality Control Handbook*, McGraw-Hill, New York, N.Y.

Juran, J. M. (1990), "Made in USA: A Break in the Clouds," summary address presented at the "Quest for Excellence" conference of 1989 in Washington, D.C., sponsored by the National Institute of Standards and Technology in conjunction with American Society for Quality Control and the American Productivity and Quality Center, Juran Institute, Inc., Wilton, Conn.

Juran, J. M. (1992), *Juran on Quality by Design*, Free Press, New York, N.Y.

Juran, J. M. and Gryna, F. M. (1993), *Quality Planning and Analysis*, (3d edition), McGraw-Hill, New York, N.Y.

Mayo, J. (1994), "Total Quality Management at AT&T Bell Laboratories," *Proceedings of Symposium on Managing for Quality in Research and Development*, Juran Institute, Wilton, Conn.

Mizuno, S. (1989), *Company-Wide Total Quality Control*, Asian Productivity Organization, Tokyo, Japan.

Morgan, M. (1990), "Quality in R&D—Fit or Folly," *Proceedings of Symposium on Managing for Quality in Research and Development*, Juran Institute, Wilton, Conn.

Perry, W. R. and Westwood, M. (1991), "Results from Integrating a Quality Assurance System with Blount's Product Development Process," *Proceedings of Symposium on Managing for Quality in Research and Development*, Juran Institute, Wilton, Conn.

Port, O. (June 10, 1996), " 'Green' Product Design," *Business Week*, McGraw-Hill, New York, N.Y.

Roussel, P. A., Kamal N. S., and Erickson, T. J. (1991), *Third Generation R&D*, Harvard Business School Press, Boston, Mass.

REFERENCES

Shear, M. (1991), "Human Factors in Basic R&D," *Proceedings of Symposium on Managing for Quality in Research and Development,* Juran Institute, Wilton, Conn.

Shipley, R. S. (1991), "Quality Improvements in the Research and Development Process," *Proceedings of Symposium on Managing for Quality in Research and Development,* Juran Institute, Wilton, Conn.

Uchimaru, K., Okamoto, S., and Kurahara, B. (1993), *TQM for Technical Groups,* (English translation), Productivity Press, Portland, Oreg.

Wiley, W. R. (1993), "Good Science Is Good Quality," *Proceedings of Symposium on Managing for Quality in Research and Development,* Juran Institute, Wilton, Conn.

Chapter 2

Bastian, R. P. and Miller, W. F. (1994), "Improving the Research Funding Process Through Process Management, Value Analysis, and Linkages to Other Processes—Lessons Learned," *Proceedings of Symposium on Managing for Quality in Research and Development,* Juran Institute, Wilton, Conn.

Block, Peter, *Flawless Consulting,* University Assoc., San Diego, Calif. 1981.

Boath, David D. (1993), "Reengineering the Product Development Process," *Proceedings of Symposium on Managing for Quality in Research and Development,* Juran Institute, Wilton, Conn.

Bywaters, David R., "Facilitation: Third-Party Therapy," *Assoc. & Society Manager,* vol. 18, no. 6, Oct/Nov, 1986, pp. 8–10.

Cole, R. M. (1990), "Quality in the Management of Research and Development," *Proceedings of Symposium on Managing for Quality in Research and Development,* Juran Institute, Wilton, Conn.

Harman, Keith A., Facilitator Kaisen Teams, *Journal for Quality & Participation,* Dec. 1989, pp. 86–87.

Holmes, J. D. and McClaskey, D. J. (1992), "Improving Research Using Total Quality Management," *Proceedings of Symposium on Managing for Quality in Research and Development,* Juran Institute, Wilton, Conn.

Juran, J. M. (August 1986), "The Quality Trilogy," *Quality Progress,* American Society for Quality Control, Milwaukee, Wis.

Juran, J. M. (1989), *Juran on Leadership for Quality,* Free Press, New York, N.Y.

Juran, J. M. (1990), "Made in USA: A Break in the Clouds," summary address presented at the "Quest for Excellence" conference of 1989 in Washington, D.C., sponsored by the National Institute of Standards and Technology in conjunction with the American Society for Quality Control and the

REFERENCES

American Productivity and Quality Center, Juran Institute, Inc., Wilton, Conn.

Juran Institute (1991), "TQM Implementation Road Map," Juran Institute, Wilton, Conn.

Konosz, D. L. and Ice, J. W. (1991), "Facilitation of Problem Solving Teams," *Proceedings of Symposium on Managing for Quality in Research and Development,* Juran Institute, Wilton, Conn.

Main, J. (1994), *Quality Wars,* Free Press, New York, N.Y.

Menger, E. L. (1993), "Evolving Quality Practices at Corning Incorporated," *Proceedings of Symposium on Managing for Quality in Research and Development,* Juran Institute, Wilton, Conn.

Rogers, Everett M., and Shoemaker, F. Floyd, *Communication of Innovations,* 2d ed., The Free Press, New York, 1971.

Taylor, D. H. and Jule, W. E. (1991), "Implementing Total Quality at Savannah River Laboratory," *Proceedings of Symposium on Managing for Quality in Research and Development,* Juran Institute, Wilton, Conn.

Webster's Ninth New Collegiate Dictionary, Merriam-Webster Inc., Springfield, Mass., 1988.

Yoest, D. T. (1991), "Comparison of Quality Improvement Team Training Methods and Results in a Research and Development Organization," *Proceedings of Symposium on Managing for Quality in Research and Development,* Juran Institute, Wilton, Conn.

Zeidler, P. C. (1993), "Using Quality Function Deployment to Design and Implement a Voice Response Unit at Florida Power & Light Company," *Proceedings of Symposium on Managing for Quality in Research and Development,* Juran Institute, Wilton, Conn.

Chapter 3

Boath, D. (1992), "Using Metrics to Guide the TQM Journey in R&D," *Proceedings of Symposium on Managing for Quality in Research and Development,* Juran Institute, Wilton, Conn.

Cole, R. M. (1990), "Quality in the Management of Research and Development," *Proceedings of Symposium on Managing for Quality in Research and Development,* Juran Institute, Wilton, Conn.

Ferm, P., Hacker, S., Izod, T., Smith, G. (1993), "Developing a Customer Orientation in a Corporate Laboratory Environment," *Proceedings of Symposium on Managing for Quality in Research and Development,* Juran Institute, Wilton, Conn.

REFERENCES

Garfinkel, M. (1990), "Quality in R&D," *Proceedings of Symposium on Managing for Quality in Research and Development,* Juran Institute, Wilton, Conn.

Hersh, J., Backus, M., Kinosz, D., Wasson, A. (1993), "Understanding Customer Requirements for the Alcoa Technical Center," *Proceedings of Symposium on Managing for Quality in Research and Development,* Juran Institute, Wilton, Conn.

Juran, J. M. (1964), *Managerial Breakthrough,* 1st edition (2d edition: 1995), McGraw-Hill, New York, N.Y.

Juran, J. M. (1989), *Juran on Leadership for Quality,* Free Press, New York, N.Y.

Juran, J. M. (1992), *Juran on Quality by Design,* The Free Press, New York, N.Y.

Juran, J. M., editor in chief (1995), *A History of Managing for Quality,* ASQC, Quality Press, Milwaukee, Wis.

Kaplan, R. S., Norton, D. P. (1992), "The Balanced Scorecard—Measures That Drive Performance," *Harvard Business Review,* January–February, Harvard Business School Publishing, Boston, Mass.

Lander, L., Matheson, D., Ransley, D. (1994), "IRI's Quality Director's Network Takes R&D Decision Quality Benchmarking One Step Further," *Proceedings of Symposium on Managing for Quality in Research and Development,* Juran Institute, Wilton, Conn.

Luther, D. B. (1993), "Advanced TQM: Measurements, Missteps, and Progress Through Key Result Indicators at Corning," *National Productivity Review,* vol. 12, no. 1 (winter 1992/1993), New York, N.Y.

Marien, B. (1991), "Incorporating Quality into the Performance Management Process for R&D at Olin," *Proceedings of Symposium on Managing for Quality in Research and Development,* Juran Institute, Wilton, Conn.

Matheson D., Matheson, J., Menke, M. (1994), "SDG's Benchmarking Study of R&D Decision Making Quality Provides Blueprint for Doing the Right R&D," *Proceedings of Symposium on Managing for Quality in Research and Development,* Juran Institute, Wilton, Conn.

Menger, E. (1993), "Evolving Quality Practices at Corning Incorporated," *Proceedings of Symposium on Managing for Quality in Research and Development,* Juran Institute, Wilton, Conn.

Rocca, C. J. (1991), "Rochester Excellence . . . Customer Satisfaction," *Proceedings of Symposium on Managing for Quality in Research and Development,* Juran Institute, Wilton, Conn.

Van der Hoeven, B., Whetten, J. (1993), "Continuous Quality Improvement at Los Alamos," *Proceedings of Symposium on Managing for Quality in Research and Development,* Juran Institute, Wilton, Conn.

REFERENCES

Wasson, A. (1995), "Developing and Implementing Performance Measures for an R&D Organization Using Quality Processes," *Proceedings of Symposium on Managing for Quality in Research and Development*, Juran Institute, Wilton, Conn.

Wiley, W. R. (1993), "Good Science Is Good Quality," *Proceedings of Symposium on Managing for Quality in Research and Development*, Juran Institute, Wilton, Conn.

Chapter 4

Fried, L. K. (1993), "AT&T Transmission Systems ISO 9001 Registration: The R&D Compliance Experience," *Proceedings of Symposium on Managing for Quality in Research and Development*, Juran Institute, Wilton, Conn.

Gibbard, H. F. and Davis, C. (1993), "Implementation of ISO 9001 in an R&D Organization," *Proceedings of Juran Institute's IMPRO® Conference*, Juran Institute, Wilton, Conn.

Holmes, J. D. and McClaskey, D. J., "Improving Research Using Total Quality Management," Juran Institute's *1992 Symposium on Management for Quality in Research and Development*, Transactions, June 16, 1992.

ISO 9000 Registered Company Directory—United States & Canada, compiled and published by Quality Systems Update, Center for Energy & Environmental Management, Fairfax Station, Virginia, May 1993.

Juran, J. M. and Gryna, F. M. (1993), *Quality Planning and Analysis*, 3d edition, McGraw-Hill, Inc., New York, N.Y.

Kozlowski, T. R. (1993), "Implementing a Total Quality Process into Research and Development: A Case Study," *Proceedings of Symposium on Managing for Quality in Research and Development*, Juran Institute, Wilton, Conn.

McClaskey, D. J., "Using the Baldrige Award to Improve," *1991 ASQC Quality Congress*, Transactions, May 1991.

McClaskey, D. J. (1992), "Using the Baldrige Criteria to Improve Research," *Proceedings of Symposium on Managing for Quality in Research and Development*, Juran Institute, Wilton, Conn.

Menger, E. L. (1993), "Evolving Quality Practices at Corning Incorporated," *Proceedings of Symposium on Managing for Quality in Research and Development*, Juran Institute, Wilton, Conn.

Peach, R. W. (1994), *The ISO 9000 Handbook*, 2d edition, CEEM Information Services, Fairfax, Virginia.

REFERENCES

Roussel, Philip A., Saad, Kamal N., and Erickson, Tamara J., *Third Generation R&D,* Harvard Business School Press, Boston, Massachusetts, 1991.

Van der Hoeven, B. J. (1993), "Managing for Quality in IBM Research," unpublished paper provided by author.

Van der Hoeven, B. J. and Whetten, J. T. (1993), Continuous Quality Improvement at Los Alamos," *Proceedings of Symposium on Managing for Quality in Research and Development,* Juran Institute, Wilton, Conn.

Chapter 5

Anderson, T. and Zimmerman, K. (1995), "The Reality of the Virtual Global Laboratory," *Proceedings of Symposium on Managing for Quality in Research and Development,* Juran Institute, Wilton, Conn.

Boath, D. (1994), "Using TQM to Improve Technology Transfer," *Proceedings of Symposium on Managing for Quality in Research and Development,* Juran Institute, Wilton, Conn.

Greene, M. (1995), "Intellectual Property Management in a Dynamic Organizational Context," *Proceedings of Symposium on Managing for Quality in Research and Development,* Juran Institute, Wilton, Conn.

Holmes, J. D. and McClaskey, D. J. (1994), "Doubling Research's Output Using TQM," *Proceedings of Symposium on Managing for Quality in Research and Development,* Juran Institute, Wilton, Conn.

Kelsey, G. and Milewski, M. (1994), "Technology Transfer from an R&D Organization Perspective," *Proceedings of Symposium on Managing for Quality in Research and Development,* Juran Institute, Wilton, Conn.

Rauner, V. (1990), "Pursuing Quality in Patent Applications," *Proceedings of Juran Institute's IMPRO® Conference,* Juran Institute, Wilton, Conn.

Chapter 6

Holmes, J. D. and McClaskey, D. J. (1992), "Improving Research Using Total Quality Management," *Proceedings of Symposium on Managing for Quality in Research and Development,* Juran Institute, Wilton, Conn.

Holmes, J. D. and McClaskey, D. J. (1994), "Doubling Research's Output Using TQM," *Proceedings of Symposium on Managing for Quality in Research and Development,* Juran Institute, Wilton, Conn.

December 1995, ASQC Case Development Meeting Held at Eastman Chemical, Kingsport, Tenn., with Dr. Jerry Holmes and Mr. David McClaskey.

Chapter 7

Black, John R. (1995), "777—Designing a Revolution," *Proceedings of Symposium on Managing for Quality in Research and Development,* Juran Institute, Wilton, Conn.

Brown, Edward A. (1993), "Defining the Technology Generation Process," *Proceedings of Symposium on Managing for Quality in Research and Development,* Juran Institute, Wilton, Conn.

Coletti, John O. (1994), "Alive and Kicking . . . The Tradition Continues," *Proceedings of Symposium on Managing for Quality in Research and Development,* Juran Institute, Wilton, Conn.

Ferm, P., Hacker, S., Izod, T. P., and Smith, O. R. (1993), "Developing a Customer Orientation in a Corporate Laboratory," *Proceedings of Symposium on Managing for Quality in Research and Development,* Juran Institute, Wilton, Conn.

Hersh, Jeff F., Backus, Marilyn C., Kinosz, Donald L., and Wasson, A. Robert (1993), "Understanding Customer Requirements for the Alcoa Technical Center," *Proceedings of Symposium on Managing for Quality in Research and Development,* Juran Institute, Wilton, Conn.

Hildreth, Stephen W. (1993), "Rolling Out BPQM in the Core R&D of Lederle-Praxis Biologicals, American Cyanamid," *Proceedings of Symposium on Managing for Quality in Research and Development,* Juran Institute, Wilton, Conn.

Jensen, Ronald P. and Morgan, Martha N. (1990), "Quality in R&D—Fit or Folly," *Proceedings of Symposium on Managing for Quality in Research and Development,* Juran Institute, Wilton, Conn.

Lee, Inn Hee (1995), "R&D Strategies for Global Competition," *Proceedings of Symposium on Managing for Quality in Research and Development,* Juran Institute, Wilton, Conn.

Lo Presti, Charles A. and Mucha, John F. (1995), "Software Development in the Research Environment: Consideration for Quality Assurance," *Proceedings of Symposium on Managing for Quality in Research and Development,* Juran Institute, Wilton, Conn.

Mayo, John S. (1994), "Total Quality Management at AT&T Bell Laboratories," *Proceedings of Symposium on Managing for Quality in Research and Development,* Juran Institute, Wilton, Conn.

Menger, Eve L. (1993), "Evolving Quality Practices at Corning Incorporated," *Proceedings of Symposium on Managing for Quality in Research and Development,* Juran Institute, Wilton, Conn.

REFERENCES

Sanford, Roy and Tsiakals, Joseph (1991), "Managing Quality at Key R&D Interfaces, *Proceedings of Symposium on Managing for Quality in Research and Development,* Juran Institute, Wilton, Conn.

Sarna, Donald S. (1994), "Using Virtual Reality to Involve Customers in Product Research Development and Engineering," *Proceedings of Symposium on Managing for Quality in Research and Development,* Juran Institute, Wilton, Conn.

Van der Hoeven, Bernard J. and Whetten, John T. (1993), "Continuous Quality Improvement at Los Alamos," *Proceedings of Symposium on Managing for Quality in Research and Development,* Juran Institute, Wilton, Conn.

Wasson, A. Robert (1995), "Developing and Implementing Performance Measures for an R&D Organization Using Quality Processes," *Proceedings of Symposium on Managing for Quality in Research and Development,* Juran Institute, Wilton, Conn.

Yoest, David T. (1991), "Comparison of Quality Improvement Team Training Methods and Results in a Research and Development Organization," *Proceedings of Symposium on Managing for Quality in Research and Development,* Juran Institute, Wilton, Conn.

Zeidler, Peter C. (1993), "Using Quality Function Deployment to Design and Implement a Voice Response Unit at Florida Power & Light Company," *Proceedings of Symposium on Managing for Quality in Research and Development,* Juran Institute, Wilton, Conn.

INDEX

INDEX

INDEX